Doing Business in Beijing

2004 Edition

ChinaKnowledge Press Private Limited

www.chinaknowledge.com

KAZAKHSTAN
KYRGYZSTAN
Xinjiang
Qinghai
Tibet
INDIA
NEPAL
BHUTAN
MYANMAR
MAP of CHINA
Capital of China
Municipalities
Special Administrative Regions
Autonomous Regions
Provinces

RUSSIA
MONGOLIA
Heilongjiang
Jilin
Liaoning
NORTH KOREA
SOUTH KOREA
JAPAN
BEIJING
Inner Mongolia
Tianjin
Hebei
Ningxia
Shanxi
Shandong
Gansu
Shaanxi
Henan
Jiangsu
Anhui
Shanghai
Chongqing
Hubei
Sichuan
Zhejiang
Jiangxi
PACIFIC OCEAN
Hunan
Guizhou
Fujian
Guangdong
Taiwan
Guangxi
Hong Kong
Macau
Hainan

MAP of BEIJING

Railway

Highway

Expressway

Fangshan
District

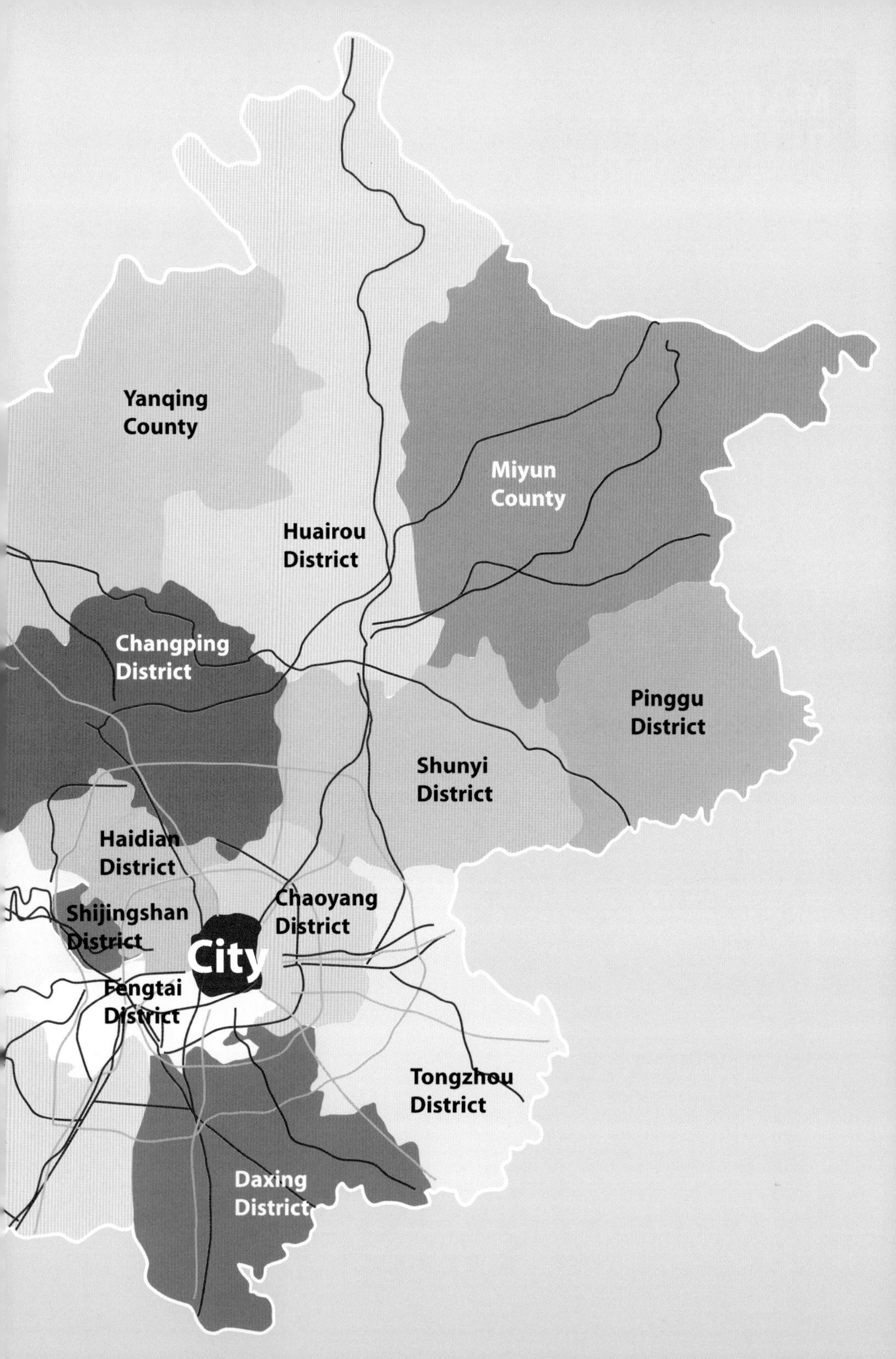
Yanqing County
Huairou District
Miyun County
Changping District
Pinggu District
Shunyi District
Haidian District
Chaoyang District
Shijingshan District
City
Fengtai District
Tongzhou District
Daxing District

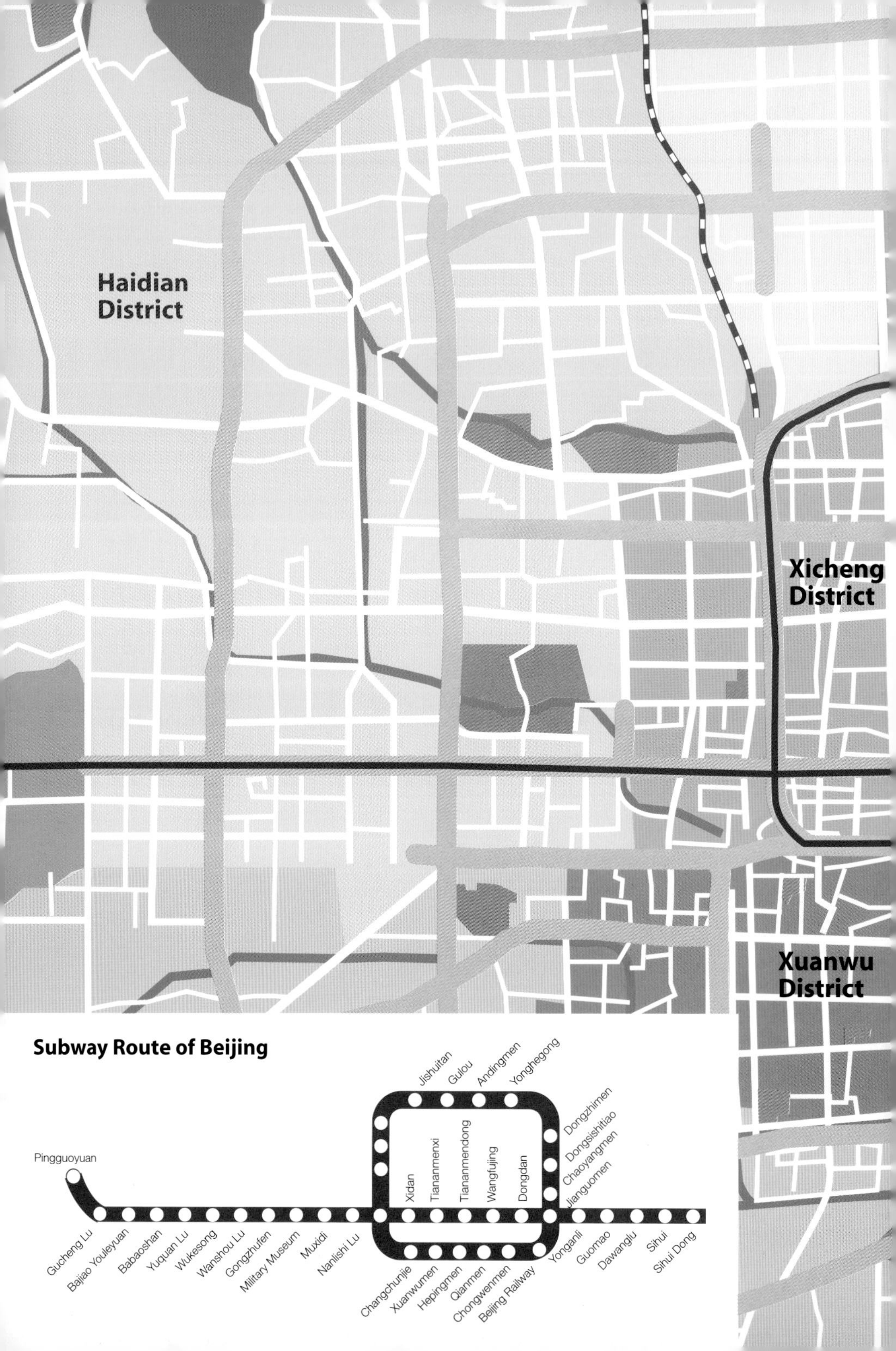
Haidian District
Xicheng District
Xuanwu District
Subway Route of Beijing
Pingguoyuan
Gucheng Lu
Bajiao Youleyuan
Babaoshan
Yuquan Lu
Wukesong
Wanshou Lu
Gongzhufen
Military Museum
Muxidi
Nanlishi Lu
Jishuitan
Gulou
Andingmen
Yonghegong
Dongzhimen
Dongsishitiao
Chaoyangmen
Jianguomen
Xidan
Tiananmenxi
Tiananmendong
Wangfujing
Dongdan
Changchunjie
Xuanwumen
Hepingmen
Qianmen
Chongwenmen
Beijing Railway
Yonganli
Guomao
Dawanglu
Sihui
Sihui Dong

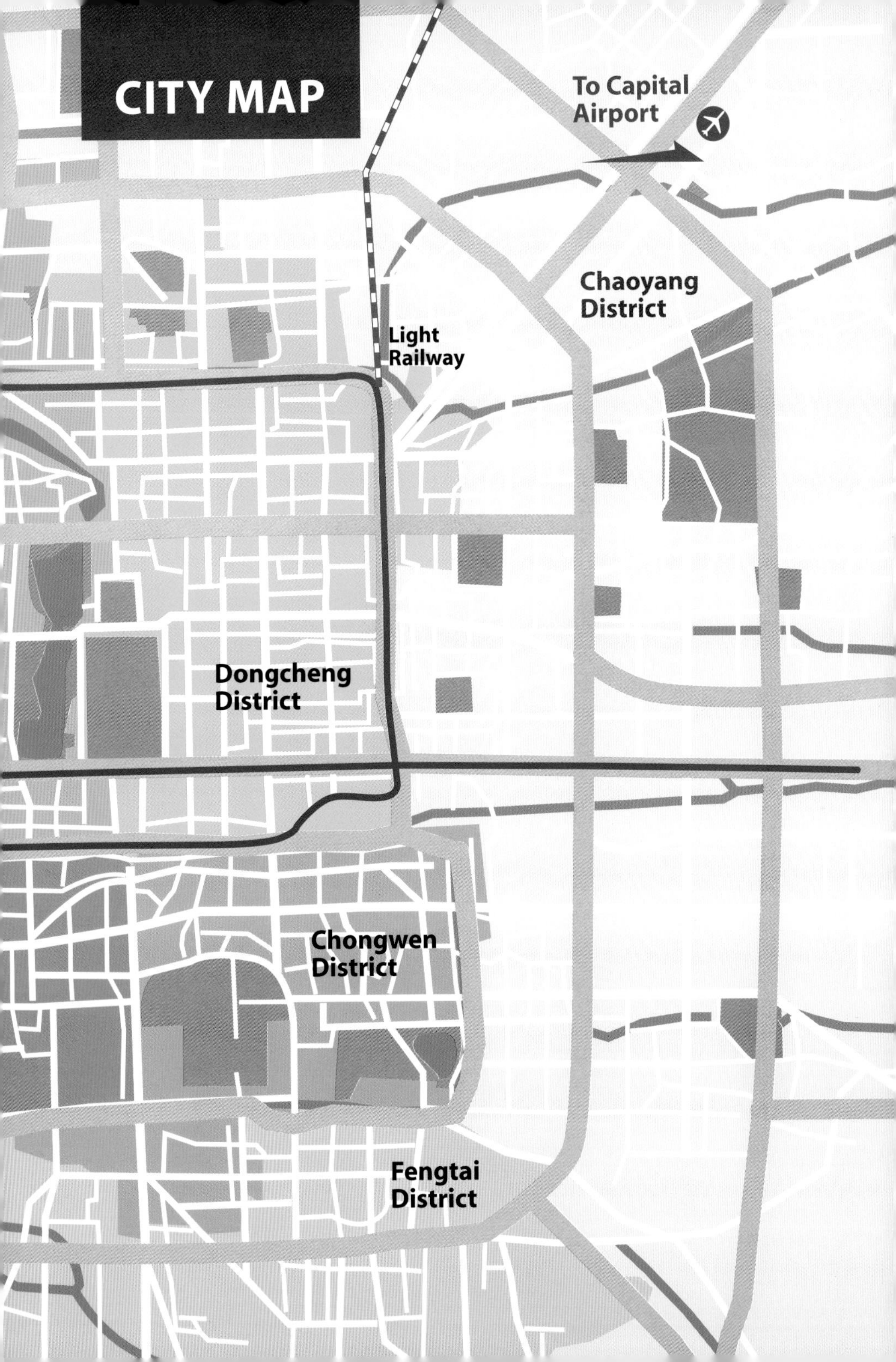
CITY MAP
To Capital
Airport
Chaoyang
District
Light
Railway
Dongcheng
District
Chongwen
District
Fengtai
District

We would appreciate it if readers could alert us as to errors and omissions by writing in to:

China Knowledge Private Limited
Doing Business in Beijing Editor
8 Temasek Boulevard
#37-01A Suntec Tower Three
Singapore 038988

ISBN 981-4163-02-3

Printed in Singapore

Foreword

In our recently-produced and launched five-episode documentary titled "Inside the World's Largest Factory", I placed Beijing in our finale episode as the capital city possesses several competitive edges over other cities in China.

Microsoft's establishment of a research laboratory, one of only three in the world, in Beijing, is testimony to Beijing's R&D capabilities and its position as the center of IT elites in the whole of China. Further confirming this status, Beijing is also host to the headquarters of Chinese IT giants Lenovo and Founder.

Just when I was writing this, I received news that our interviewee in Episode Five of our documentary, Professor Chen Chunxian had passed away at the age of seventy.

Professor Chen was the first person to set up a private enterprise in Zhongguancun, thereby laying the foundation for the "Sillicon Valley" of China to take shape. Professor Chen's early struggles with the central government to set up private enterprises in Zhongguancun reflected the foresight of the visionary pioneer. Today, local authorities are actively promoting and attracting foreign enterprises to set up in the vast country, and even larger market.

In the first six months of this year, 859 foreign-funded enterprises were registered in Beijing, and utilized FDI reached USD 1.72 billion. The two figures had risen 30.6% and 68.1% respectively compared to the same period in 2003.

Preparations for the upcoming Beijing 2008 Olympic Games saw Beijing invite bids for more than 110 projects with total planned investment of USD 12 billion. Beijing city is set to embrace athletes from around the world with warmth and hospitality. Already, people from all walks of life are working hard to learn English in order to communicate and interact with the wider world.

To internationalize, Beijing has begun inviting and recruiting, for the first time, overseas professionals into its local government.

The growth of registered enterprises has given rise to many business opportunities and encouraging governmental policies. In particular, various reform measures adopted by Beijing city have greatly reduced enterprises' costs and made the investment environment even more attractive to investors. Beijing offers unique opportunities that are not found in more than 200 cities all across China.

Like all our investment guides, "Doing Business in Beijing" brings readers comprehensive investment guidelines on setting up and expanding businesses, or investing in projects, in Beijing.

With reader-friendly maps and a useful directory, this guide also highlights notable business opportunities and latest economic data to help readers unlock the secrets of doing business in China's economic, political and cultural center.

Charles Chaw C. Loong
Managing Director
China Knowledge Press

August 2004
Singapore

北京

Doing Business in BEIJING

INDUSTRY HIGHLIGHTS

DIRECTORY

BEIJING TODAY

Remaking Beijing

Beijing, the capital of China, has nearly 14 million residents and a history of more than 3,000 years. Located in the northern part of the country, it is the economic, political and cultural center of modern China and the cradle for China's scientific advancement.

Today, Beijing is said to have embarked on an economic roller-coaster ride. The city's economy has grown at a double-digit rate annually in the past five years; its GDP grew by 10.5% in 2003 with total value reaching USD 43 billion. The old winding Hutongs (narrow lanes) have been demolished or widened. Many are encircled by an expanding chessboard of urban road-flyovers. Dilapidated houses and buildings have been replaced by modern glass-paneled high-rise buildings. Notoriously overcrowded railway stations and airports of the past are being upgraded and expanded.

Beijing has successfully earned itself the honor of hosting the 2008 Olympic Games. And the "New Beijing New Olympics" logo has now become popular everywhere. The Beijing Organizing Committee for Olympic Games (BOCOG) was established in December 2001, five months after Beijing was granted host city status. The Committee currently consists of 15 departments overseeing the improvement of environmental management and handling other related affairs.

Since then, the city has entered a period where many changes abound. Preparations for the Olympics have triggered a host of development initiatives. Now that this rare historical opportunity is in hand, Beijing is seizing it to make further progress. It is channeling great effort into building the capital into a modern global cosmopolitan city.

To meet the new challenges, Beijing has designed its commercial layout and developed its service facilities to meet international standards. The features include many malls with comfortable shopping environments, and restaurants serving up exquisite Chinese delicacies.

On the economic front, there is governmental concern over the economy over-heating, the transportation network clogging up, and hikes in costs of raw materials. Consumer prices and bank lending continue to rise rapidly in the second quarter of 2004. Beijing saw gross retail sales exceed USD 21.02 billion in 2003, an increase of 11.3% over the previous year. All indications point toward a continued boom in the economy.

In striving to run the best-ever Olympic Games in history, a team of quality personnel is being put together to undertake various projects in the organization of the Games. Both from home and abroad, there is a congregation of talent and manpower in Beijing – there is no lack of domestic and international human resources to ensure the Olympic Games run smoothly.

Infamously known for dusty winds and grey skies, the city has taken great pains to enhance its environment in creating a New Beijing. Attention is also being paid to alleviating clogged-up urban traffic by improving the city's physical infrastructure. Environment-friendly energy resources have been widely advocated; new expressways have been constructed and put into use, such as Badaling Expressway, Beijing-Shenyang Expressway, Lotus Lake East Road etc; the subway has also been upgraded and extended to Line 5.

Transportation construction and management in Beijing will be aimed at providing convenient, rapid, safe, orderly and efficient transport services. The development of railways, urban roads, expressways, inter-urban transport hubs and modern administrative systems for transport operations will be accelerated to sufficiently serve transportation needs, guaranteeing Beijing's socio-economic and urban development. This will also mean that a first-class urban transport system will be ready for the Olympic Games.

Inter-provincial passenger transport routes will be increased by 15% while expressway routes will be extended by 10%. They will reach 24 provinces, municipalities and autonomous regions and satisfy demand for long distance highway passenger transport.

An inter-urban highway passenger network connecting the whole country, with Beijing as the center, comprising expressways and high-grade highways, will soon become a reality.

Brief history

Beijing is both old and young. It is the cultural cradle of the Chinese nation and also the birthplace of human civilization. It was here that the 'Peking man' lived and multiplied in primitive communities 700,000 years ago.

Beginning to take shape during the later period of the Shang Dynasty, Beijing existed as a city more than 3,000 years ago. As a matter of fact, 2005 will be the 3050th anniversary of the founding of Beijing city.

In 352 A.D (Jin Dynasty), Beijing became the capital city of the Kingdom of Yan, the first ever established by a Chinese national minority. Later, it was chosen by one dynasty after another as their capital and turned into a central city for all nationalities across the country.

From 938 to 1123, Beijing was the capital of the Liao Dynasty and called 'Yanjing'; 1153 to 1214, it was the capital of the Jin Dynasty and was called 'Zhongdu'; 1272 to 1368, Beijing was the capital of the Yuan Dynasty and was called 'Dadu'. During both the Ming (1368-1644) and Qing (1644-1911) dynasties, Beijing was the capital and called "Jingshi".

Beijing was founded and developed with the joint effort of all the Chinese nationalities from generation to generation. It is a melting pot of time-honored Oriental Civilization and Chinese cultural heritages.

As the capital of the Liao, Jin, Yuan, Ming and Qing dynasties, Beijing witnessed centuries of prosperity, many major historical events and various national achievements.

WORLD HOTELS
STEIGENBERGER RESERVATION SERVICE

Beijing Economic Indicators 2003

General

Area of territory	16,807.8 m^2
Population	14.2 million
GDP Value	USD 43.78 billion
GDP Growth Rate	10.5%
Total Fixed Asset Investment	USD 215.71 billion (+18.9%)
Total Government Financial Revenue	USD 7.16 (+18.2%)
Total Government Financial Expenditure	USD 8.92 (+17.3%)
Total Retail Sales	USD 191.67 billion (+14.5%)
Unemployment Rate	1.43% (+0.08%)

Foreign Trade

Total Trade Volume	USD 18.93 (+34.8%)
Total Exports	USD7.37 billion (+24.9%)
Total Imports	USD 11.57 billion (+42%)

Investment

Actual Foreign Direct Investment	USD 2.15 billion (+19.8%)
Investment Contract Value	USD 3.27 billion (+16.5%)
Number of Contracts Signed	1,360 (-0.7%)

Industry

GDP of Primary Industry	USD 9. 53 billion (+3.3%)
GDP of Secondary Industry	USD 129.85 billion (+11.9%)
GDP of Tertiary Industry	USD 221.82 billion (+10%)
Total Industrial Output	USD 367.72 billion (+15.9%)
Total Agricultural Value Added	1.15 billion (+3.3%)
Total Construction Value	USD 3.4 billion (+11.6%)

Consumer Market

Retail Sales of Consumer Goods	USD 23.2 billion (+14.5%)
Foodstuff	USD6 billion (+6.7%)
Clothing	USD 2.55 billion (+11.8%)
Daily Use Commodities	USD 13.7 billion (+18.9%)
Consumer Price Index	2%
Annual per capita Urban Disposable Income	USD 1,678 per year (+11.4%)
Annual per capita Rural Income	USD 785 (+10.5%)
Per Capita Living Expenses	USD 1,345 (+8.2%)
Total Sales of Vehicles	408,000 units
Total Value of Sales of Vehicles	USD3.69 billion (+51.2%)
Total Sales of Residential Property	USD 9.54 billion (+10.1%)
Expenses on Education	RMB 971 per capita (+10.3%)

Banking and Insurance

Total Bank Saving Deposits	USD2.22 billion (-7.3%)
Total Bank Loans	USD 13.7 billion (+23.6%)
Total Insurance Premium	USD 0.34 billion (+20.7%)
Total Indemnity Paid	USD 5.8 million (+2.3%)

Source: Beijing Statistics Bureau (www.bjstats.gov.cn) and Ministry of Commerce of China (www.mofcom.gov.cn)

As an ancient cultural city, Beijing has produced many eminent personalities whose achievements have added splendour to the national history and enriched the world's cultural treasure house. At the same time, many outstanding figures from the West, such as Marco Polo and Matteo Ricci from Italy, travelled to China and lived for many years in Beijing, contributing to the cultural exchanges between the East and West.

Marco Polo came to China in 1275 during the Yuan Dynasty. Marco Polo's travel experiences provided the West with one of the first glimpses into China.

Matteo Ricci came to China in 1582 and arrived in Beijing in 1601. While doing missionary work, he also introduced the Western natural sciences to China, bringing with him the 'Great Map of Ten Thousand Countries' and translating Euclid's 'Elements' into Chinese, in collaboration with the Chinese scientist Xu Guangqi.

Beijing was renamed Beiping in 1928, when the Republic of China moved its capital to Nanjing.

With the founding of the People's Republic of China in 1949, Beijing became its capital and entered a new epoch.

While Beijing has had relations with foreign countries on the principle of mutual benefit for some time, it was only in the late 1970s that Beijing came into full contact with the outside world, as a result of economic reforms and the open policy carried out throughout the country.

Today, the city is speeding up its efforts in this direction by drawing on the fruits of human civilization and learning other countries' advanced methods of management and administration, so as to achieve better and faster results in its own development.

Beijing has undergone big changes in recent years and is heading for all-round modernization. Beijing is rising as a metropolitan city, where ancient Chinese civilization meets with modern achievements of human society, creating new spirit and charm.

Beijing 2008 Olympics

On July 13, 2001, Beijing was selected by the International Olympic Committee to host the 2008 Olympic Games. Beijing's successful bid is both a triumph for the Chinese leadership and a boost to the national pride. While this poses a great challenge to the people of China, it also brings tremendous business opportunities and pushes the nation's development into the new economy.

As the host of the 2008 Olympics, Beijing will benefit considerably from massive investment spending in the pipeline and numerous job opportunities the event will create. In the run-up to 2008, Beijing plans to spend a total of USD 34 billion on the Olympic Games, including USD 22 billion earmarked for modernizing the nation's capital. In one of the most ambitious infrastructure projects so far, Beijing will build extensive Olympic-related sports venues and associated facilities, enhance its transportation and telecommunications networks and install environmental protection systems.

While a small part of the planned infrastructure projects are financed by Beijing Organizing Committee for Olympic Games (BOCOG), the rest are financed by the Chinese National Government, Beijing Municipal Government and private investors within and outside China.

To meet international standards, the design, construction and management of most of the Olympic-related infrastructure facilities, including the Olympic Park, have been put up for international bidding. Action plans have been drawn up for the overall organization of the Olympic Games and nine specific planning areas.

The hosting of the Olympics will also have a significant impact on generating awareness of Beijing city, and will help accelerate the growth of its tourism industry. Judging from the experience of previous host cities of the Olympics, particularly in the case of Sydney, tourist arrivals in Beijing could increase by 20% during the year of the Games, which would provide a strong boost to retail sales in the city. According to rough

Revenue Generated by Sydney Olympics 2000

Source: IOC

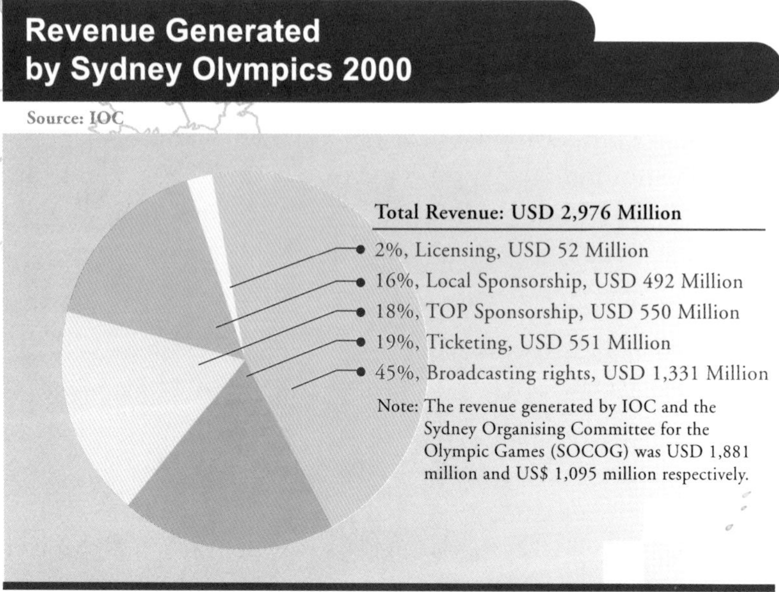

estimates, increased infrastructure spending and the gain in tourism income would add an average of about two to three percentage points per year to Beijing's GDP growth in the next seven years. In 2003, Beijing's economy had grown by 10.5%.

More resources and talent needed

Over the next few years, Beijing will commit more resources and talents to prepare itself for the hosting of a successful Olympic Games. Opportunities abound for a wide range of businesses in the run-up to 2008.

After the strategic preparatory phases which were completed in June 2003, plans for the construction of Olympic facilities, infrastructure and marketing programs have been put into operation. The development phase is scheduled for the period between July 2003 and June 2006. During this period, the task set forth in the "10th Five-year Plan" will be completed. The construction of Olympic venues, other related facilities and preparation in other areas will be in full swing.

By June 2006, major construction projects involving Olympic venues and facilities will be completed and basic preparations finished. The improvement and operation phase will run from July 2006 to the opening of the 2008 Olympic Games. During this phase, venues will be examined and improved; and test events would be conducted to ensure smooth operations. All services should run smoothly.

Key infrastructure projects

The infrastructure projects in the pipeline for Beijing 2008 Olympics will translate into a host of investment opportunities for the business community.

Natural environment and infrastructure development

Considerable improvement in the ecological environment of the city is needed to achieve the goal of a green Olympics. Focus will be placed on the prevention of air pollution and the protection of potable water sources. This will be done through economic restructuring, increased use of cleaner high quality energy resources, establishing a more restrictive emission standard and strengthening ecological protection and construction.

Besides preventing pollution by coal burning, pollution by automobile emission has to be reduced as well. From 2003, a standard parallel to the European Standard II regarding the pollutant emission of new vehicles has been in place, and before 2008, a standard parallel to the European Standard III will be put into effect.

By 2007, 90% of all buses and 70% of all taxis will use clean fuel. The development of new technologies, such as electrical automobiles, will be pushed forward. Stricter control on particle pollution will also be required at all construction sites to meet requirements for environmental protection.

Open grounds in urban areas will also be covered by trees or grass, and the cleaning of main motorways in the urban area will be mechanized. Emission of industrial pollutants will be reduced by exercising control on total emission volume. All key enterprises will be required to practise clean production and introduce the ISO 14001 environment management system in their offices. Special attention will be given to pollution control in metallurgical, chemical, electricity and cement industries.

In an effort to move pollutant-emitting enterprises from the urban districts, by 2008, the chemical industrial zone in the Southeast suburbs and some 200 polluting enterprises within the Fourth Ring Road will be relocated. The Capital Iron & Steel Plant will reduce its steel production by 2 million tons and its production structure will be readjusted.

Urban transport development and management

Construction of new road networks and improvement of traffic management in Beijing will be promoted. These projects will aim at providing convenient, quick, safe, orderly, efficient services. The construction of the rail transport system, urban road transport systems, inter-city transport systems, and city transport hubs will be accelerated. These will provide favorable conditions for further socioeconomic and urban development of Beijing as well as first-class urban transportation services for the Olympic Games.

Construction of the urban rail transport network comprises such projects as Beijing Urban Light Rail, Ba-Tong Subway Line, Subway Line No. 5, Subway Line No. 4, Olympic Subway Line, and the fast rail from Dongzhimen to Beijing Capital International Airport. By 2008, 148.5 km of new rail transport will be added, reaching a total of 202 km.

New expressways including the Fifth Ring Road, the Sixth Ring Road, Beijing-Miyun Road, and a number of first and second grade motorways will be completed. By 2008, the length of expressways in the whole city will reach 718 km, motorways will reach 14,700 km, and road density will reach 87.3 km per km^2. The density of urban streets will increase in the course of renovating the old city.

By 2007, the construction and expansion of 318 km of urban streets will be completed. In order to satisfy special demands before, during and after the Olympic Games as well as the needs of the city's future development, the Beijing Capital International Airport will be expanded, making it a large hub for international as well as domestic air traffic.

Development of IT systems

In applying IT extensively to urban development to build a "Digital Beijing", focus will be on the "Digital Olympics" program and the building of a strong telecommunications infrastructure and network system, in order to create a favorable IT environment and provide excellent information services. By 2008, information services will be inexpensive, rich in content, free of language barriers, and available to anyone, at any time and anywhere.

Some landmark IT buildings will be built, which can serve as multi-functional centers for the Olympic Games. To ensure access to radio broadcasts of news and information on the Olympic Games, overall planning and management of radio frequencies will be strengthened. A technical support system for radio management will be established in Beijing to facilitate the overall improvement of frequency management, radio signal monitoring, radio interference analysis and radio equipment testing ability. Comprehensive measures will be taken to provide a clean electromagnetic environment so as to ensure the smooth operation of all radio communication devices. Advanced communications facilities will be built to provide a broadband digital communications system that is reliable, flexible, expandable, reusable, and adaptable to new technologies.

Focus will also be placed on the development of the software for management systems and information service systems related to the Olympic Games. Weather forecasting and monitoring will be reinforced to provide timely and accurate meteorological services for large-scale gatherings and sports events. E-commerce services covering ticketing, the tourism, merchandizing, shopping, projects tendering, and procurement will also be provided. Artificial intelligence technologies will be used in an effort to overcome the "language barrier" during the Olympic Games. Smartcard technology will also be used to provide participants with safe and convenient services in accreditation, security check and payment, etc. A card-based payment network and a favorable card-based payment environment will be established. In addition, facilities will be provided for various personalized information services.

Sports venue

37 stadiums are planned for use for the 28 sporting events in the 2008 Olympic Games. Olympic venues will be situated in six cities: Beijing, Shenyang, Qinhuangdao, Tianjin, Qingdao and Shanghai. 27 sports

Olympic Green

The Olympic Green, located on the north end of the central axis of the city, occupies an area of 1,135 hectares, which contains a forest park of 680 hectares and a central area of 405 hectares for the Games. The Olympic Green, supplemented by the venues and facilities for the Asian Games, will boast convenient traffic systems, high population, good urban infrastructure, and well developed service facilities for commercial and cultural activities. In the planning of the Olympic Green, emphases are placed on the long-term development of the city and the material and cultural needs of the residents, making it a multi-functional public center for sports, meetings, exhibitions, entertainment and shopping, with broad spaces and landscaped surroundings.

The major venues to be built in the Olympic Green include:

National Stadium

Seating capacity: 80,000 people

It will be the venue for the opening and closing ceremonies, athletics and football events.

National Indoor Stadium

Seating capacity: 18,000 people,

It will be the venue for gymnastics, handball, and volleyball events.

National Swimming Center

Seating capacity: 18,000 people

It will be the main venue for swimming competitions. It will serve as a public sports center after the Olympic Games.

Other related facilities to be built in the Olympic Green include:

Olympic Village

With complete supporting facilities, the Olympic Village will contain 360,000 m^2 of apartments available to the athletes, coaches and team officials during the Games. These apartments will be sold as commercial housing after the Games.

Other facilities

A number of other buildings will also be planned and built in the Green, which will serve as the competition venue for table tennis, badminton, fencing and wrestling and as the Main Press Center (MPC) and the International Broadcasting Center (IBC). After the Games, these buildings will be turned into convention and exhibition centers and cultural facilities, such as the Capital Youth Palace and Urban Planning Exhibition Hall, etc. In addition, other supporting service facilities will also be available for accommodation, commerce, and offices, etc.

events will take place in 32 stadiums located in Beijing. Sailing and preliminary matches for football will take place in five venues outside Beijing.

The 32 stadiums in Beijing are sited in the following areas: Olympic Green Western Community District, University District and Northern Tourist District. The whole layout is described as “one center with three districts” (literal Chinese translation).

The Olympic Green will be the “main and central district” where the Games will take place. With 13 sports venues for the Olympic Games, it is the area where major sports events will take place and 70% of the gold medals will be awarded.

Nine stadiums are located in the “Western Community District”. The new project, Wukesong Sports Center, will be a place for residents in Southwest Beijing to conduct their cultural and sports activities. Four stadiums are located in the “University District” including the Capital Stadium which will be used by universities and the local community for their cultural and sports activities. Two stadiums, situated in the "Northern Tourist District" including Beijing Countryside Horse Racetrack, will try to facilitate tourism in the suburban area after the Olympic Games. In other areas, four stadiums will be expanded and renovated, e.g. Workers' Stadium, in order to create a favorable environment for the cultural and sporting needs of the community's residents.

Investment policies

Due to higher investment demand, longer construction cycles and lower rating standards, the city government will finance many infrastructure construction projects. This creates significant barriers for investors from home and abroad, resulting in a large gap between infrastructure construction and the needs of local economic development.

In order to change the status and accelerate deregulation in infrastructure construction, Beijing Municipal Government has recently established a mechanism granting appropriate compensation to domestic and foreign investors who invest in infrastructure construction in the city. Meanwhile, the prices of infrastructure products, which were impractical, will be rectified gradually.

1. Diversified investment sources. Any business that has the financial resources to enter into the industry, no matter whether it is state-owned or private, domestic or international enterprise, may seek to become an investor in certain infrastructure projects in Beijing. For some infrastructure projects, competitive bidding will be adopted in the selection of investment partners.
2. In case the current rate is unable to reach the designated level, favorable policies will be offered to those infrastructure projects financed by enterprises selected via competitive bidding. Meanwhile, franchise rights may be granted to enterprises by the government. The preferential policy involves exempting investors from some taxes and charges in selected infrastructural projects.

Financial Center
中关村 金融中心
Zhongguancun Financial Center
Tower A is ready for you
World-renowned architects KPF, first project in Beijing
150 meters, West Beijing's tallest office tower
At 100,000 m², ZGC Square is home to Asia's largest garden plaza
Tower C of ZGC Financial Center --an independent commercial space
Hotline
8610-82626622
8610-82628822
www.sciencepark.com.cn
Developer: Beijing Science Park Development Co. Ltd.
Architect: Kohn Pederson Fox Associates PC
效果图

3. In order to substantively carry out preferential policies for infrastructure construction, there is the need to ensure reasonably attractive returns to investors who invest in infrastructure projects in Beijing. The Beijing Municipal Government will adopt the following measures:
   a) The government will establish a compensation fund to fill in the gap between the contract price and the government-set price. The compensating approach will see the government define the quality of services/products, technical specifications as well as the production capacity. It will undertake to purchase, and determine the compensation as per the contract price. The government will take into account the demand patterns of end-users, and set the prices of services/products accordingly.
   b) In order to balance construction funds or budget, depending on specific infrastructure projects, the Beijing Development and Planning Commission will, after substantive study in collaboration with related authorities (such as urban planning and land administration) propose the granting of rights to investors to use land specially allocated for development and construction of high profit returns projects.
   c) Upon examination by the relevant authorities and approval by the Municipal Government, fixed-term franchise rights will be granted to the investors on operating such business activities as advertisements in the infrastructure projects financed and operated by them. Investors will also be encouraged to develop culture and sports businesses, tourism and entertainment in conjunction with the infrastructure projects under construction.
   d) Under the condition that is statutorily permitted, the government will assist investors in applying for loans from foreign governments and international financial organizations etc and support them in capital securitization.
   e) For projects that need a large amount of investment that is difficult to be recovered in the short term, the government may be involved in the investment and operation by contributing a certain proportion of capital stocks.
   f) The government will coordinate various public facilities for

investors during project construction and operation.

4. In order to provide immediate access to infrastructure projects and other investment-bidding projects, the Beijing Municipal Government has assigned the Beijing Development and Planning Commission and the Municipal Economic Information Center to undertake and develop, respectively, the "Beijing Investment Platform". Its main functions are to facilitate on-line inquiries about Beijing's investment bidding projects and related policies and regulations as well as to publicize bid invitation information to attract interested investors and enhance the transparency of government contract-awarding.

Olympic marketing plan

The Beijing Organizing Committee for the Olympic Games (BOCOG) launched on 1 September 2003 the marketing plan of the Beijing 2008 Olympic Games. The marketing plan of Beijing Olympics forms the basis for both domestic and overseas companies to take part in the broadcasting, ticketing, sponsorship and licensing programs of the Beijing 2008 Olympic Games

The marketing plan of the Olympics is actually a partnership between the Olympic Movement and the business community. While the International Olympic Committee (IOC) manages a series of Olympic marketing programs to solicit support for the Olympic Movement and the Olympic Games in terms of technology and capital, the global business community also finds the marketing programs an effective marketing platform for their companies.

Television broadcast partnership - The Olympic Games is the most-watched sporting event in the world. Since the Seoul Olympics in 1988, the number of countries televising the Games has increased from 160 to 220 in the 2000 Sydney Olympics. The long-term broadcasting rights strategy developed by the IOC is now the most important source of the Olympic marketing revenue.

Olympic Games ticketing - In 2000, more than 6.7 million tickets were sold in the Sydney Olympics. USD 551 million in revenue was generated.

Corporate sponsorship - Sponsorship is a relationship between the Olympic Movement and corporations. There are different levels of sponsorship entitling companies to different marketing rights in various regions, category exclusivity and the use of designated Olympic images and symbols. Companies can also become suppliers to the Olympic Movement, providing the Olympics with the necessary support and products. In return, suppliers at different levels are granted the corresponding marketing rights.

Olympic licensing - Licensing programs are agreements that grant rights of use of Olympic marks, imagery, themes, including emblems and mascots, to companies to produce products commemorating the Olympic Games. The company, or licensee, pays a royalty fee for the rights of use which is usually between 10% and 15% of product sales revenues.

Three-tier administrative structure of Olympic marketing – IOC, OCOGs and NOCs

The administration of Olympic marketing is a three-tier structure, each having its own corresponding marketing program within specific boundaries.

The highest level is the International Olympic Committee (IOC). The IOC, as the holder of the rights to the Olympic Games and the Olympic symbols, is responsible for the overall direction and management of Olympic marketing programs. Marketing programs directly under the IOC are those worldwide programs such as worldwide sponsorship and broadcasting.

The second tier is the Organizing Committee for the Olympic Games (OCOGs) and the third tier is the National Olympic Committees (NOCs). Under the direction of the IOC, the OCOG manages the Olympic Games marketing programs that are targeted at the Olympic host country. The NOCs manage national Olympic marketing programs that are targeted at consumers in the home countries.

The three tiers of Olympic marketing structure take charge of different types of programs.

1. Sponsorship

There are three levels of sponsorship programs.

Worldwide sponsorship, also known as the Olympic Partner Program (TOP), was created and is directly managed by the IOC. TOP partners are multinational organizations which will provide direct support, services or expertise for the staging of the Games. Agreements with these multinational organizations are on a four-year term, including one Olympic Winter Games and one Summer Games. The TOP partners, in return, are granted exclusive marketing rights, including the use of all Olympic imagery, and opportunities within their designated product category. They may exercise these rights on a worldwide basis.

Olympic Games sponsorship, also known as OCOG sponsorship, is managed by the OCOG under the direction of the IOC. These programs are not for implementation worldwide, but are targeted within the host country of the Olympic Games. Olympic Games sponsors, or OCOG sponsors, are granted marketing rights within the host country or territory only.

National sponsorship, or NOC sponsorship, is managed by local Olympic Committees that support sports development in their country and their Olympic teams. These programs grant marketing rights within the NOC country or territory only.

So far, nine international corporations have signed contracts to become IOC's TOP partners. They are Coca-Cola, General Electric, John Hancock, Kodak, Panasonic, Samsung Electronics, Schlumberger, Swatch and Visa International. Reportedly, IOC hopes to invite more companies (including Chinese enterprises) to participate in the partner program in addition to the existing nine TOP partners.

As for sponsors, the Beijing Olympics marketing plan has not placed any special restrictions on their industry category. Sponsors can come from any industry provided that the category does not contradict the Olympic spirit and is in line with the actual needs of the Games and the marketing rules. However, according to common practice, there is usually only one sponsor in each category, creating exclusive marketing opportunities for the sponsoring company. Sponsors to BOCOG can enjoy various rights and benefits, including:

- Use of BOCOG and/or COC marks and designations for the purposes of advertising and marketing promotions;
- Product/service exclusivity in specific categories;
- Hospitality opportunities at the Olympic Games;
- Preferred option to purchase TV ad space and billboards during the Games period;
- Preferred option to purchase sponsoring opportunities of cultural programs and signature events such as the Torch Relay; and
- BOCOG sponsor recognition programs and acknowledgements.

The following criteria will be applied in the process of selecting sponsors:

Corporate strength and accountability – Companies must be prestigious enterprises, enjoying market leadership, boasting good growth prospects, financial strength, and the ability to generate adequate cash flow in order to meet the sponsorship investment requirements.

Quality and reliability of product/service – Companies should be able to supply sufficient top-notch and reliable products/technology/service as required to ensure the sound operation of the Games.

Financial pledge/investment – Companies should make competitive financial offers, which is one of the key criteria for selecting sponsors.

Brand alignment – Companies must possess a good reputation and social image, identify with and boost the ideals of the Olympic Movement and the concepts of the Beijing Olympic Games. In addition, their products should be environment-friendly.

BOCOG will recruit sponsors in different ways, including open recruitment, selective recruitment (i.e. sending out invitations to companies satisfying the necessary technical requirements) and individual recruitment (i.e. direct negotiations with individual companies).

2. Licensing

Similar to the sponsorship program, the licensing program also has a three-tier structure.

The first tier is the IOC licensing program. The IOC operates a limited worldwide licensing program in certain categories such as film, video games and other multimedia opportunities.

The second tier is OCOG's granting of licensees the rights to use OCOG or Olympic Games marks to create souvenirs or merchandise relating to the Olympic Games for sale to the public. The merchandise is usually of a festive or commemorative nature, such as pins, T-shirts and caps.

The third tier is NOC's granting of licensees the rights to use NOC or national Olympic team marks to create souvenirs relating to the national Olympic team.

The licensing program of the Beijing Olympics will serve to promote the Olympic image with an appealing blend of Chinese culture and Beijing characteristics. Major licensed product categories include sporting goods, cultural products, leisure goods, arts and crafts, and souvenirs. The program will adopt a segmented market strategy, ensuring that Beijing Olympics-licensed products will be available in a broad range of styles and prices targeting different consumer groups. Where fees are concerned, licensees have to pay a minimum guarantee and a royalty advance to BOCOG.

BOCOG will take into account the following factors in selecting licensees:

- Licensees will be selected based on market research, qualification assessment, and first-hand investigation;

- The overall investigation will cover financial status, production capacity, quality control, design ability, environmental protection, anti-counterfeit measures, marketing strategy, distribution channels, after-sale services, logistics, etc;
- Licensees should have the financial ability to pay guarantees and royalties on time.

Licensees should maintain good performance as the contract term may vary and contract renewal is subject to prior performance. This will help achieve the "Made-in-China = High Quality" objective.

Beijing Organizing Committee of the Games of the xxix Olympiad (BOCOG)

Office: 24 Dongsishitiao Street, Beijing, China, 100007

Tel: (8610) 6528 2009

Fax: (8610) 6528 2008

Email: 2008@beijing-olympic.org.cn

Olympic lodging agreement

The Beijing Organizing Committee for the Games has signed the Olympic Lodging Agreement with seven five-star hotels. They are Beijing Hotel, China World Hotel, Grand Hotel Beijing, Hong Kong Macau Center Swissotel, Beijing International Hotel, Kunlun Hotel and Crowne Plaza Park View Wuzhou Beijing.

According to the agreement, the seven hotels will provide accommodation to accredited people from the Olympic Family, the sponsors and the media. At the time of the Games, the seven hotels are to keep a total of 3,500 rooms available to BOCOG while accommodating other guests.

Currently, Beijing has more than 90,000 rooms in 600 star hotels, not including more than half a million beds in about 4,000 hotels, hostels, inns and training centers that are not star-graded. Beijing committed itself in its bidding documents that it will have 130,000 rooms in 800 star-graded hotels by 2008.

Beijing's star hotel rooms were set to increase by 7% every year till 2008. The additional rooms will be made available by renovating and expanding existing rooms and building new ones. It can be expected that the city will provide proper and adequate accommodation for all of the estimated 800,000 athletes, journalists, spectators and tourists who will come to Beijing for the Games.

GEOGRAPHY

Location

Situated in the northeastern part of China and elevated 43.5m above sea level, Beijing is an independently administered municipal district. The climate in Beijing is defined as "continental monsoon", with cold and dry winters. January is the coldest month (-4°C), while July is the warmest (26°C). Winter usually begins towards the end of October. The summer months, June to August, are wet and hot, contributing to about 40% of the annual precipitation.

Lying in the northern part of the North China Plain, Beijing is surrounded by mountains on the west, the north and the northeast. Topographically, the northeastern part of the city is high, the southwestern part is low, and the southeastern plain tilts gradually downward to the Bohai Sea.

Major rivers flowing through Beijing include Yongding River, Chaobai River, North Canal and Juma River, originating in the northeastern mountainous areas of Beijing. These rivers flow through rugged mountains towards the southeastern plain of Beijing, finally joining the Bohai Sea. The southeast section of Beijing is 150 km away from the Bohai Sea.

As the capital city of China, Beijing is also at the center of the national transportation and communication network. There are eight national truck railways radiating from Beijing in all directions, reaching Shanghai (1,660 km), Harbin (1,490 km), Guangzhou (2,650 km), and Urumchi (3,840 km) directly.

Topography

Beijing is situated at the northern edge of the North China Plains; the territory descends from northwest to southeast. Slopes of the Xishan, Jundushan and Yanshan Mountain surround the city's west, north and northeast. Badaling, a part of Jundushan Mountain is famous for the section of Great Wall within the municipality. The peak of the municipality, Mt. Dongling, stands at an altitude of 2,303 m, sharing a border with Hebei in the west. Hilly lands, with a total area of 10,417.5 km^2, account for nearly 62% of the municipal territory. The area supplies mineral deposits like coal and iron ore, as well as construction materials like granite and marble.

The southeast of Beijing, Beijing Crescent Plain, is a piece of alluvial land between 20-60 m above sea level, tilting gradually to the sea. The Peking Man, who was discovered at Zhoukoudian in the southwest, lived here 230,000-600,000 years ago. With an area covering 6,390.3 km^2, the plain makes up 38% of Beijing. The average altitude of the urban area is about 44 m.

Area

The total land area of Beijing is 16,807.8 km^2, less than 0.18% of the national total or roughly three times of Shanghai. This includes 16 districts and two counties. Total urban built-up area is now 490 km^2, or 2.9% of the city's total.

The city center of Beijing is defined by a set of ring roads. The 62.5 km^2 downtown area is bounded by the 2nd Ring Road in the east and west and by the city moat in its northeast stretch. The area encircled by the 3rd Ring Road is about 158 km^2, and that by the 4th Ring Road is approximately 290 km^2.

According to the Beijing urban development master plan, the total planned area of the city will be 750 km^2, up to Dingfuzhuang in the east, Shijingshan in the west, Nanyuan in the south and Qinghe in the north.

Population

Some 14.2 million people are registered as permanent residents of Beijing. These, plus a floating population of an estimated 3 million, make the population density in the urban sector of the municipality 28,300 people per km^2.

The local population consists of all the 56 ethnic groups of the Chinese nation. Buddhism, Taoism, Islam, Catholicism and Christianity are the more popular religions in the Chinese capital, of which Buddhism, Taoism and Islam have exerted a great influence on the history and culture of Beijing. There are 103 sites for religious worshipping in the city, and 320,000 Beijing residents embrace some religion or other.

People's livelihood

In 2003, disposable incomes for Beijing residents averaged USD 1,786 per capita, an increase of 11.4% over the previous year. With advancements in the economy and overall improvement in living standards, Beijing people's demand for intellectual and cultural activities is constantly on the rise. Many of them now pay more attention to self-improvement than in the past. For this reason, participation in various technical training courses has become increasingly popular. In recent years, there has been a great increase in per capita expenses on education and recreational activities. Domestic travel in China as well as outbound tours are becoming increasingly popular.

Healthcare and social security

In the arena of healthcare and medical services, Beijing has attained the advanced standards of developing countries. Doctors in Beijing have scored several world-leading achievements in medicine, and their fields of practice include neurosurgery, ophthalmology, otolaryngology and orthopedics.

Along with the economic restructuring in urban areas, Beijing has embarked on a comprehensive reform of its social security system, and has instituted the old-age pension system, the unemployment insurance system and the health insurance schemes for urban retirees.

Currently, some 51.1% of Beijing families have insured themselves against various personal risks. Among them, 69.6% have taken out personal insurance accounts, 53.4% endowment insurance, 47.4% life insurance, and 38.3% and 29.3%, insurance against major diseases and accidents respectively.

Culture and education

Beijing is home to a great number of top writers and artists. Many of its excellent films and TV programs, plays and literary works have won various top prizes in the country. It boasts first-class museums and many valuable cultural relics. It has reaped remarkable achievements in art, mass culture, cultural market and facilities building, journalism, radio, and television broadcasting, etc.

Beijing's education system has developed well. Currently, there are 73 institutes of higher learning with over 457,353 students.

Over the past two decades, schools of higher learning in Beijing have produced nearly 620,000 graduates. In basic education, there are 977 high schools with 630,000 students and 1652 primary schools with nearly 546,530 pupils. The figures suggest that 99.95% of the younger population enjoy proper education.

Climate

Beijing belongs to the warm temperate zone with semi-humid continental monsoon climate characteristics. Summer is usually hot and rainy, winter cold and dry, and spring and autumn are short. Average annual temperature ranges from 10 to 12°C. Average temperature in January and July ranges from 7 to 4°C, and 25 to 26°C, respectively. Extreme temperatures recorded are 42°C highest and 27.4°C lowest.

Rainfall occurs unevenly during the year, but 75% of precipitation occurs in summer, usually with rainstorms in July and August. Annual rainfall averages 600 mm, making Beijing one of the wettest areas in North China. However, the southern part of Beijing is sometimes afflicted by drought, flood, dust and sand. Mud avalanches sometimes occur in the north-western mountainous area during summer hard rains. The frost-free period in Beijing lasts 180-200 days beginning from early April.

GOVERNMENT

Communist Party of China

As stated in the Constitution of the People's Republic of China – the state's fundamental law – China is a socialist state led by the Communist Party of China (CPC).

Founded in 1921, the CPC had led the Chinese people to overthrow the rule of imperialism, feudalism and bureaucrat-capitalism in the past, and had defended the country's independence and security since the founding of P. R. China in 1949. In an era of socialist economic development, CPC's mission focuses on developing a prosperous and competitive economy. The Third Plenary Session of the 11th Central Committee of the Communist Party of China, held in December 1978, formally determined shifting the party's focus to economic modernization and set the policy for reform and opening up to the outside world.

In Beijing, the Municipal Committee of CPC is the paramount authority. It exercises great influence and power in the city's political and economic developmental progress, and oversees social stability and security. The Municipal Congress of the Party is usually held once every five years and exercises power via its Standing Committee when it is not in session. Accordingly, there is a committee or sub-committee in every district or county.

The mayor of Beijing is Mr Wang Qishan. He was made deputy secretary of the CPC Beijing Municipal Committee and acting mayor of Beijing in

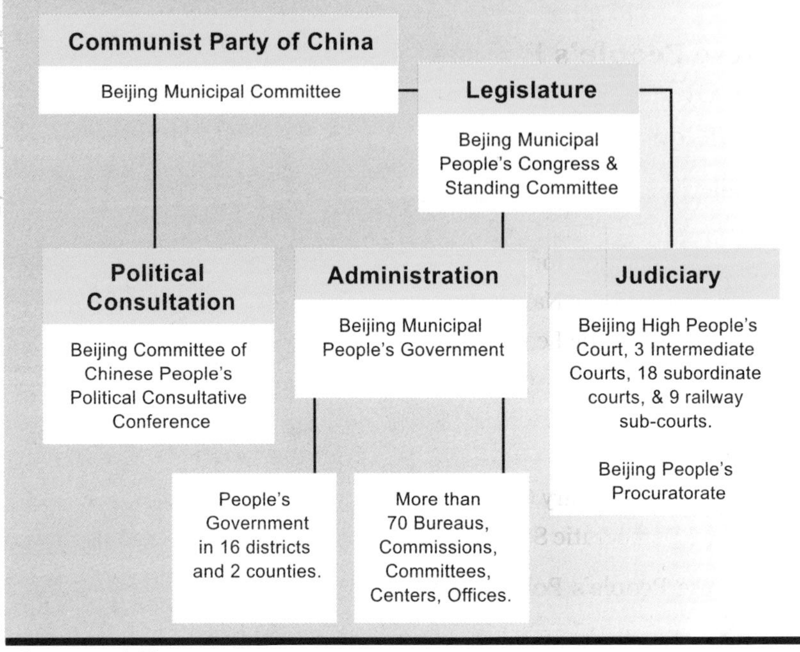

Source: www.beijing.gov.cn

April 2003. In 2004, he was appointed mayor by the Beijing Municipal People's Congress. He is also chairman of the organizing committee for

Beijing's new mayor

Wang Qishan, 55, was appointed Beijing Mayor by the Beijing Municipal People's Congress in 2004.

Born in July 1948, Wang is a native of Tianzhen in Shanxi Province, north China. He joined the Communist Party of China (CPC) in 1983. In 1969, he was sent to the countryside to work as a farmer in the neighboring Shaanxi Province. He served the Shaanxi Provincial Museum in 1971-1973, graduated from the History Department of Northwest China University in 1976, and began to work in the Institute of Modern Chinese History of the Chinese Academy of Social Sciences in 1979.

Wang worked in the rural policy and development research centers of the Secretariat of CPC Central Committee and the State Council between 1982 and 1986. He served as general manager and Party secretary of the China Rural Trust and Investment Company in 1988. He was appointed as vice president of the Construction Bank of China in 1989, and the Beijing Olympic Games.

Chinese People's Political Consultative Conference (CPPCC)

Besides the CPC, there are also eight non-Communist democratic parties ("participating political parties") in China, each with an established committee in Beijing:

- China Association for the Promotion of Democracy
- China Democratic National Construction Association
- China Democratic League
- Chinese Peasants and Workers' Democratic Party
- China Zhigong Party
- Jiusan Society
- China Revolutionary Committee of the Kuomintang
- Taiwan Democratic Self-governance League

The Chinese People's Political Consultative Conference (CPPCC) is the main political platform for these parties to communicate with the ruling party, express their political concerns, exercise democratic practices and participate in policy-making activities related to economic and political reforms.

became vice governor of the People's Bank of China in 1993. Wang became president of the Construction Bank of China in 1994 and was elected president of the Chinese Investment Society in 1995.

Two years later, Wang became a member of the Standing Committee of the CPC Guangdong Provincial Committee, and was elected vice governor of Guangdong Province in 1998. He was appointed director of the Economic Restructuring Office of the State Council in 2000, and secretary of the CPC Hainan Provincial Committee in 2002-2003. He was elected chairman of the Standing Committee of the Hainan Provincial People's Congress in January 2003. In April that year, Wang was made acting mayor of Beijing and deputy secretary of the CPC Beijing Municipal Committee. He is also chairman of the organizing committee for the Beijing Olympic Games slated for 2008. He is an alternate member of the 15th CPC Central Committee and member of the 16th CPC Central Committee.

Source: Xinhuanet

The Beijing Committee of CPPCC currently has 718 members, including CPC members, members of the eight democratic parties and other independent individuals. There are 10 specific sub-committees, 2 offices and 1 administrative department set up under Beijing Committee of CPPCC.

Website: www.bjzx.gov.cn/

People's Congress

The People's Congress is the nation's legislative body and constitutes the basic political system of China. Administrative organs, the judiciaries and the procuratorates at various levels are established by People's Congresses, to which they are answerable and by which they are supervised.

Beijing Municipal People's Congress (BMPC) is the organ of state power of Beijing. It is elected every five years and usually meets once a year. The Standing Committee of BMPC convenes meetings. When the Standing Committee deems it necessary or 1/5 of the members request for it, meetings can also be called at short notice. However, meetings can only be held when more than 2/3 of the representatives are present. The BMPC exercises local legislative power. Its functions include:

- formulating and promulgating local rules and regulations;
- ensuring that the Constitution, state laws, administrative regulations and the decisions made at the state level are abided by and implemented, and that state plans and budget are carried out;
- reviewing and approving Beijing's economic and social development plan, municipal budget and reports concerning its implementation;
- discussing and deciding on key issues pertaining to politics, economy, science, culture, public health, environmental and resource protection, civil affairs, and ethnic minorities;
- electing or recalling chairman, vice chairmen, secretary general and members of the Standing Committee of BMPC, mayor, vice mayors of Beijing Government, president of Beijing High Court,

procurator-general of Beijing High Procuratorate, and municipal representatives to the National People's Congress;

- hearing and reviewing the work reports made by the Standing Committee of BMPC, the Municipal Government, Beijing High Court and Beijing High Procuratorate, and modifying or annulling inappropriate decisions made by them.

The Standing Committee of BMPC consists of the chairman, vice chairmen, secretary-general and a number of members, who are elected from among BMPC members and should not hold posts in other state administrative organs, judiciaries or procuratorates. They serve five-year terms and meet at least once every two months. During the adjournment of BMPC, the Standing Committee exerts power on its behalf. The Standing Committee comprises eight working committees with specific functions, an administrative department and three offices.

BMPC candidates, who must be above the age of 18, are nominated on a constituency basis. Political parties and people's organizations can also recommend candidates on a collective or individual basis. The minimum number of BMPC members is 350 with every additional member per 25,000 in the increased population. The current 11th BMPC has a total of 763 members.

Website: www.bjrd.gov.cn/

Government agencies

The Beijing Municipal People's Government is the administrative organ of the capital city. It exercises administrative functions via various bureaus and commissions. The People's Government has more than 50 bureaus and commissions under its charge, and leads 18 subordinate governments at district or county level.

Website: www.beijing.gov.cn

Economic Development Administration

Beijing Development and Planning Committee

After some adjustments and reorganization of its duties in 2002, the Committee now takes care of the following:

- drawing up medium- and long-term strategic plans for urban, economic, and social development;
- setting targets and forecasts, and supervising annual economic and social development;
- coordinating financial organizations in Beijing;
- planning and financing key public projects and the total volume of fixed asset investment, approving and reporting to the State Council regarding large-scale constructions;
- making policies for better allocation of FDI inflows, approving foreign-funded projects and reporting to the State Council;
- analyzing demand-supply conditions, planning key agricultural exports and imports etc.

Beijing Development and Planning Committee
2 Fuxinmen South Avenue, Xicheng District
Tel: (8610) 6641 0901
Email: gmbgs@bjpc.gov.cn
Website: www.bjpc.gov.cn/

Beijing Economic Commission

The Commission has also undergone some changes in its functions recently. Its major responsibilities now include:

- promulgating and implementing industrial development laws, rules, regulations and policies at municipal level in order to conform to national industrial policies;
- studying, formulating and adjusting municipal industrial structure;
- setting targets for the development of industry; coordinating supplies of energy and basic materials; handling key problems encountered in local industry development;
- guiding the investment of industrial enterprises and commercial

banks; announcing industrial catalogue of investment regularly; organizing and implementing key municipal projects;

- directing inflows of foreign investments and loans in local industry; encouraging local enterprises to engage in international operations and economic cooperation;
- encouraging local high-tech, energy-saving, and pro-environment industry development;
- guiding and monitoring state-owned enterprises in restructuring or selling shares to foreign investors etc.

Beijing Economic Commission
4 Gongti North Road
Caoyang District, Beijing 100027
Tel: (8610) 8523 5626
Fax: (8610) 8523 5889
Email: bjec@bjec.gov.cn
Website: www.bjec.gov.cn/

Beijing Industrial & Commercial Administration (BICA)

The BICA is responsible for market supervision and administration of trademarks and contracts in Beijing. It currently administers more than 290,000 state-owned and collective enterprises, 130,000 private companies, 8,000 foreign-invested enterprises (FIEs), 7,000 representative offices of foreign companies, and over 280,000 sole proprietors. The scope of duties of the BICA includes:

- promulgating and implementing industrial and commercial administration laws, rules, regulations and policies;
- registration of industrial and commercial enterprises or sole proprietors, checking and ratifying registered company names, and issuing certificates upon approval;
- monitoring misdemeanors in local market, such as monopoly, illegal competition, fraud, smuggling, etc;
- dealing with customers' complaints and protects customers' rights;
- monitoring and administrating advertisement distribution and the companies' conducts;

- protecting copyright of registered brands, monitoring the use and printing of brands etc.

Beijing Industrial & Commercial Administration
Tel: (8610) 8269 0904, 8269 0900
Website: www.hd315.gov.cn/

Beijing Commerce Commission

The Commission looks after commodity circulation and social services in the municipality. Its functions are as follows:

- studies, drafts and implements local rules, regulations and policies related to commerce;
- does market research and prepares and implements developmental plans for commerce; analyzes and forecasts market situation of commodity circulation, restaurants, and social services, and disseminates relevant information;
- administers auctions, circulation of used products, leasing, recycling and large-scale trading fairs and exhibitions;
- encourages innovative ways in marketing;
- guides foreign investment, trade and technology transfer in commerce etc.

Beijing Commerce Commission
3 Taijichang Avenue
Dongcheng District, Beijing 100744
Tel: (8610) 6308 8189
Fax: (8610) 6512 4791
Email: bjsw@bjsw.gov.cn
Website: www.bjsw.gov.cn/

Beijing Municipal Foreign Economic Relations & Trade Commission

For foreign investors who want to set up business in Beijing, the Commission is the most important authority to be acquainted with. In general, the Commission does the following:

- implements laws, regulations and policies related to foreign investment;

- formulates strategic plans on FDI utilization;
- reviews applications of foreign-funded projects, approves the establishment of FIEs (except financial institutions);
- administers foreign economic cooperation and import/export of technology;
- examines and permits local enterprises' right for foreign trade and allocates relevant quotas;
- oversees and coordinates Customs operations in Beijing, and drafts relevant rules and regulations for Beijing;
- reviews overseas trips of municipal delegation and invites foreign businessmen to Beijing.

Beijing Municipal Foreign Economic Relations & Trade Commission
190 Chaonei Avenue
Beijing 100010
Tel: (8610) 6523 6688
Email: bjfetc@bjfetc.gov.cn
Website: www.bjfetc.gov.cn/

Beijing Foreign Investment Service Center

The Center was established in 1988 by the Beijing Municipal Government as a non-profit organization providing comprehensive and professional services, such as business setup application and consultation, for both domestic and foreign investors. Besides promoting Beijing to potential foreign investors, the Center also does the following:

- introduces partners for foreign investors and does market research and project assessment;
- drafts business proposals, feasibility studies, contracts for foreign investors, and applies on behalf of them for registration with various authorities and subsequent amendments and changes;
- provides consultation and planning services for FIEs in corporate management, operations and public relationship;
- assists foreign companies in finding office space and manpower;
- represents clients in litigation, arbitration and special liquidation, and handles complaints filed by FIEs;

- assists government's institutions and development zones in attending economic conferences, seminars, trade shows and exhibitions;
- represents and assists FIEs in advertising;
- appraises assets, reviews accounts and reports, and verifies capitalization of FIEs;
- provides consultation and one-stop services for real estate projects etc.

Beijing Foreign Investment Service Center
3 & 4 F Furama Plaza
8 Chaoyangmen North Avenue
Beijing 100027
Tel: (8610) 6554 3151, 6554 3166
Fax: (8610) 6554 3161
Email: guosong@bj.china.com
Website: www.fdibeijing.org.cn

Urban planning and construction

Beijing Municipal Commission of Urban Planning

As Beijing is the capital city of China, the Commission also acts as the Capital Layout and Construction Commission Office. The main responsibilities of the Commission are as follows:

- conducting research on urban and rural planning and construction; promulgation of related policies; participation in the city's economic and social development planning;
- promulgation and modification of municipal rules and regulations pertinent to urban planning;
- implementation of urban master planning, district planning, controllable detailed planning, and urban design in Beijing;
- site selection for projects, issuing land use permit and license for construction, and review of initial design of the projects;
- review of the qualifications of domestic and foreign surveyors and designers;
- urban survey and management of GIS system etc.

Beijing Municipal Commission of Urban Planning
60 South Lishi Road
Beijing 100045
Tel: (8610) 6802 0689
Fax: (8610) 6512 7141
Website: www.bjghw.gov.cn/

Beijing Construction Committee

The main responsibilities of the Committee are as follows:

- to study and draft local rules and regulations related to construction, overall construction of urban development, and utilization of building materials;
- to supervise civil engineering and organize, implement and coordinate key construction projects in Beijing;
- to review and approve housing and other infrastructure construction projects of the central government and military forces in Beijing;
- to oversee and ensure construction engineering quality and safety;
- to administer the overall construction industry in Beijing;
- to manage the use of construction materials, construction machinery and crane equipments etc.

Beijing Construction Committee
5 Guanglian Road
Fengtai District, Beijing 100055
Tel: (8610) 6395 1166
Email: bjjs@bjjs.gov.cn
Website: www.bjjs.gov.cn/

Beijing Land Resources and Housing Board (BLRHB)

The BLRHB looks after the rightful use of land and the property market in Beijing Municipality. Specifically, it does the following:

- drafts and implements rules and regulations pertaining to land use, mineral resources, housing management and reform;
- sets and amends planning on land use, mineral resources development, geological disaster prevention, and housing reform;

- protects cultivated land and organizes land resources surveys and statistics;
- monopolizes land market, implements paid land transfer system, and price, sells or leases state-owned land use right;
- registers and administers real estate ownership; administers municipal property market such as sale, rent, exchange, brokerage and evaluation of properties etc.

Beijing Land Resources and Housing Board
1 Nanweizi Hutong, Nanheyan Avenue, Dongcheng District
Website: www.bjgtfgj.gov.cn/

Beijing Municipal Engineering Administration Committee

The Committee is responsible for civil mechanical and engineering projects in Beijing, which include the construction and maintenance of urban streets, roads, bridges, tunnels, and piping works.

Beijing Municipal Engineering Administration Committee
80 Xi'dan North Avenue
Xicheng District, Beijing 100032
Tel: (8610) 660 1988
Website: http://www.bjmac.gov.cn/

Beijing Traffic Administration

The Traffic Administration is in charge of the planning, administration and maintenance of transportation facilities in the municipal territory, including highways, roads, waterways, subways, public traffic routes, stations and interchanges, etc.

Beijing Traffic Administration
2 Huaibaishu Street, Xuanwu District, Beijing 100053
Website: www.bjtb.gov.cn/

Beijing Finance Administration

The Finance Administration is responsible for municipal fiscal planning and budgeting, implementation of national fiscal policies, administration of municipal government's purchases, and collection and distribution of fiscal revenues.

Beijing Finance Administration
15 Fucheng Road
Haidian District, Beijing 100037
Tel: (8610) 6842 3355
Website: www.bjcz.gov.cn

Beijing Press and Publishing Administration (Beijing Copyright Bureau)

The Administration is the authority governing the local press and publishing industry, and administers copyright in the name of Beijing Copyright Bureau. It supervises publishing activities (publishing, printing, duplication and distribution) in Beijing, and regulates publication, audio-visual product, e-publishing markets.

Beijing Press and Publishing Administration
24 Heping Street, Zone 11
Chaoyang District
Beijing 100013
Tel: (8610) 8425 1187
Fax: (8610) 8425 1189
Website: www.bjppb.gov.cn

Beijing Statistics Bureau

The Bureau collects, analyzes and disseminates statistical information on Beijing's economic and social development.

Beijing Statistics Bureau
2 Huaibei Street
Xuanwu District, Beijing 100053
Tel: (8610) 6354 5252
Website: www.bjstats.gov.cn

Judiciary

Court

The Beijing municipal court system consists of Beijing High People's Court, three intermediate courts, 18 subordinate courts in each district or county and six railway transportation sub-courts.

The courts deal with civil, criminal, economic and administrative cases at different levels. Generally, cases with significant impact on the city will be tried first at the high court, and cases exceeding a certain amount of value are brought to intermediate courts for the first trial, e.g. RMB 1 million for civil cases, RMB 1.5 million for real estate cases, or RMB 500, 000 for cases involving overseas parties. Both the high court and intermediate courts handle appeals against decisions made by lower courts.

Beijing People's High Court
215 Xiheyan Chongwenmen, Beijing 100051
Tel: (8610) 6529 0467
Website: www.bjgf.gov.cn/

Procuratorate

Beijing People's Procuratorate reports to the Municipal People's Congress and its Standing Committee. Its main duty involves investigation and prosecution of government officials engaged in corrupt practices, embezzlement, and any misconduct; prosecution of criminal cases; and supervision over courts' decisions in Beijing.

Beijing People's Procuratorate
12 Shijinshan Road
Shijinshan District
Tel: (8610) 6868 2000
Website: www.bjjc.gov.cn/

INFRASTRUCTURE

Introduction

Beijing is the capital city of China, and it has long enjoyed great development due to its importance in politics, science, culture and the national economy. Beginning in the 1950s, the municipality has carried out large-scale infrastructure construction, which has been the cornerstone of the national economy as well as social progress. The focus of these infrastructure projects is not only on transportation, but environmental protection as well. This is particularly true after China's entry into the World Trade Organization (WTO), and Beijing's successful bid for 2008 Olympics.

Tenders invited: USD 7.2 billion Infrastructure Projects

The Beijing Municipal Government presented 50 infrastructure projects worth USD 7.2 billion to Chinese and foreign enterprises at a recent promotional fair. The Chinese Government announced that the projects involved sewage treatment, expressways, metro line construction and water supplies.

The Beijing Municipal Government also issued a new regulation – the Regulation on Chartered Operations of Beijing Urban Infrastructure Facilities to further encourage private and foreign investment in Beijing's infrastructure. According to the new regulation, private and foreign-funded enterprises will be allowed to conduct chartered operations in infrastructure facilities, including water, gas and heating supplies, sewage treatment and solid waste disposal, public transport, such as expressways, subway lines, light rail system and bus routes.

The possible forms of investment are build-operate-transfer (BOT), transfer-operate-transfer (TOT) and chartered operations of public services.

Source: Xinhuanet, June 2004

Land transportation

The Beijing subway project started in 1965. The first stretch was from Beijing Railway Station and *Pingguoyuan*, and includes today's western branch of Line 1 and the southern part of Line 2. In 1987, the 16-km circle line was completed and both lines started operating simultaneously.

In the 1990s, the eastern extension of Line 1 was built – the so-called Fu Ba Line – to Sihuidong (formerly known as Ba Wang Fen). It opened in October 1999. The new section was 13.5 km long and was eventually connected to the western section of Line 1 in January 2000. This project had been upgraded to ATO operation. Now the local government is embarking on a new project for further extension to the east.

The entire Line 1 is now 38 km long and provides transfer to Ring Line 2. Ring Line 2 is 16 km long. The total network operating in 2000 is around 54 km. Most stations have central platforms and are 118 m long, but only 10 stations have escalators. To prepare for future extensions of the network (eight lines), five stations have already been built as transfer stations, namely, *Xizhimen*, *Dongsishitiao*, *Jianguomen*, *Yonghegong* and *Jishuitan.*

The metro system will be enhanced by plans to build subway, light rail and suburban trains. Construction work for Line 13, or the City Rail project, began at the end of 1999. Phase 1 of the 43-km-long line was completed and opened for operation in 2001. Phase 2 will be ready in 2005.

Another plan involves extending Line 1 by around 17 km. Subway Line 5 is already being extended by 27.7 km. Construction of an 18.9-km-long elevated light metro began two years ago. When completed, it will link the eastern suburb of Tongzhou to the subway terminal at Sihuidong.

The Beijing Metro transports over 460 million passengers a year, or 10% of total transportation volume. The Beijing Municipal Government will spend USD 446 million by 2007 to remove hidden dangers in its subway system. The large-scale subway safety project aims to improve fire-prevention facilities in the subways.

Operating hours: 5:10 am-11:40 pm, 3-4 minutes' waiting time per train during peak hours, 8 minutes during off-peak hours

Fares: RMB 2 or 3 depending on traveling distance

Railway

The railway service in Beijing has developed rapidly and is very extensive. Beijing has five railway stations. Railroad lines run to almost every provincial capital, and to all of China's province-level administrative areas except Tibet, Hainan and Taiwan.

The Beijing Railway Station and Beijing West Railway Station are the two major ones, and the latter is the largest railway terminal in Asia. Both the two main stations have left-luggage facilities, ATMs, tourist information, shops and restaurants. All express trains have four different classes of carriage, namely, the soft sleeper, soft seat, hard sleeper, and hard seat, which actually apply to the whole Chinese railway system. Tickets can be bought at the foreigners' booking office at each station; and passports are required for ticket purchase. Reservations, especially for sleepers, should be booked at least two or three days in advance.

Tickets for international railway routes may be bought through China International Travel Service (CITS) (Tel: 86-10-66011122) or the International Train Booking Office at the Beijing International Hotel, Jianguomenwai Avenue (Tel: 86-10-65126688).

Beijing Railway Station

Beijing Railway Station (Tel: 86-10-51019999) serves railroad routes to the north and east of Beijing. Trans-Manchurian services to Moscow (journey time of around six days) and Trans-Mongolian trains to Ulan Bator and Moscow (journey time around five days) leave from Beijing Railway Station, as do trains to Pyongyang in North Korea (journey time around 25 hours).

Beijing West Railway Station

Beijing West Railway Station Beijing West Railway Station (Tel: 86-10-51827188), the newer and much larger railway station takes travellers to the south and west. Trains to Hong Kong (journey time around 27 hours) and Hanoi, Vietnam (journey time around 43 hours) leave from Beijing West Railway Station.

Journey times for domestic services to Beijing are as follows:
- Harbin – 14 hours
- Shanghai – 13 hours
- Xi'an – 15 hours
- Guangzhou – 24 hours

Beijing - Kowloon Through Train 2003

Destination Kowloon-Beijing	Train No. T98
January	Even
February	Odd
March	Odd
April	Even
May	Even
June	Odd
July	Odd
August	Even
September	Odd
October	Odd
November	Even
December	Even

Odd - Odd number dates, e.g. 1st Dec, 3rd Dec, 5th Dec, 7th Dec etc.
Even - Even number dates, e.g. 2nd Dec, 4th Oct, 6th Dec, 8th May etc.

Some of the most popular routes include Beijing to Shanghai (13 hours). There is also a route on alternate days between Beijing and Hong Kong. The journey is about 27 hours and passengers choose their own class of carriage: hard sleeper, soft sleeper and deluxe soft sleeper.

Tickets for these routes should be bought through China International Travel Service and China Youth Travel Service.

Destination Beijing-Kowloon	Train No.T97
January	Odd
February	Even
March	Even
April	Odd
May	Odd
June	Even
July	Even
August	Odd
September	Even
October	Even
November	Odd
December	Odd

Odd - Odd number dates, e.g. 1st Dec, 3rd Dec, 5th Dec, 7th Dec etc.
Even - Even number dates, e.g. 2nd Dec, 4th Oct, 6th Dec, 8th May etc.

The train (Beijing West – Kowloon) comprises 12 carriages. The De Luxe carriage has eight cabins, the three Soft Sleeper carriages have nine cabins each, and the five Hard Sleeper carriages have 11 cabins each. The rest are café and luggage carriages.

It is worth mentioning that there are some differences in fare charges in Beijing and Hong Kong. In China, children who are less than one meter tall travel free of charge, but they do not get a bed. Children who are between 1 and 1.40 meters tall pay a children fare.

In Hong Kong on the other hand, children under five years of age travel free of charge, but they do not get a bed. Children between five and ten years old pay a children fare.

There are also two direct trains from Shenzhen to Beijing daily. Train No. T108 departs at 1337 hrs and arrives at 1335 hrs the next day; train No. T106 departs at 2355 hrs and arrives at 0554 hrs two nights later. It is recommended that travellers buy tickets at CTS Hong Kong or inquire at the counter in Shenzhen. As for fare charges, Hard Seats are HKD 306 each, Hard Sleeper HKD 508 each, Soft Sleeper HKD 306 each, Hard Sleeper HKD 508 each and Soft Sleeper HKD 752 each.

Journey Schedule (*day after departure)

Station	Train No. T97 (Beijing-Kowloon)	Train No. T98 (Kowloon-Beijing)
Beijing West	10:06am depart	6:05pm arrive
Zhengzhou	3:54pm arrive	12:16pm arrive
Hankou	9:09pm arrive	7:01am arrive
Wuchang	9:36pm arrive	6:34am arrive
Changsha	1:29am arrive	2:42am arrive
Shaoguan	7:06am arrive	9:08pm arrive
Guangzhou	10:10am arrive	6:00pm arrive
Dongguan	11:57am arrive	4:14pm arrive
Kowloon, HK	1:10pm arrive	3:00pm depart

(No stopover is allowed for this route.)

Adult fares:

De Luxe (1/2) class	USD 166
Soft (1/4) class	USD 133
Hard (2/6) class	USD 88

Children fares:

De Luxe (1/2) class	USD 114
Soft (1/4) class	USD 90
Hard (2/6) class	USD 62

Highway/Expressway

Beijing has a well-developed highway network that conveniently links the capital city to regions throughout the country. At end-2002, total highway length reached 4,200 km. With the opening of new highways and expressways, Beijing strives to serve more people with better service. Beijing now has extensive and specialized highway and expressway transportation network and has also opened more than 100 cargo transportation routes and 500 passenger lines to cities all around China.

More than 12 expressways and highways have been newly built or upgraded. In 2001, the highway network transported 161.65 million passengers, and 280.7 million tons of freight, an increase of 24.5% freight volume over the previous year.

Famous expressways include Beijing-Tianjin-Tanggu Expressway, Beijing-Shijiazhuang-Taiyuan Expressway, Beijing-Shenyang Expressway and Beijing-Chengde-Zhangjiakou First Class Road. Using the highway and expressway network, it is convenient for travelers to get in and out of the city. For instance, it takes only 1 hour 30 minutes to drive from Tianjin to Beijing; 3 hours 30 minutes to drive from Chengdu to Beijing and 6 hours to drive from Taiyuan to Beijing.

One important project is the 1,262 km Beijing-Shanghai Expressway. Starting operations on 19 December 2000, it has four lanes and even six lanes in some sections of the expressway. The great expressway connects Beijing to Tianjin, Hebei, Shandong, and Shanghai. There are 11 tollgates on the trunk line, one within the Beijing region, two each in Hebei, Tianjin and Shandong, three in Jiangsu and one in Shanghai.

Various coach services are available in Beijing. While coach and bus travel could be very slow and rather uncomfortable, bus tickets are cheaper than rail fares and easier to obtain due to the lower demand. There are few facilities at the bus stations and tickets should be purchased at specified ticket offices. Generally, the four main long-distance bus stations in Beijing are situated on the perimeter of the city in the direction of their destination.

Dongzhimen, Dongzhimen West Street, serves the northeast area such as Chengde; Haihutin, Nanyuan Road, serves the south area; Beijiao (also known as Deshengmen) is for the north area; and Majuan, Guangqumenwai Avenue, serves the east area. In addition, buses to Tianjin depart from Zhaogongku, near the intersection of South 3rd Ring East Road and Puhuangyu Road.

Urban public transport

City bus

Public bus is the most popular transportation means for the locals in Beijing. City buses run from 5 am to 11 pm, and are very crowded, particularly in the peak hours of 0700 hrs and 0830 hrs in the morning and 1700 hrs and 1830 hrs in the evening.

There is also a limited night service between 2300 hrs and 0530 hrs of the next day. Fares are between RMB 1 and RMB 2 within the city (or between RMB 2 to RMB 10 for suburban bus routes). Air-conditioned buses within the city cost between RMB 2 and RMB 8, depending on the traveling distance. It is important to have the destination written in Chinese characters, as the driver and the ticket seller generally do not know much English.

In 2002, Beijing had a fleet of over 13,000 buses, which accounts for 89% of the city's total. The annual capacity is 3.94 billion people. There are two ticket-sellers who serve passengers at the front and back entrances/ exits respectively. Taking these buses in the dusk, one could view the brilliant scene of Tian'anmen Square and Tian'anmen Rostrum bathing in the colors of the sunset. Air-conditioned buses of No. 808, 801, 802 and 803 traverse the busiest streets of Beijing.

Double-decker buses offer travelers the chance of a better view of the fast changing city. Right now, there are four routes. Tickets cost RMB 2 each.

- Route No. 1 – Beijing West Railway Station to Bawangfen along Chang'an Avenue.
- Route No. 2 – Qianmen to Dongdan, Yonghe Gong Lamasery, the Chinese Ethnic Culture Park and the Asian Games Village.
- Route No. 3 starts from Jijia Temple, passing by the Grand View Garden, Jinsong, the Jingguang Center and the Agricultural Museum before arriving at the Lufthansa Shopping Center.
- Route No. 4 – starts from Beijing Zoo, to the Beijing Exhibition

Center, Yuetan Park, Fuxing Overpass and Qianmen Commercial District.

The mini bus is an alternative to expensive taxis and crowded public transport. Running on a regular schedule, these small vans guarantee each rider a seat even in the rush hour and stop on request anywhere along the route. Fares vary from RMB 1 to RMB 6. Their routes match those of the large public buses.

Taxis

Foreign visitors rarely attempt the public transport system, in particular the bus system, unless they have a good understanding of Mandarin Chinese. Other than the subway, travel by taxis is by far the easier option.

There are presently more than 65,000 taxis on the roads of Beijing, 6,000 of which are installed with detection systems. Taxis in Beijing are actually reliable, plentiful, and safe. Taxis wait around major department stores, hotels and railway stations and could be hailed on the street. Taxis in Beijing are mostly small, red hatchbacks or saloons and, generally, the smaller and older the car, the cheaper the fare.

Taxi journeys are metered, and it is wise to watch the meter carefully. All taxis have a sticker in the back window that indicates the rate per kilometer but the usual rate is RMB 10 for the first three km and RMB 1.2 to 1.6 per kilometer thereafter. There will be a 20% surcharge after 11 pm. It is important to write the destination in Chinese characters. Maps and written addresses or business cards are the best tools to direct taxi drivers, as few are able to speak English. Tips are not mandatory but always welcome.

Limousines

CITS, at CITS Building, Fuxingmennei Avenue arranges limousine services, the fare being USD 90 per day within the city limits.

Civil aviation

Capital International Airport

The Capital International Airport is located 27 km northeast of downtown Beijing and is undoubtedly China's top air hub. Built at a cost of around RMB 1.1 billion, the new, bright and beautiful international terminal opened in September 1999. It is a welcome replacement to the former facility, which started operation in the 1950s, and had become increasingly cramped, given the ever-rising passenger volume to China.

The new state-of-the-art terminal is able to handle 190,000 flights, 35 million passengers, and 780,000 tons of cargo a year. With 98 international, 21 regional and 757 domestic air routes, the airport links Beijing to 54 cities in 39 countries worldwide. More than 40 foreign airlines have set up their booking offices in Beijing.

Its four-storey terminal (including the basement level) has an area of 336,000 m^2, which is three times the size of the former terminal, and there is more emphasis now on passenger comfort. The complex also has a large-scale public parking building and a cargo

Travel information

From Beijing Capital Airport to	
Bangkok	4hrs 45mins
Hong Kong	2hrs 50mins
Kuala Lumpur	5hrs
Seoul	1hrs 50mins
Vancouver	10hrs 30mins
Singapore	7hrs 55 mins
Tokyo	3hrs 10mins
Melbourne	13hrs 15 mins
Sydney	16hrs 30mins
Frankfurt	8hrs 10mins
Paris	8hrs 25mins
London	10hrs 45mins
Rome	13hrs
Los Angeles	14hrs 30mins
Moscow	8hrs 25mins
Osaka	5hrs 5mins
Nagoya	2hrs 35mins
Stockholm	9hrs 10mins
New York	15hrs
Detroit	12hrs 55mins
Toronto	16hrs 20mins
Guangzhou	2hrs 40mins
Shanghai	1hr 40mins
Xiamen	2hrs 45mins
Dalian	1hr 10mins
Shenzhen	2hrs 40mins

It is convenient for travelers to book air tickets in Beijing. Most airlines have sales offices at the China Aviation Building near Xidan.

station. Electronic display boards are installed throughout the airport, providing arrival and departure information in both Chinese and English. The Unisys Airport Passenger Processing System (APPS) is used at the airport.

It is convenient for travelers to book air tickets in Beijing. Most airlines have sales offices at the China Aviation Building near Xidan.

Travelers will be able to stay in touch with the world via multimedia payphones conveniently located throughout the terminal. A phone card, available at airport counters, is required to make calls. Free baggage carts are available at the concourse outside the departure hall. The airport offers Smart Locke lockers for passengers to store their luggage. The lockers are located on the second level. There are 12 ATMs and four auto cash exchange machines conveniently located throughout the terminal which accept various cards such as Cirrus, American Express, Visa, Visa Interlink and MasterCard.

The following banks have booths at the airport for foreign currency exchange, namely, Bank of China, the Industrial and Commercial Bank of China, the Agricultural Bank of China, and the China Construction Bank. Some of these banks also provide cash advances to Visa cardholders. The ATM machines are open 24 hours a day while the bank booths are open during normal flight arrival and departure hours.

At the airport, facilities are available such as bureaux de change, duty free stores, as well as shops, cafés, restaurants, left-luggage and tourist information counters. In addition, there are four business centers, three in the Domestic Hall and one in the International Hall on the second floor. All have Internet facilities installed.

The Airport – City shuttle buses are available every 30 minutes from 0530 hrs to 1900 hrs between the China Aviation Building on West Chang'an Boulevard and the airport; and every hour from both the China Art Gallery and Zhongguancun to the airport. The bus fare is RMB 16, and the journey time is around 45 minutes. These shuttle buses take three routes into the city. The most popular is to Xidan in downtown Beijing, a short walk from the Forbidden City. The other routes are to Gongzhufen in southwest Beijing and to Zhongguancun in northwest Beijing. For passengers choosing to take taxis, the taxi fare is approximately RMB 80.

Urban construction

Urban construction in Beijing has developed well, and this is particularly true of late, ever since China's entry into WTO and Beijing's successful bid for 2008 Olympics. Local government has focused its urban construction plans on developing functional infrastructure, and a large part of infrastructure projects are to do with water resources, energy, transportation, posts and telecommunications, and raw materials management and development.

Beijing plans to spend a total of USD 35 billion on the construction of Olympics-related infrastructure, including USD 23 billion for modernizing the municipality. The Olympics-related infrastructure program is one of the most ambitious and impressive one Beijing had ever undertaken. The program will include extensive construction of sports venues and facilities,

Digital Beijing

In terms of the construction of an information infrastructure in Beijing, it is sometimes said that a digital Beijing is being created. Modern digital information and Internet technologies are being adopted to enhance the efficiency of the management mechanism. In fact, efficiency has become an important focus and developmental aim.

For example, if an enterprise wishes to apply for an operation license, it could visit the Internet for relevant offices and authorities and download the appropriate application forms. Completed application forms can then be sent back electronically. Only a few working days are needed for approval. The increasing use of the Internet has greatly enhanced administrative efficiency.

IT-related infrastructure and telecommunications play a role in the construction of a digital Beijing. In fact, high-speed broadband and a computer network are under construction. In addition, Beijing has also established a database, which is based on the General Information System (GIS). A recent survey showed that around 80% of daily information is related to government services, thus the compilation of a general information database is of great importance for the construction of a digital city.

major enhancements to transportation and telecommunications networks, and further installation of environmental protection systems.

To accelerate economic development, Beijing is determined to improve infrastructure construction and environmental protection. The city had completed over 60 major construction projects in 2001, with a total investment commitment of RMB 128 billion, or USD 15.4 billion. One major project is the construction of an information superhighway, with the application of information and on-line technology in all managerial areas.

In accordance with the master plan, Beijing will invest RMB 180 billion or USD 21.8 billion, in the construction of local infrastructure facilities during the five-year period from 2001 to 2005. Major investments will be put into the construction of traffic facilities and energy-related projects.

The traffic facilities include a network of urban light railways, subways and highways. Energy-related projects include the second Shaanxi – Beijing gas transmission line, the Inner Mongolia – Beijing high voltage electricity transmission route and a thermal power plant in suburban Beijing. Beijing has worked hard and will continue to do so to improve

Using a digital platform, anyone can visit a shopping mall without stepping out of the house. Detailed information about the mall and its tenants, products and services will be available electronically.

Undoubtedly, establishing a government information center is the prime condition for a digital Beijing, and Beijing has plans to set up an information management center. In doing so, information could be collated and integrated with efficiency, and to a unified standard. With the help of modern technology such as e-government, e-business and the like, Beijing is confident of achieving further improvement in the construction of infrastructure.

Source: www.beijing.gov.cn

urban construction, to protect ancient cultural relics and to enhance environmental-friendly construction.

To enhance improvements in infrastructure, environmental protection has become a big concern for the municipal government. Emphasis has been placed on preventing air and water pollution, and several major infrastructure projects are engaged in controlling pollution. Large-scale wastewater and rubbish treatment plants have been completed. In the near future, Beijing will also demolish and rebuild three million m^2 of worn-down housing blocks.

As part of the master plan, the investment commitment specified in environmental protection is as much as RMB 45 billion, or USD 5.4 billion. More and more trees and grass have appeared along the city streets. By 2005, greenery will make up 48% of the city.

ADMINISTRATIVE AREAS

Overview

Beijing comprises 18 administrative areas, of which 16 are districts and 2 are counties. It is often divided into four groups, namely, four urban districts, four suburbs, eight outer suburbs and two counties.

Population and land area of Beijing administrative areas

Region	Population (1,000)	Area (km²)	Population density
Central Districts	**2,394**	**87.1**	**27,486**
Dongcheng	630	24.7	25,506
Xicheng	786	30.0	26,200
Chongwen	412	15.9	25,912
Xuanwu	566	16.5	34,303
Urban Districts	**4,392**	**1,282.8**	**3,424**
Chaoyang	1,552	470.8	3,297
Fengtai	836	304.2	2,748
Shijingshan	335	81.8	4,095
Haidian	1,669	426.0	3,918
Suburb Districts	**3,749**	**11,122.3**	**337**
Mentougou	234	1,331.3	176
Fangshan	747	1,866.7	400
Tongzhou	603	870.0	693
Shunyi	540	980.0	551
Changping	436	1,430.0	305
Daxing	535	1,012.0	529
Pinggu	389	1,075.0	362
Huairou	265	2,557.3	104
Suburb Counties	**688**	**4,315.6**	**159**
Miyun	418	2,335.6	179
Yanqing	270	1,980.0	136
Beijing	**11,223**	**16,808**	**668**

Source: Beijing Statistic Bureau, 2001. Population refers to registered residents.

Central Business District

Beijing unveiled plans in 1993 to create a bustling, glittering Central Business District (CBD) in its eastern rim, in a bid to become a commercial metropolis on top of being China's political and cultural center.

The District is a special business zone where many facilities such as office buildings, hotels and apartments are built for financial, business, trade, information and intermediary agencies, with complete municipal works, as well as transportation and communications infrastructure to facilitate business activities.

The location of the district is between Chaoyangmen in the north and Jianguomen in the south, and between the East Second Ring Road in the west and the East Ring Road in the east. In the years since 1993, people in Beijing have witnessed the transformation of the district and enjoyed the multi-functional, Internet-linked one-stop services it provides, state-of-the-art facilities, complete services and a pleasant environment.

The district is in a favorable position to develop foreign trade and exchange activities. It is indeed a central district for international business activities in Beijing and the entire country. It has given top priority to the development of four service industries, namely, information services centering on communications, Internet, news media and information consultation; financial services such as banking, insurance, securities, trust, investment and funds; intermediary agencies of financial accounting, auditing, appraisal and legal services; and new services of vocational training, conferences and exhibitions, and international business.

The four industries have thrived, meeting the demands of the various international businesses in the city and around the world.

There are several so-called business circles in Beijing, including those around the China World Trade Center, Chaoyangmen Wai Avenue, the Lufthansa Center and the Asian Games Village.

The China World Trade Center business circle, centering on the planned Golden Cross, has become the golden area in Beijing, possessing economic strength and the most modern business buildings. The regions around Chaoyangmen Wai Avenue and the Lufthansa Center have huge development potential with the high concentration of department stores, financial institutions and office buildings. Taking 10 years to build, the Asian Games Village business circle is in north Beijing.

Three-dimensioned traffic network

The district boasts a complete three-dimensioned traffic network based on road, railway and air transport. It has built more than 1,000 km of highways, with a density rate of twice the city's average.

More than 30 overpasses connect the Second, Third and Fourth Ring roads, and four expressways lead to the suburban districts of Changping, Tongzhou and Shunyi, and the neighboring city of Tianjin. The railway to Baotou, Chengde, Guangzhou and Qinhuangdao pass through the district. The Capital International Airport lies in the northeast of the district.

Overseas cooperative partners

To accelerate construction of the major items in the CBD, the Beijing Municipal Government will help enterprises involved in CBD construction find overseas cooperative partners and offer them preferential policies in raising funds, project registration, getting approval for projects and relocation of plants. In contrast to CBDs in the US and Hong Kong, Beijing's will be more resident-friendly as office buildings are to be interspersed with apartment blocks, condominiums and cultural facilities.

The general design of the CBD includes one overall plan and four special ones. The overall plan covers distribution of space and use of land; the four special plans are for environment and scenery, transportation, telecommunications network and infrastructure construction. Beijing had invited well-known designers, architects and related experts from

Beijing's new satellite towns

In order to mitigate population pressure in downtown areas, Beijing is building several new-style satellite towns, each designed to accommodate half a million population.

Beijing Municipal Committee for Development and Reform is in charge of developing education, culture, hygiene and commerce in the satellite towns and expanding the various facilities for boosting social investments.

Several satellite towns with favorable locations, good industrial foundations and living environment will be selected through public bidding. The new towns will serve as important centers for diverting industries and population from the downtown areas while at the same time providing more employment opportunities for farmers who wish to move to the city areas.

Beijing has decided on the grand design of the new satellite towns, which it described as "two axes - two zones - multi-centers".

"Two Axes" represent the cross axes formed by Beijing's traditional middle axis and Chang'an Avenue, the essence of Beijing. "Two Zones" mean the "southern development zone" which starts from the north along Huairou and Miyun with Shunyi, Tongzhou and Yizhuang as key areas, and the "western ecological zone" which includes Yanqing, Changping, Liangxiang and Huangcun. "Multi-centers" refer to the construction of several comprehensive service districts in the downtown areas including the CBD, Olympic Park and Zhongguancun, and of several new towns in the areas covered by both the city and the "Two Zones".

home and abroad to appraise the numerous proposals. The final design was the culmination of the contributions of many famous experts.

To create an environment for modern international business activities, priority will be given to the construction of information networks, roads and facilities for water and power supply. The roadway area of the CBD will make up as much as 39% of its total, linking it to the rest of the city in all directions.

Together with the development of traffic facilities that include railways, pedestrian pathways and parking areas, the CBD designers have devised macro and micro plans as well as short-term and long-term plans for the development of transportation infrastructure.

These include the plan for construction of two metro lines. In the underground core area, shops, garages and walkways will be connected to each other. An initial plan for building an information network, Digital

CBD, has been made by Beijing Telecom and related departments.

The CBD design is of international standard, as it had been repeatedly discussed and improved by foreign experts. It is also economically viable, as the use of existing buildings and those to be constructed are fully taken into consideration. In regard to transportation, the design will suit the traffic situation several decades from now. The CBD will combine the functions of business, culture, science and technology, recreation and residence into one.

The construction of the CBD is not only intended for the development of real estate but also for the long-term economy. Based on the system of land purchase and reserve, the city government would control land development and ensure the project is undertaken in an orderly way. One-third of the land is already in the hands of developers, and the rest of the land will be auctioned to other developers.

Beijing's CBD will formulate special policies to absorb talented people, in the hopes of making itself an international talent market. With its entry into the WTO, China will have a greater demand for international business talents. A survey by the Ministry of Personnel of China showed that business professionals are listed second among the 10 most badly needed professionals in China. The manager of the Beijing Personnel Market believes that the CBD will become home to a large number of such people. To achieve this goal, Beijing will relax policies on residence permit and schooling for business professionals and their families who are from outside Beijing.

Central Districts

Traditionally, the four districts of Dongcheng, Xicheng, Chongwen and Xuanwu form the central part of Beijing.

Dongcheng District

Fast Facts

Dongcheng 2001	Figure	%
GDP	3,541.3	12.6
Primary	-	-
Secondary	423.7	5.2
Tertiary	3,117.7	13.7
Total Industrial Output (RMB mil)	754.3	-8.9
Export (RMB mil)	11.52	-0.2
New FDI projects	49	-
Contractual FDI (USD mil)	247.6	-
Utilized FDI (USD mil)	200.6	-

Source: www.bjdch.gov.cn

Dongcheng is best known as Beijing's heartland where the Forbidden City, the spectacular imperial palace for the Ming and Qing Dynasty, is located. It is said to be the best-preserved site of classical Chinese architecture and is listed by UNESCO as a World Cultural Heritage. The Palace Museum (http://www.dpm.org.cn) attracts millions of people all over the world every year.

The famous Tiananmen ("Gate of Heavenly Peace") Square, the current Beijing Municipal Government, and 100 over national-level authorities are located in this district.

Situated to the east of Beijing city, Dongcheng is one of the districts with the highest population density, with more than 25,500 residents per km^2. It has been a commercial center for hundreds of years. Famous commercial districts include Wangfujing, Beijing Station, Longfu Temple, Dongdan and Dongsi etc. Wangfujing is dubbed the "Golden Street" of Beijing as shopping centers, hotels, serviced apartments and all sorts of shops are found here.

The existing total gross land area of this modernized shopping paradise is about 1.8 million m^2. The magnificent Oriental Plaza, the largest building cluster in Asia with total area of 900, 000 m^2, is located just at the beginning of the Street. Other places most patronized by shoppers and visitors include the Dong'an Market, Sun Dong An, Beijing Department Store, Donglaishun Restaurant for Muslims and Wangfujing Bookstore.

With the large number of tourist arrivals in the district every year, the tertiary sector now accounts for 88% of Dongcheng's economy, and the share is still increasing. In 2001, the district's GDP rose by 12.6% and FDI inflow increased 31% to USD 247.6 million.

The district government now stresses the development of modern services and high-tech industries with the hopes of making them future growth engines for Dongcheng. IT companies, banking and insurance institutions with international exposure, R&D and sales centers, headquarters of large technological enterprises are widely encouraged. Effort will be put into the development of three areas within the district, namely, Wangfujing Commercial Center, East Second Ring Business Area, and a Cultural Tourism District around the Yonghe Palace.

Dongcheng District Government
6 Yuqun Hutong
Dongcheng District
Tel: (8610) 6403 4477
Website: www.bjdch.gov.cn

Xicheng District

Fast Facts

Xicheng 2001	Figure	% (+/-)
GDP (RMB mil)	5,007.6	10.3
Primary	-	-
Secondary	310.5	10.3
Tertiary	4,697.0	10.3
Total Industrial Output (RMB mil)	958.0	31.0
Export (RMB mil)	54.2	379.2
New FDI projects	29	-
Contractual FDI (USD mil)	34.5	-
Utilized FDI (USD mil)	157.6	-

Source: www.bjxch.gov.cn

Literally meaning "west of the city", Xicheng is located west of Beijing. It plays host to the city's top-level authorities such as the Central Committee of CPC, the State Council, the Standing Committee of National People's Congress, the Central Military Commission, the China People's Political Consultative Conference and numerous minister-level organizations. Zhongnanhai, situated west of the old imperial palace, is the political center of the whole of China.

As the ancient Yongding River used to run through this area, the district has a few lakes and ponds including Zhongnanhai and Beihai. Xicheng also boasts a spectrum of sightseeing spots such as Beihai and Jingshan Park, Beijing Zoo, White Clouds Taoist Monastery, White Pagoda, and former residences of eminent personalities like Mr. Lu Xun and Mr. Guo Moruo.

Industries in the Xicheng District include printing, garment, arts and crafts, food and automotive maintenance. But with 55% of its territory within the Second Ring Road, Xicheng represents a typical urban economy. While 94% of its economy is contributed by the tertiary sector, more than half of total value-added comes from the financial industry.

There are many financial institutions in Xicheng District. The headquarters of major national financial institutions, namely, People's Bank of China (PBOC), Bank of China (BOC), Industrial & Commercial Bank of China (ICBC), Agricultural Bank of China (ABC), China Construction Bank (CCB) and People's Insurance Company of China are all located in Xicheng District. The Financial Street, lying in the western part of the district, had begun development in 1993. With total planned area of 103 hectares and 2 million m^2 of floor space, the Street is aiming at becoming the national center for banking and finance.

Xicheng District Government
27 Erlong Road, Xicheng District
Tel: (8610) 8806 4341
Fax: (8610) 8806 4312
Email: zhengfb@mail.bjxch.gov.cn
Website: www.bjxch.gov.cn/

Chongwen District

Fast Facts

Chongwen 2003	Figure	%
GDP (RMB million)	8,640	15
Primary	-	-
Secondary	2,310	20.2
Tertiary	6,330	13.2
Total Industrial Output (RMB mil)	2,605	22.76
Export (USD mil)	32	12.3
New FDI projects	20	-
Contractual FDI (USD mil)	50.6	-27.6%
Utilized FDI (USD mil)	42.9	39.3%

Remark: GDP figures inclusive of that contributed by enterprises above district level.

Source: www.cwi.gov.cn

In terms of size, Chongwen is the smallest administrative area in Beijing. Named after the demolished Chongwen Gate, the 15.9 km^2 district borders Dongcheng in its north and is separated from Xuanwu District in its west by the southern extension of the axis of Beijing city.

Occupying one-sixth of the district's territory, Tiantan ("Temple of Heaven") used to be a place where emperors prayed for good harvests. Other attractions include Zhengyang Gate, Beijing Amusement Park, Longtan Park and Beijing Museum of Nature etc. With a long history stretching over five dynasties, many brand-names have originated from this area such as Quanjude and Bianyifang Roasted Duck, Gongdelin Vegetarian Restaurant, Douyichu and Yueshengzhai. Modern shopping malls are also abundant, including Tianqiao Department Store, Jinlun, New World, and Qianmen Commercial Center.

Chongwen also has many sporting facilities such as Beijing Stadium, International Tennis Center and Bicycling Field, and looks set to benefit from the exposure given to the 2008 Olympics.

In 2001, total GDP of Chongwen rose by 11.1% to USD 303 million, of which 22.8% came from state-level or municipal enterprises. The tertiary sector accounted for 86.8% of the GDP. Four pillar industries contribute nearly 40% to the local economy. These are real estate, pharmaceuticals, sports and culture & tourism, increasing by 26.4%, 13.1%, 10.8% and 25% in 2001, respectively.

Chongwen District Government
32 Fortune Avenue
Tel: (8610) 6711 2184
Website: www.cwi.gov.cn/

Xuanwu District

Fast Facts

Xuanwu 2001	Figure	%
GDP (RMB mil)	1,882.2	2
Primary	-	-
Secondary	484.2	0.1
Tertiary	1,398.0	2.7
Total Industrial Output (RMB mil)	610.6	0.1
Export (RMB mil)	97.0	363.2
New FDI projects	22	-
Contractual FDI (USD mil)	690.0	-
Utilized FDI (USD mil)	36.0	-

Source: www.bjxw.gov.cn

West to Chongwen and south to Xicheng lies Xuanwu District, one of the four central districts of Beijing. Out of its 566,000 population, nearly 30,000 belong to Hui, a minority of Muslims in China, forming the largest Hui settlement in Beijing. The district is also the most populated area of Beijing, with more than 34,000 residents per km^2.

With a long tradition of doing business, Xuanwu boasts venerable brand names with profound cultural and historical heritage, such as Tongrentang Pharmaceuticals, Neiliansheng Shoe, Ruifuxiang Silk, Liubijiu Sauces and Pickles, and Zhang Yiyuan Tea. Most are in the famous Dashilan business area. Niujie Mosque, Liulichang, Fayuan Temple, Taoran Pavilion and Daguan Garden are all visited by many.

In the period of 1991-2001, the average annual growth rate of Xuanwu was 9.5%. In 2001, total GDP of the district reached RMB 13.66 billion (USD 1.6 billion), a 9.3% increase over the previous year. With RMB 9.8 billion (USD 1.2 billion) of value added, the tertiary sector accounted for 72% of local economy.

Future development of Xuanwu focuses on four functional sub-districts specializing in trade and commerce, business office, cultural tourism and residential districts, and encourages five industries, namely, modern services, trade, real estate and construction, cultural tourism and high-tech industry.

Xuanwu District Government
68 Guang'anmen South Street
Tel: (8610) 6352 9714
Fax: (8610) 6352 9714
http://www.bjxw.gov.cn

Urban Districts

Chaoyang District

Fast Facts

Chaoyang 2001	Figure	%
GDP (RMB mil)	10,100.0	13.7
Primary	250.0	-2.1
Secondary	2,400.0	16.2
Tertiary	7,450.0	13.6
Total Industrial Output (RMB mil)	8,253.5	11.8
Export (RMB mil)	238.3	-2.8
New FDI projects	227	-
Contractual FDI (USD mil)	170.5	-
Utilized FDI (USD mil)	153.9	-

Source: www.bjchy.gov.cn

With a total area of 470.6 km², Chaoyang is the largest district within Beijing's urban area. The territory is endowed with eight creeks and varied topography like plains, terraces and hills, giving Chaoyang a beautiful natural scenery and expansive landscape. Statistics show the total population of the district might have surpassed 2.29 million, among which a quarter households are not registered.

Chaoyang has been an industrial base of electronics, textile, machinery and automobile. Its strength is also shown in commerce, finance, tourism, logistics, high-tech industries, real estate and modern agriculture.

According to the district government, the GDP of Chaoyang has already exceeded RMB 5 billion (USD 603,800) in 2001. However, a comparison with the municipal statistics reveals that the majority is contributed by municipality or state-level enterprises and the GDP of local enterprises is around RMB 10 billion (USD 1.2 billion).

Chaoyang is also a place for intensive international communication. Currently, it hosts more than 60% of total foreign business establishments in Beijing, over 3,000 FIEs, more than 50 foreign-funded hotels and apartments, many expatriate clubs and associations, 167 international news agencies, and two-thirds of the 158 Fortune 500 MNCs that already have set-ups in Beijing. Moreover, foreign embassies, are also located in the district.

In the new millennium, three hot spots will make the district even more outstanding and brilliant – the development of Beijing new CBD (central business district), the hosting of the 2008 Olympics, and the development of Beijing Electronics City.

A 3.99-km^2 area in Chaoyang was designated by the municipal government in 1998 to be the future CBD of Beijing (http://www.bjcbd.gov.cn). The Olympic Garden, with a total area of 12.15 km^2 and 14 sports venues will be established in the northwest part of the district (http://www.beijing-2008.org). The 10.5-km^2 Beijing Electronics City lies at the conjunction of the Fourth Ring Road and Airport Expressway and has become the industrial base of telecommunications, software, monitor, kinescope, digital audio-visual products and new components.

The Capital International Airport is located in the northeast of Chaoyang. A number of expressways, trunk roads and railways run through the district, further increasing its accessibility. Famous existing sites in Chaoyang include the Asian Games Village, Beijing Worker's Stadium, International Exhibition Center and National Exhibition Center of Agriculture.

Chaoyang District Government
Tel: (8610) 6509 4288
Fax: (8610) 6509 0287
Website: www.bjchy.gov.cn

Fengtai District

Fast Facts

Fengtai 2001	Figure	%
GDP (RMB mil)	5,367.6	19.0
Primary	162.4	-10.0
Secondary	1,522.7	14.9
Tertiary	3,682.6	22.5
Total Industrial Output (RMB mil)	7,026.1	30.9
Export (RMB mil)	22.0	0.1
New FDI projects	35	-
Contractual FDI (USD mil)	59.1	-
Utilized FDI (USD mil)	18.6	-

Source: www.bjft.gov.cn

Fengtai is the southwestern gateway to Beijing. The West Beijing Railway Station and a number of regional cargo stations are located in this district. The Second, Third and Fourth Ring Roads as well as expressways to Shijiazhuang and Tianjin all run through Fengtai. The anti-Japanese War (1937-1945) was first started in Lugouqiao, a town in the central part of the district.

The economy of Fengtai has been developing rapidly in recent years. In 2001, its GDP accelerated by an astonishing 19% over the previous year. The GDP of the tertiary sector, including real estate, commerce, service and tourism saw exceptional growth, accounting for almost 70% of the local economy. As Fengtai opens more to foreign capital, FIEs are making greater contributions to Fengtai's modernization.

Fengtai is the largest floricultural base of Beijing. It also provides Peking ducks, rice, vegetables, egg, milk and fruits for Beijing residents. Tourism sites in the district include Dabaotai Han Mausoleum, Relics of Jin Capital and a World Park.

Zhongguancun Science Park, Fengtai Zone, was approved as a state-level high-tech park in 1994 and was subsequently opened to APEC member nations. The park has already formed a cluster of industries led by optical electromechanical integration, IT, biopharmaceuticals and environmental protection technologies. It is made up of three parts, namely, the 5-km^2 scientific city, a science and technology street and an incubation center.

Fengtai District Government
2 Wenti Road, Fengtai District
Tel: (8610) 6381 2244-8233
Website: www.bjft.gov.cn

Shijingshan District

Fast Facts

Shijingshan 2001	Figure	%
GDP (RMB mil)	2,427.1	68.6
Primary	17.0	-13.7
Secondary	998.5	273.3
Tertiary	1,411.7	22.5
Total Industrial Output (RMB mil)	2,163.4	54.2
Export (RMB mil)	43.2	-12.7
New FDI projects	16	-
Contractual FDI (USD mil)	20.2	-
Utilized FDI (USD mil)	-	-

Source: www.bjsjs.gov.cn

Shijingshan lies in the west part of Beijing. The district is the heavy industry base for the capital city as a large number of municipal or state-level enterprises such as Capital Steel, Shijingshan Power, and Beijing Heavy Electrical Machinery are all located here. As a result, steel, electricity and machinery form the mainstay of the local economy.

However, promising industries like IT, new building materials, biopharmaceuticals and pro-environment instruments are emerging in Shijingshan. As the district enhances its urbanization level and improves service standards, the potential for investment is growing.

As early as 2001, the total GDP of Shijingshan had exceeded RMB 20 billion (USD 2.4 billion). Contributions from large state-owned enterprises made up the biggest share.

Major attractions in the district include Shijingshan Amusement Park, Badachu Park, Laoshan motorcycle racing field, Beijing Shooting Range and Fahai Temple. The subway runs though the territory and ends at Pingguoyuan. Shijingshan Road is actually the western extension of Chang'an Road, the longitudinal axis of Beijing.

Website: www.bjsjs.gov.cn

Haidian District

Fast Facts

Haidian 2001	Figure	%
GDP (RMB mil)	34,441.1	22.5
Primary	176.2	-15.9
Secondary	16,320.4	5.5
Tertiary	17,944.6	44.5
Total Industrial Output (RMB mil)	40,165.7	-16.3
Export (RMB mil)	1,798.0	-33.0
New FDI projects	350	-
Contractual FDI (USD mil)	477.4	-
Utilized FDI (USD mil)	260.0	-

Source: www.bjhd.gov.cn

Haidian is best known for its many top Chinese universities and high-tech industries in the Zhongguancun area which is dubbed the "Silicon Valley" of China. Started from the Zhongguancun Street of Electronics and designated as the location for China's first state-level high-tech park in 1988, Haidian is now Beijing's leading district in terms of high-tech industries. Shangdi Information Industrial Base and Zhongguancun Avenue Economic Belt of Technology are two important zones for the incubation of high-tech start-ups in Haidian. Zhongguancun IT Festival is held in the district on a regular basis.

The district's high-tech development is fully backed by over 50 Chinese universities, 41 research institutes of Chinese Academy of Science and numerous corporate R&D centers across this region. Peking University, Tsinghua University, Founder, Lenovo and Stone Group are all based in Haidian. Having the largest population in Beijing, the district has more than 200,000 professionals and technicians.

The district's economy is strongly supported by the four pillar industries of IT, optic electromechanical integration technologies, new materials and bio-pharmaceuticals. In recent years, the bio-pharmaceutical industry has achieved robust growth.

A large number of banks and security firms have also set up their branches or subsidiaries in Haidian, hence boosting its financial sector significantly. According to the Haidian district government, local GDP rose by 19.4% to RMB 33.56 billion (USD 4.05 billion) in 2001, of which RMB 31.0 billion (USD 3.7 billion) was value-added achieved by high-tech enterprises. The most remarkable growth was registered in the tertiary sector. During the same period, 350 FIEs were newly registered in Haidian and USD 260 million was utilized.

Haidian also boasts rich cultural and natural tourism resources, such as the Summer Palace, Yuanming Garden, Xiangshan Mountain, Beijing Botanic Garden, Phoenix Hills, Biyun Temple, Temple of Big Bell, and CCTV Tower etc.

Moreover, Haidian is also replete with modern shopping malls and service outlets. These include Shuang'an Market, Modern Plaza, Cuiwei Plaza, Haidian Theatre and more than 1,000 clinics, hospitals and healthcare centers.

Website: www.bjhd.gov.cn

Suburban Districts

Mentougou District

Fast Facts

Mentougou 2001	Figure	%
GDP (RMB mil)	2,403.3	18.8
Primary	52.1	5.4
Secondary	788.3	11.2
Tertiary	1,562.8	23.6
Total Industrial Output (RMB mil)	2,025.7	10.7
Export (RMB mil)	65.5	-28.7
New FDI projects	17	-
Contractual FDI (USD mil)	19.9	-
Utilized FDI (USD mil)	3.5	-

Source: www.bjmtg.gov.cn

Located in the hilly area of west Beijing and bordering Hebei Province, Mentougou has abundant natural resources. Coal, limestone, granite and marble top its list. Glazed products have been the specialty of the district for more than 600 years.

As the upper stream of Yongding River runs down and cuts through Mentougou, it is bestowed with beautiful scenery and biological diversity. The area is sometimes called the “Natural Museum in North China”. Today, 36.5% of the territory is green. However, not so long ago, the district was notorious for its poor sanitary conditions.

There are four development zones in Mentougou, including two industrial parks, a biological tourism zone and a special farming zone. The former two are the four-km^2 Shilong Industrial Park and a 30-ha New Construction Materials Industrial Park.

Mentougou has grown much during the past few years. In 2001, its GDP increased by 18.8% and the share of primary sector dropped to a mere 2% of the local economy.

Mentougou District Government
Tel: (8610) 6982 0430
Fax: (8610) 6982 0430
Website: www.bjmtg.gov.cn

Fangshan District

Fast Facts

Fangshan 2001	Figure	%
GDP (RMB mil)	9,417.8	11.7
Primary	960.4	16.2
Secondary	4,095.9	11.9
Tertiary	4,361.5	10.5
Total Industrial Output (RMB mil)	7,830.5	14.5
Export (RMB mil)	544.0	48.4
New FDI projects	15	-
Contractual FDI (USD mil)	32.7	-
Utilized FDI (USD mil)	20.1	-

Source: www.bjfsh.gov.cn

Located in the southwest corner of the municipality and upper reaches of the Juma River, Fangshan is made up of mountains, hills and plains. It has rich mineral deposits like coal and marble. High quality white marble from Fangshan was even used for building the Imperial Palace. Therefore, the district is also called the “hometown of construction materials”.

Zhoukoudian, the home to Peking Man, is located in the district. It has been listed by UNESCO as a World Cultural Heritage Site. More than 500 other cultural relics can be found across the region.

In 2001, the district achieved GDP of RMB 9.4 billion (USD 1.14 billion), up 11.7% over 2000. Most recently, real estate development and construction industry have become the growth engines of Fangshan’s economy. There are nine industrial parks in the district and emphasis is put on the development of Liangxiang High-tech Park where more than 305 enterprises are already in operation.

As agriculture is an important component of the local economy, Fangshan has set up many agricultural and aquaculture zones to better utilize its abundant resources of crops and fruits. The famous Liangxiang chestnuts are produced in Fangshan.

Fangshan District Government
1 Zhengtong Road
Tel: (8610) 89350 0494
Website: www.bjfsh.gov.cn

Tongzhou District

Fast Facts

Tongzhou 2001	Figure	%
GDP (RMB mil)	6,715.8	17.6
Primary	1,149.3	7.7
Secondary	2,500.0	29.3
Tertiary	3,066.4	13.1
Total Industrial Output (RMB mil)	6,557.7	15.1
Export (RMB mil)	1,009.3	40.2
New FDI projects	32	-
Contractual FDI (USD mil)	28.1	-
Utilized FDI (USD mil)	61.7	-

Source: www.bjtzh.gov.cn

Tongzhou lies on the alluvial plain formed by the Yongding River and Chaobai River. It has served as the southeast gateway to Beijing since the Sui Dynasty when the Grand Beijing – Hangzhou Canal was put into operation. Today, Tongzhou is equipped with a developed transportation network that comprises expressways from Beijing to Tianjin, Shenyang and Harbin, the Sixth Ring Road, national highways and railways. Being 20 km away from downtown Beijing, Tongzhou is an important satellite city of Beijing.

As the "East Beijing Granary", Tongzhou supplies wheat, rice and corn to the capital city. It is also the top supplier, among all the administrative areas in Beijing, of beef produce and freshwater fish. Machinery, textile, printing, construction materials, foodstuff and art & crafts form the mainstay of the economy.

In 2001, GDP grew by a significant margin of 17.6%. Value added of secondary industries increased even more vigorously up 29.3% over the previous year. Growth in the tertiary sector was largely constituted by real estate development.

An open economy has taken shape in Tongzhou. Important areas for investment include a 7-km^2 Beijing Optical-Mechanical Industrial Park (http://www.bjoip.com.cn) in Ciqu; a 6.75-km^2 Tongzhou Distribution Park and a 7.32-km^2 environment protection industrial park in Majuqiao; a 175-ha Central Industrial Park and a 203-ha chemistry park in Zhangjiawan; and the Yongle Economic Development Zone in Yongledian. Most of them are municipal-level industrial parks.

Tongzhou District Government
Tel: (8610) 6951 2345
Website: www.bjtzh.gov.cn

Shunyi District

Shunyi District

Shunyi 2001	Figure	%
GDP (RMB mil)	11,604.6	14.9
Primary	1,934.3	12.8
Secondary	5,577.1	7.1
Tertiary	4,093.1	28.6
Total Industrial Output (RMB mil)	20,254.8	-15.0
Export (RMB mil)	6,181.1	4.2
New FDI projects	50	-
Contractual FDI (USD mil)	60.3	-
Utilized FDI (USD mil)	113.7	-

Source: www.bjshy.gov.cn

Shunyi is another granary in Beijing. Important agricultural supplies include wheat, corn, rice, peanut, sesame, meat, egg, duck, fish and vegetables. Township and village enterprises have developed rapidly; they now form a cluster of industries including textile and garment, machinery, construction, construction materials and brewery.

As more than 100 FIEs are located in Shunyi, export from the district has far exceeded that of any other suburban district. In 2001, its GDP reached RMB 11.6 billion (USD 1.4 billion), up 14.9%. The tertiary sector grew particularly fast, up 28.6%, making a crucial contribution to strong economic growth.

The district has a land transportation network radiating from the center of Shunyi. Two railways, National Highway No.101 and the planned Sixth Ring Road of Beijing run through the district.

Shunyi has developed a number of industrial parks to leverage on the Capital International Airport. Tianzhu Airport Industrial Park, which includes an export-processing zone, sits on a 6.6-km^2 area along the Airport Expressway. To date, companies like JVC, Sony, Panasonic, Seiko, SMC, Citizen, Samsung, Airbus, Ericsson and Crown Can have all moved in.

Another municipal-level industrial park, Linhe Industrial Zone, located at the northeast end of the airport is designated as the microelectronics production base in North China. In 2003, Shunyi attracted 75 foreign-funded projects with total FDI of USD 2.57 billion.

Shunyi District Government
5 Fuqian Middle Street
Tel: (8610) 6944 3080
Website: www.bjshy.gov.cn

Changping District

Fast Facts

Changping 2001	Figure	%
GDP (RMB mil)	6,628.5	14.1
Primary	510.4	3.1
Secondary	2,610.2	17.6
Tertiary	3,507.9	13.3
Total Industrial Output (RMB mil)	8,159.9	39.1
Export (RMB mil)	663.0	1.9
New FDI projects	40	-
Contractual FDI (USD mil)	15.9	-
Utilized FDI (USD mil)	13.9	-

Source: www.bjchp.gov.cn

West to Shunyi lies Changping district. It has become a major satellite town for Beijing for promoting tourism and higher education. More than two-thirds of the district are hilly area; it also has rich reserves of natural resources such as raw construction materials, non-ferrous metal and mineral water resources. The district is also a key provider of agricultural products and resources to urban residents. The Beijng – Badaling Expressway and a few railway lines run through Changping.

As a famous tourism site, Changping is home to many natural scenic spots, such as Tiger Valley, Duijiu Valley, the Peach Blossom Valley, the White Sheep Valley, the Big Goat Mountain and 78 protected cultural relics, including three national-level relics and three municipal-level cultural treasures.

The Thirteen Ming Mausoleums, with total area spanning over 120 km^2, is a well-preserved group of ancient imperial tombs in China and has joined the World Cultural Heritage list. Juyongguan is a key pass of the Great Wall located in northwest Changping. Other attractions include Nine Dragon Amusement Park, Wax Figure Palace of Ming Emperor, Python Mountain National Forest Park, International Shooting Range and China Aviation Museum.

Real estate, commerce and tourism are important components of the economy. The GDP of Changping was around RMB 6.6 billion (USD 797 million) in 2001.

The future development of Changping will be focused on the development of the so-called "three parks and three zones". These are Changping Zone of Zhongguancun Science Park, a Biological Park, Little Tangshan Exemplary Park of Modern Agriculture, a tourism zone, a residential zone and Shahe university education zone.

Changping District Government
19 Zhengfu Street, Changping District
Tel: (8610) 8974 1792
Website: www.bjchp.gov.cn

Daxing District

Fast Facts

Daxing 2001	Figure	%
GDP (RMB mil)	6,279.5	17.5
Primary	1,226.5	10.2
Secondary	2,107.8	20.7
Tertiary	2,945.3	18.6
Total Industrial Output (RMB mil)	8,461.6	20.5
Export (RMB mil)	907.3	6.0
New FDI projects	40	-
Contractual FDI (USD mil)	21.1	-
Utilized FDI (USD mil)	55.2	-

Source: www.bjdx.gov.cn

In January 2001, Daxing became a district of the municipality. Located in south Beijing, Daxing enjoys great advantages of flat lands and an extensive river system. It used to be an agriculture-dominant economy and an important supplier of crops and non-staple food to Beijing. The district has been hosting a major Watermelon Festival every year since 1988. Pears, grapes, flowers, black bone chicken and cows are all specialties of Daxing.

The strategy of the district's development is focused on four districts. A modern urban zone will be set up in a 5.75-km^2 area near Huangcun. The south part of the district aims to develop a comprehensive industrial park focusing on the deep processing of agricultural products and the utilization of advanced technologies in agriculture.

The west of Daxing will become an industrial belt along Beijing–Kaifeng Expressway comprising a number of towns and development zones. The north part of Daxing, or Yizhuang, was allocated as a part of the state-level Beijing Economic & Technological Development Zone (www.bda.gov.cn) in 1994. It has already attracted over 270 FIEs with contractual FDI of more than USD 2.7 billion, including Nokia, Lucent, Honeywell, Amcor, Bayer, Messer, Schneider, ABB, SMC, Shiseido and Coca Cola etc.

Year 2001 saw Daxing's GDP soar 17.5% to RMB 6.3 billion (USD 760 million) and the development of industrial sectors registered above 20% growth. Construction, real estate and industries engaged in advanced technologies have become hot sectors in the district's economy.

Daxing District Government
15 Xingzheng Street
Tel: (8610) 6120 8500
Website: www.bjdx.gov.cn

Pinggu District

Fast Facts

Pinggu 2001	Figure	%
GDP (RMB mil)	3,645.1	10.1
Primary	847.7	11.8
Secondary	1,403.5	4.0
Tertiary	1,393.8	15.8
Total Industrial Output (RMB mil)	4,845.4	8.1
Export (RMB mil)	109.0	17.5
New FDI projects	14	-
Contractual FDI (USD mil)	23.0	-
Utilized FDI (USD mil)	13.9	-

Source: www.bjhd.gov.cn

Located in the east of Beijing, Pinggu is the only administrative district of Beijing that borders Tianjin. The district is mainly made up of hilly areas and plains. It is rich in water, mineral and biological resources. Gold, silver, iron, manganese, granite and barite deposit can be found here.

Production and export of fresh and dried fruits form an important part of Pinggu's economy. The district has been the largest supplier of peach, chestnut, cherry and apple to Beijing for 12 consecutive years. The primary sector as a whole accounted for 23% of local GDP in 2001, up 10.1% over 2000, representing considerable growth in this sector. The secondary and tertiary sectors share the rest almost equally. Major industries include garment, wool knitting, foodstuff, brewery, deep processing of agricultural products, fine chemicals and electronics.

There are a few major industrial parks in Pinggu. The 2.47-km^2 Binhe Industrial Park was among the first batch approved by the municipal government in 1991. It has so far attracted about 200 enterprises, 32 of which are foreign-funded. Xinggu Economic Development Zone is a 5-km2 industrial park approved by the Beijing municipal government in 1993. A prestigious Taiwanese food manufacturer, Want Want Group, has established a subsidiary there. Others include Yukou Industrial Park and

Changxing Industrial Development Zone in Machangying Town.

Major attractions include Jingdong Canyon, Jinhai Lake, and Hudongshui.

Pinggu District Government
Tel: (8610) 89980025
Fax: (8610) 89980026
Website: www.bjpg.gov.cn

Huairou District

Fast Facts

Huairou 2001	Figure	%
GDP (RMB mil)	4,332.1	14.2
Primary	420.6	9.2
Secondary	2,352.6	15.6
Tertiary	1,558.9	13.7
Total Industrial Output (RMB mil)	9,023.1	8.3
Export (RMB mil)	487.3	18.2
New FDI projects	30	-
Contractual FDI (USD mil)	54.0	-
Utilized FDI (USD mil)	46.3	-

Source: www.bjhd.gov.cn

With a territory covering 2,128.7 km², Huairou is the single largest administrative area in Beijing. However, it maintains the smallest population in the municipality, only 265,000 or just 104 people per km². One of the youngest districts in Beijing, Huairou was approved as a district by the State Council on 30 December 2001.

The narrowly-shaped district extends 128 km from the north to the south with 88.7% covered by mountains and hills that form a natural barrier in the north of Beijing. Huairou is an important source of water for Beijing, with its 22 reservoirs and 774 springs. Besides crops and chestnuts, it has the largest plantation area of American ginseng in China.

Agriculture accounts for one-tenth of the local economy with ginseng, chestnut and fish taking the lead. As the district is Beijing's water catchment area, pollution-free industries are encouraged. Currently, food and beverage, automobile and accessories, packaging and printing form the mainstay of Huairou's economy. In 2001, the secondary sector had a share of 54% in local GDP, up 15.6%. Leveraging on its scenic natural landscapes and cultural heritage, Huairou has no lack of tourist spots for its many visitors and its tourism industry looks set to attract investors.

There are a number of industrial parks in Huairou, mostly located in the southern part of the district. Yanqi Industrial Park, for instance, is a municipal-level industrial park. It has a total development area of 9.6 km^2.

Huairou District Government
15 Fuqian Street
Tel: (8610) 6965 514
Fax: (8610) 6964 7788
Website: www.bjhr.gov.cn

Suburban Counties

Fast Facts

Miyun 2001	Figure	%
GDP (RMB mil)	4,334.8	20.8
Primary	781.3	15.9
Secondary	2,064.4	26.5
Tertiary	1,489.0	16.2
Total Industrial Output (RMB mil)	6,744.8	26.9
Export (RMB mil)	562.4	31.4
New FDI projects	31	-
Contractual FDI (USD mil)	28.5	-
Utilized FDI (USD mil)	19.5	-

Source: www.bjmy.gov.cn

Miyun County

Miyun is the second-largest administrative area in Beijing. 95% of its 2,336 km^2 territory is a water conservation area and 10.1%, or 23,000 ha, is covered by water. The famous Miyun Reservoir, with a total volume of

4.375 billion m^3, is the largest one in North China and the most important water source for Beijing. Lakes, waterfalls and natural or cultural scenic sites are abundant in the county. Simatai Great Wall, Bailong Pool, Heilong Pool and Yunmeng Mountain are some famous ones.

Mineral resources are rich in the county. Deposits include lead, aluminum, tungsten, gold, silver and iron. Miyun has an exposed area of 368 km^2 of granite, making exploration very convenient. Malacolite, amphibolite and high-quality construction materials are plentiful too.

The county is connected to downtown Beijing by two railways and one highway.

Miyun Industrial Park (www.bmida.com) is a 16-km^2 municipal-level industrial park. It has been designated as an industrial base for university technological achievements by the Ministry of Education, and a National Torch Plan High-tech Industrial Base by the Ministry of Science & Technology. In addition, it is also the planned Beijing Software Base, Beijing Bio-engineering and Pharmaceutical Industrial Base, and a high-tech incubation center in Beijing. More than 120 enterprises have set up their businesses in the park.

Year 2001 saw Miyun's GDP soar tremendously, up 20.8% from the previous year, mostly contributed by the secondary sector that accounted for 47.6% in local economy and increased by 26.5%. Pollution-free industries like food processing, textile and garments, machinery and hardware form the core of local industry.

Miyun County Government
30 Gulou South Street, Miyun County
Tel: (8610) 6904 2356
Website: www.bjmy.gov.cn

Yanqing County

Fast Facts

Yanqing 2001	Figure	%
GDP (RMB mil)	2,494.7	14.3
Primary	806.7	4.7
Secondary	816.6	16.5
Tertiary	871.7	22.5
Total Industrial Output (RMB mil)	2,127.2	12.8
Export (RMB mil)	272.1	16.8
New FDI projects	4	-
Contractual FDI (USD mil)	1.1	-
Utilized FDI (USD mil)	0.9	-

Source: www.bjyq.gov.cn

Yanqing enjoys much attention as it plays host to the Badaling Great Wall, which has been accepted as a part of the World Cultural Heritage. The Great Wall is easily accessible at Badaling Town. With other famous tourist spots like Longqing Canyon, Songshan Natural Protection Park and Kangxi Pasture, the county receives more than 6 million visitors from all over the world every year. As Yanqing has a continental monsoon climate, it is an ideal summer resort. Led by booming tourism, the tertiary industries in total achieved 22.5% growth in 2001.

Located in the mountainous southwest of Beijing, three-quarters of the 1,980-km^2 wide territory is hilly area. Forest and woods have 55.4% coverage of the county. Yanqing is also a vegetable base during off-peak seasons. The primary sector accounts for almost one-third of the local economy. Guanting Reservoir is a major water resource for Beijing.

In recent years, industry in Yanqing has made considerable progress. Yanqing Industrial Park and Badaling Industrial Park have already attracted 450 enterprises. Foodstuff and brewery, wool knitting, building materials and pharmaceuticals are the mainstay of local industry. By the end of 2001, the secondary sector accounted for 32.7% in Yanqing's GDP. However, FDI penetration in the county remains low.

Two railways and one national highway run through the hilly county. Badaling Express is in full operation and it only takes 50 minutes to reach downtown Beijing.

Yanqing County Government
Tel: (8610) 6914 3015
Website: www.bjyq.gov.cn

FOREIGNERS IN BEIJING

The foreign community

With the rapid development of the Chinese economy and its adoption of open policy, a growing number of foreigners are now working and living in China. Figures show Beijing is home to more than 60,000 foreigners.

At present, approximately 16,000 foreigners in Beijing have work permits. Most of them are expatriates, while many others work for local organizations and enterprises.

Beijing has friendship ties with 124 capitals or big cities in 72 countries, and enjoys twin-city relationships with 27 cities in 24 countries. Beijing plays host to 150 embassies, 18 representative offices of international and regional organizations, and 190 bureaus of foreign news organizations. All in, 6,314 foreign companies have set up representative offices in the Chinese capital.

Figures released by the Municipal Statistics Bureau reveal that 1.85 million overseas travelers visited Beijing in 2003. With numerous foreign embassies and international companies, Beijing has the largest group of foreign nationals among all Chinese cities. This is expected to increase as a result of China's WTO entry and the preparations for the 2008 Summer Olympic Games.

Hotel accommodation

Beijing has over 50,000 hotels, resorts and inns of various kinds. 614 of these are star-rated, offering over 100,000 rooms and suites. Many of these hotels are operated by international hotel management corporations. The number and variety of hotels in Beijing mean visitors to the city have no lack of options for a place that meets their specific needs.

A free hotel reservation service is available for the reservation of the finest hotels and accommodation in Beijing. Various accommodation options

Beijing and its Sister Cities

	City	Country	Date of Sister City Relationship Establishment
1	Tokyo	Japan	14-03-1979
2	New York	U.S.A	25-02-1980
3	Belgrade	Yugoslavia	14-10-1980
4	Lima	Peru	21-11-1983
5	Washington D.C.	U.S.A	15-05-1984
6	Madrid	Spain	16-09-1985
7	Rio de Janeiro	Brazil	24-11-1986
8	Ile-de-France	France	02-07-1987
9	Köln	Germany	14-09-1987
10	Ankara	Turkey	20-06-1990
11	Cairo	Egypt	28-10-1990
12	Islamabad	Pakistan	08-10-1992
13	Jakarta	Indonesia	08-10-1992
14	Bangkok	Thailand	26-05-1993
15	Buenos Aires	Argentina	13-07-1993
16	Seoul	South Korea	23-10-1993
17	Kiev	Ukraine	13-12-1993
18	Berlin	German	05-04-1994
19	Brussels	Belgium	22-09-1994
20	Hanoi	Vietnam	06-10-1994
21	Amsterdam	Holland	29-10-1994
22	Moscow	Russia	16-05-1995
23	Paris	France	23-10-1997
24	Rome	Italy	28-05-1998
25	Gauteng	South Africa	06-12-1998
26	Ottawa	Canada	18-10-1999
27	Canberra	Australia	14-09-2000

are available for business, leisure and holidays. Brochures of the hotels are provided, together with room rates, hotel packages, special offers and other accommodation in Beijing. People can also enjoy real-time booking facilities which sometimes come with remarkable discounts.

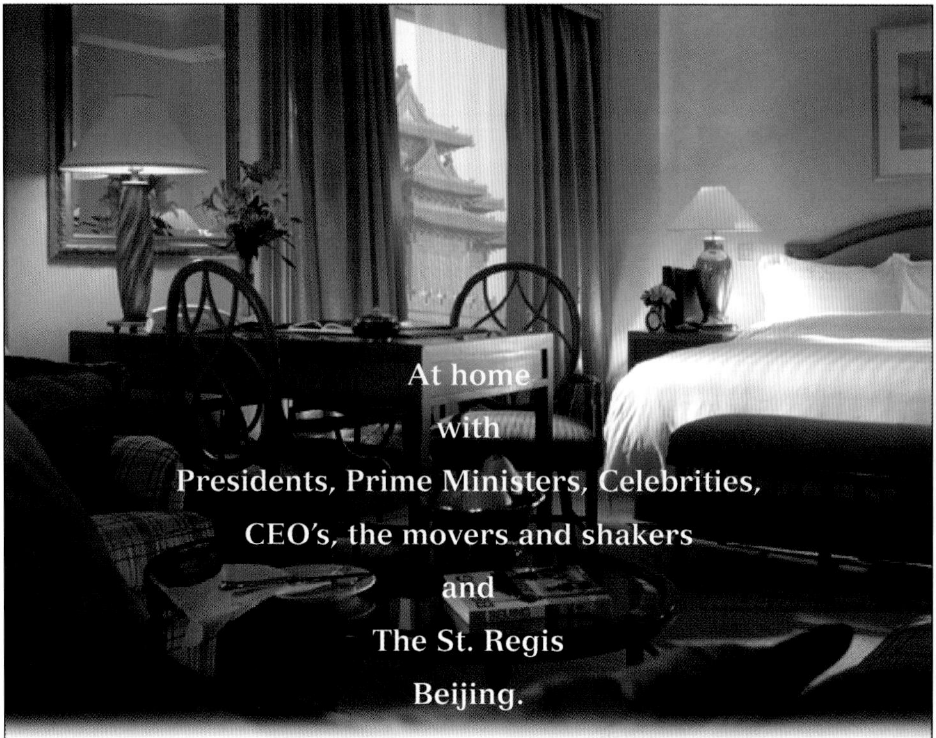

Star hotels

Beijing is the capital city of China, and it is known for the accommodation services it provides. For both luxury hotels and budget accommodation in Beijing, choices are plentiful and range from three-star to five-star hotels.

Five-star hotels

Beijing boasts a number of internationally well-known hotels. The following are some highly-recommended ones.

ANA Beijing New Century Hotel is located in northwest Beijing, at 6 South Capital Gymnasium Road, in Haidian District. It is 45 minutes from Beijing's Capital International Airport and 25 minutes from downtown areas by car. It is close to the Beijing Zoo, the National Library, Capital Stadium, The Summer Palace, Zhongguancun, Beijing University and other famous universities.

Famed for its beautifully landscaped gardens and excellent service, **Shangri-La Hotel Beijing** is located in the western part of Beijing. From the hotel, it is a mere 30-minute drive to Beijing's commercial and business center. There are as many as 657 guest rooms, each having all the creature comforts of a real home. Visitors can enjoy a fine variety of food from seven different restaurants. For banquets, conferences and meetings, the Shangri-La Hotel is certainly an ideal venue. It also provides guests with a 24-hour business center offering a full range of professional services. Undoubtedly, the Shangri-La Hotel is a delightful place to relax and conduct business.

Guests at **The China World Hotel** enjoy its beautiful surroundings and easy access to many local monuments and historical sites as well as main business and shopping districts. As part of the China World Trade Center, the hotel offers unrivaled access to Beijing's most sophisticated conference and exhibition facilities. The 738 rooms and suites of the hotel offer panoramic views of the city, and are equipped with modern amenities. The hotel has a world-class fitness center, a business center and some of the finest restaurants Beijing has to offer. Staying at the China World Hotel is indeed a unique and pleasurable experience.

Wangfujing Grand Hotel is located in one of Beijing's busiest business areas. This modern and luxurious hotel provides services for business, conferences and leisure.

Located at the center of the city, guests at the **Grand Hotel Beijing** can see from the terrace of the Grand Hotel the golden-glazed rooftops of the Forbidden City glittering in the sunlight and Chang'an Avenue. With plush interiors and an imperial ambience, the Grand Hotel promises a lavish and posh experience.

Zhaolong Hotel is located in Chaoyang District. The hotel is adjacent to Beijing's Embassy District. The Hotel is 17 minutes to the Capital International Airport by taxi, 15 minutes to Tiananmen Square, and 10 minutes to the downtown area. It is located close to museums, parks and other tourist attractions.

Four-star hotels

In addition to five-star hotels, Beijing also has a wide variety of four-star ones. Some of the more noteworthy ones are as follows.

Beijing Continental Grand Hotel is located in the Asian Games Village. It is 20 km from Beijing's Capital International Airport in the east, 9 km south of Tiananmen Square, 10 km from the Summer Palace and 80 km from the Badaling section of the Great Wall. The hotel is situated close to Beijing Recreation Center, a top fitness and entertainment center, as well as Beijing International Convention Center.

Beijing Continental Grand Hotel provided accommodation to domestic and overseas guests for the Asian Games, the International Entomology Conference, the International Parliamentary Union Conference and the

4th World Conference on Women. The president of the World Bank, the president of the International Olympic Committee, as well as Nobel Prize Winners have all been guests at the hotel.

Radisson SAS Hotel Beijing is located in Chaoyang District. The hotel is adjacent to the China International Exhibition Center. 20 minutes by taxi from the Capital International Airport, the Radisson SAS Hotel Beijing is 15 minutes to downtown Beijing and close to major commercial districts and embassies.

Holiday Inn Hotel belongs to yet another famous hotel chain. The Holiday Inn Lido-Beijing Hotel was the first Holiday Inn hotel in China. Established in 1984, the hotel is the proud winner of numerous international service and hospitality awards. The Hotel is located in a commercial-residential complex that houses a large number of Beijing's foreign community and multinational companies.

Settling in

Visas

L-visas for single or multiple entries for tourists are valid for 30 to 60 days. F-visas for business travel can be valid for up to six months but may require the visitor to leave every 30 days. They are good for single, double or multiple entries. Those seeking business visas must obtain official invitation from a government office or a company authorized by the Ministry of Foreign Affairs.

Green Cards

Beijing implemented a green card system in 2003 to grant permanent resident status to foreigners. Senior managers, investors, and other professionals would be considered first. Foreigners with such green cards enjoy preferential treatment, such as visa-free access for multiple entries into China.

This program is aimed at attracting more foreigners, especially high-level professionals and investors. Aside from Shanghai and Beijing, several other cities are also considering similar programs.

Beijing's Capital International Airport

Beijing's Capital International Airport is one of China's major gateways. Electronic display boards are installed throughout the airport, providing arrival and departure information in both Chinese and English. The Unisys Airport Passenger Processing System (APPS) is used at the airport. APPS enables airport personnel to use intuitive Windows-type graphical screens, enabling them to check in passengers and baggage, and complete reservations and departure control processes more quickly and efficiently.

Beijing is served by international carriers such as Northwest, United, Canadian Airlines, Japan Airlines, ANA, SAS, Dragon Air, Lufthansa, British Airways, Malaysian Air, Austrian Airlines, Air France, Alitalia, Korean Air, Pakistan Airlines, Singapore Airlines, Thai International, Air China, China Southern, and China Northern.

Travelers will be able to keep in touch with the world via multimedia payphones conveniently located throughout the terminal. A phone card, available at airport counters, is required to make calls. While travel books or maps might be scarce at the airport, tourist information and maps can be found at the front desks of most hotels.

Banks & ATMs

There are more than 12 ATMs (available 24 hours) and four auto cash exchange machines conveniently located throughout the terminal and they accept Cirrus, American Express, Visa, Visa Interlink and MasterCard.

Travel tax

Travelers departing Beijing on an international flight must pay a RMB 90 airport construction tax. Those flying to domestic destinations must pay RMB 50. Payment must be made at counters in the departure area prior to checking in for your flight. Remember to keep your receipt in the event that verification is needed.

Taxi services

The airport is 26 km, or 40 minutes, from the center of Beijing. Modes of transport (available during normal flight arrival and departure times) include bus and taxi. The airport bus is available on the lower level just outside the Arrivals area. There is just one government-run airport bus shuttle. Many hotels run their own airport shuttle bus services. Taxis are available on the lower level just outside the Arrivals area.

When arriving at the airport, avoid drivers who approach you in the terminal or outside the terminal. These drivers will almost always quote a price that is triple or more than the actual price. There is a taxi line just outside the terminal. Remember to insist that the driver use his meter; and make sure that the driver puts down the flag. This is to avoid drivers who say they forgot to put down the flag and ask for a ridiculous amount of money. The cost to midtown Beijing is normally around RMB 70 depending on the type of taxi, plus RMB 15 for the highway toll. There is no need to tip taxi drivers in Beijing unless they render extra assistance such as carrying your bags.

Most of the better hotels provide a card with the taxi's license plate when you get into a taxi at the hotel's front door. Retain this card should you need to be in touch with the driver, or his taxi company, or just in case you might have left something behind in the taxi. If you lose something and do not have the number of the taxi, you could try either your destination or departure point as it is not unusual for taxi drivers to turn lost goods in at these places. It is advisable to always carry the name of your hotel and any destination in Chinese because very few drivers in

Beijing speak English. You can ask the staff at the front desk of your hotel to write your destination in Chinese.

Banking hours

Banking hours vary from bank to bank in Beijing. However, most Chinese banks are open from 9 a.m. to 4 p.m. or 5 p.m. and have branches that are open on Saturdays and Sundays.

Paying taxes with bankcards

In the past, only two kinds of cards issued by the Industrial and Commercial Bank of China (ICBC) may be used for foreigners to pay tax. Now, foreigners may use various bankcards issued by the Bank of China, Agricultural Bank of China, China Construction Bank, China Bank of Communications and ICBC.

Credit cards

In Beijing, most major credit cards including American Express, Diner's Club, Federal Card, JCB, MasterCard and Visa are accepted at major hotels, restaurants and shops.

Tipping

Tipping is generally not expected in mainland China.

Electricity

The voltage is 220 volts, 50 cycles. Most luxury hotels have built-in converters in bathrooms for shavers, hair dryers, etc.

Time zone

GMT +8 hours. The whole of China is set to Beijing Time.

Business hours

Offices in Beijing generally open from 8:30 a.m. to 6 p.m., with a lunch break of about an hour. Government-stipulated workdays are from Monday to Friday. Shops generally open at 9 a.m. and close between 7 p.m. and 9 p.m.

Business attire

Normal Western business attire is considered appropriate for doing business in China.

People

Beijing people are quite friendly and outgoing in dealing with foreign guests. However, they are often quite reserved and cautious when dealing with foreigners in formal situations or in initial business relationships.

Driving

If you wish to drive, a Chinese driving license is required. Driving is illegal for visitors holding tourist visas. Holders of Resident Permits may apply for a Chinese driving license but again this is really not to be recommended. Driving is chaotic as many road-users pay little attention to rules and regulations and accidents are frequent. Road signs are mainly in Chinese script, though there are signs with the English translation in some places. Basically, foreigners who wish to travel by car in China are recommended to hire a car and a local driver, which is inexpensive and much more convenient.

Getting legal aid

For foreigners with little awareness about Mandarin Chinese and happen to have queries about Chinese law, what they could do is certainly more than just wait. Calling for legal aid is possible.

An English-language legal service hotline is available for foreigners in Beijing. English-speakers may dial 1600148 and then follow the instructions for legal consultation, provided in English. Follow-up legal services could also be arranged for foreigners if they find the consultation satisfactory.

The local government hopes that the English-language hotline will provide foreigners in Beijing with effective legal help. In fact, having the hotline is considered as a local effort to make foreigners feel at home during their stay in Beijing. At least 16 lawyers who speak fluent English serve at the hotline at any one time, more than half of them have doctorates or master's degrees.

The hotline is open from 9:00 am to 5:00 pm Monday through Friday. The number is a nationwide hotline where people could get free and handy legal advice. Figures from the Beijing Bureau of Justice indicate that some 590,000 people have called the hotline for legal advice in the first three years that it was launched.

Housing costs

Home to 14.2 million residents, Beijing has been in the midst of a property boom for nearly two decades, with spiraling prices amidst the plentiful construction of high-rise office towers and apartment blocks. The influx of job-seeking locals and business-dealing foreigners has kept demand for housing hot. Beijing's successful bid for the 2008 Olympics and China's entry into the WTO guarantee the acceleration of newcomers adding to the housing crunch.

For most foreigners in Beijing, prices have risen even faster, due to the existence of foreign communities. Every city has areas where foreigners tend to live and play, but Beijing's foreign communities are different. As early as the 12th century, Arab traders were forced to live apart from the regular Chinese population. Until the mid-1990s, the Beijing government had strictly regulated the places where foreigners and overseas Chinese could live. Much land in Chaoyang District, where many foreign embassies are located, has been designated for foreigner-occupied residential areas. The cost of such land is inevitably high, as a result.

On 1 September 2002, the regulation on housing that separates foreigners and locals was cancelled. With the regulatory change, foreigners have much wider range of choices when looking for a house to buy. The original regulation restricted foreigners to only buying or renting properties that should be specially approved, while locals had choices about any property on the market. Under the new regulations, the special term requiring foreigners to get approval will disappear for all sales permission certificates. People with earlier-edition certificates could change for new ones in authorization offices.

Also, sales contracts for property would be unified. In other words, foreigners may buy any kind of property in Beijing. The approved new regulation will certainly affect the market, in terms of supply, demand as well as price. Finally, chances will increase for foreign investment, as many foreigners have expressed interest in buying what local people could buy. In the near future, more and more foreigners would buy their own properties in Beijing on the same terms as locals, enjoying good quality as well as relatively low prices.

Schooling

In recent years, the growing number of foreigners entails growing demand for international schools for their children. In fact, Beijing saw an increasing number of international primary and secondary schools emerging to meet the needs of foreign children. Most of the teachers at these schools are from overseas.

Beijing BISS International School

Beijing BISS International School was founded in 1994 to serve the expanding Beijing expatriate community's need for international education. The school is a non-profit, co-educational English-language school with classes from Kindergarten level to Grade 12.

BISS is the first International School licensed by Beijing Educational Commission, an associate member of the European Council of International Schools (ECIS) and is accredited by the Western Association of Schools and Colleges (WASC). The school has been growing very fast, mirroring the rapid development of Beijing in the last few years. From 30 students in 1994, the School has expanded to over 500 students from 50 different countries today.

BISS hires highly experienced and qualified teaching faculty members from Africa, Australasia, Europe and North America. The diverse international background of these faculty members ensures the international character of the school, and gives students a well-rounded education.

Beijing BISS International School
No. 17, Area 4 Anzhenxili
Chaoyang District, Beijing
P. R. China 100029
Tel: (8610) 6443 3151
Fax: (8610) 64435156

International School of Beijing (ISB)

The American Embassy in Beijing originally established ISB as an elementary school. It then became truly international in nature, merging with small elementary schools from the British and Australian Embassies and thus earning its name in 1980. Children from the Canadian and New Zealand Embassies also joined the new school at this time.

The school (grades K to 8) moved to the Lido Hotel Complex in the spring of 1988. Many changes took place soon after. Children representing other national groups were offered opportunities to apply for enrollment to the ISB. Increased numbers of ESOL students (children whose first language was not English) were enrolled, and additional instruction in English Language was offered. Finally, the secondary school began to take shape.

Today, ISB is a fully accredited, private, non-sectarian, co-educational, college preparatory day school with English instruction for children from grades PK (Pre-Kindergarten) through comprehensive International High School. All students at the ISB engage in the Chinese Language Program from kindergarten to Grade 12. The curriculum focuses on integrating China Studies into all academic program areas. In addition, the ISB offers a technology program designed to assist students as a learning tool.

International School of Beijing
No. 10 An Hua Street
Shunyi District, Beijing
P. R. China 101300
Tel: (8610) 8046 2345
Email: admissions@isb.bj.edu.cn
Website: www.isb.bj.edu.cn

Other international schools in Beijing

There are many other international schools in Beijing, some of which are as follows.

New School of Collaborative Learning
Shangdi West Road, Haidian District

International Montessori School of Beijing
7 Sanlitun North Street, Chaoyang District

Beijing Yew Chung International School
Honglingjin Park, No 5 Houbalizhuang, Chaoyang District

International Study Group
1311 Sanlitun Street, Chaoyang District
Tel: 6532-2293

German School
Lido Complex, Chaoyang District

Japanese School
Lido Complex, Chaoyang District

Spanish Educational Study Group
Heping Jie Beikou, Huixin East Street, Chaoyang District

Pakistan College of Beijing
Embassy of Pakistan
1 Dongzhimenwai Avenue, Sanlitun, Chaoyang District

L'Ecole Francaise de Pekin (French School of Beijing)
13 Sanlitun East 4th Street, Chaoyang District

Montessori Kindergarten
China World Trade Center, South Lodge

Beijing Oxford Baby Bilingual Kindergarten
Asian Games Village North Gate, Bldg 308
Chaoyang District

Beanstalk Kindergarten
Sino-Japanese Youth Exchange Center
40 Liangmaqiao Road, Chaoyang District

Leisure

Events and festivals

Chinese New Year, or Spring Festival, starts on the first day of the lunar calendar, usually in February. Although officially it last only three days, many people take a week off work. Beijing is probably at its prettiest on 1 May, the Labor Day holiday. For the whole month of May, the city (especially Tiananmen Square) is decorated with flowers.

The Lantern Festival is also a good time to visit Beijing. People walk the streets at night carrying colored paper lanterns. It falls on the 15th day of the first month of the lunar calendar. Qingming Festival or Tomb Sweeping Day is a day for worshipping ancestors; people visit the graves of their relatives and tidy up the area. It falls on 5th April in most years. The Mid-Autumn Festival (Moon Festival) is the time to eat and to give mooncakes.

City life

A bike tour allows foreigners to experience the city as locals do and gives them access to the narrow, spidery hutongs. In winter there are many ice-skating venues around the city, including Beihai Lake, Kunming Lake, Zizhuyuan Park and the moat around the Forbidden City. Flying kites is an old tradition in China and in Beijing, one can do this at the Tiananmen Square. Kites are available for rent in the Square itself.

The arts and culture scene is very much alive in Beijing. Theater performances for example, are popular in Beijing. Capital Theater is located in the busy Wangfujing Avenue, and presents modern drama performances by the Beijing People Art Troupe. Beijing Music Hall stands in Xinhua North Street, and plays host to symphony concerts, solo concerts, choral concerts and so on.

In addition, Beijing Exhibition Hall Theatre showcases synthetic concert and ballet plays. Poly International Theatre mainly presents operas of

various kinds by foreign art groups. Chang'an Theatre hosts performances such as Beijing Operas and various kinds of folk art forms.

There are also many sports places in Beijing. The Olympic Sports Center is the place where China held the 1990 Asian Games. It is now the biggest and best sports venue in Beijing. Many foreigners as well as locals go there for a swim or to play various ball games. Beijing International Golf Court and Beijing International Tennis Center are another two busy sport venues.

Popular bowling alleys in Beijing include Apolo Entertainment City, which is located in the Friendship Palace of Friendship Hotel, New Century Hotel Bowling Center, Holiday Inn Hotel Bowling Center and so on. As for song-and-dance entertainment places, popular joints include Jackson Dance Hall, Eden Nightclub, Chang'an Entertainment City, Beijing International Club and so on.

Sightseeing

Beijing, having been the capital for many feudalistic dynasties, is particularly rich in historical and cultural attractions. It offers an extensive range of choices to wow tourists coming from across the country and abroad. A rough count shows that more than 7,300 sites in Beijing have been consistently drawing tourist dollars, creating hence a burgeoning tourism industry with over 450 tourist agencies and 5,000 tourist guides, offering special tourist services in over 20 foreign languages. In 2003 alone, 1.85 million foreign guests plus 87.37

million fellow countrymen visited Beijing, raking in high revenues for the city.

Forbidden City

Built on more than 72 ha and comprising more than 800 buildings and 9,000 rooms, the Forbidden City, or Imperial Palace, is located in the heart of Beijing. As the largest imperial residential-cum-administrative palace in the world, it has the best-preserved collection of ancient Chinese architecture. The seat of supreme power in China for five centuries before China's last emperor was ousted in bourgeois democratic revolutions, the grandeur and imposing presence of the Forbidden City is a sight to behold.

Truly in a league of its own, the Forbidden City sits regal among lush, landscaped gardens and bears numerous rooms containing exquisite

furniture and state-of-the-art artwork. The exhibits in the Forbidden City are the priceless legacies of the Chinese civilization in the Ming (1368-1644) and Qing (1644-1911) dynasties.

Summer Palace

Situated in the outskirts of the city is the Summer Palace, which used to be the holiday resort for emperors and queens. It is famous for its lake, gardens and hills. The palace was badly damaged by Anglo-French troops during the Second Opium War in 1860 and a full restoration was interrupted by the disintegration of the Qing Dynasty and civil rebellions. The beautiful Kunming Lake, which takes up three-quarters of the park, attracts visitors all year long. The main building is the poetically named Hall of Benevolence and Longevity, and along the north shore is the picturesque 700-meter-long Long Corridor decorated with many mythical paintings.

Tiananmen Square

Across from the entrance to the Forbidden City is the Tiananmen Square. The 880-meter-by-500-meter world's largest city square was mooted by the late Chairman Mao Zedong, the founder of the People's Republic of China. In the Chairman Mao Memorial Hall right in the middle of the Square lies the body of the late leader in a crystal coffin. Between the Hall and Tiananmen (Gate of Heavenly Peace) is the Monument of the People's Heroes. On the sides of the Square are the Museums of Chinese Revolutionary History and Chinese History.

The Great Wall of China

The Great Wall of China has undergone many restorations in the past and present. Originally built 2,000 years ago in the Warring States Period (770-722 BC) and then in the Qin Dynasty (221-206 BC) subsequently, it was a foreboding fortress against the marauding northern nomadic tribes. This seemingly old-fashioned defense system served as an effective frontier against invasions from the north for a long period of time. Construction continued up to the Ming Dynasty, when the Great Wall became the largest and longest military structure in the world.

Its historical and strategic importance seems to be matched only by its architectural value. Today, it is a tourist attraction known the world over. With a total length of over 6,000 km, it extends from the Jiayu Pass in Gansu Province in the west to the mouth of the Yalu River in Liaoning Province in the east. What lies north of Beijing is a small section of the meandering Great Wall. Today, the majority of visitors come to Badaling, Mutianyu and Shimatai to experience firsthand the splendor of the UNESCO-listed world cultural heritage.

Tiantan

Tiantan literally means the Temple of Heaven. It is set in the 267-hectare Tiantan Park and was originally used as a holy stage for solemn rites and rituals. Famous buildings in the park include the Round Altar, the Imperial Vault of Heaven and the Hall of Prayer for Good Harvests, which were recognized as communicative interfaces between the gods and mortals. For ancient emperors, it was the place where they held ceremonies to show their respect for the heavens. The buildings are carefully designed and the original construction is closely related to fengshui (geomancy), numerology, cosmology and religion.

Beijing handicrafts

Jade Carving

Jade carving appeared first in the Shang and Zhou dynasties about 3,000 years ago. The materials used for jade carving included all kinds of hard stones, such as jadeite, nephrite, red agate, white agate, crystal, amethyst, coral, ruby and sapphire. It is a special skill to capitalize on the natural color of a piece of jade to create an effective design. So the most expensive ones are not those of one single color, but those of multiple colors.

Skilled carving enhances the different colors in an object. Jade carvings are popular among the Chinese people. There are also other jade items of highly practical use, such as rings, bead-necklaces, earrings, pendants, seals and cigarette holders.

Carved Lacquer Ware

Lacquer ware originated in the Han Dynasty more than 2,000 years ago, but it only reached Beijing about 1,000 years later, in the Tang Dynasty. Techniques improved throughout the Yuan and Ming dynasties.

There are two types of carved lacquer ware – metal and non-metal roughcast. The former has an enamel lining, and the latter has a lacquer lining. Many layers (up to a few hundred) of lacquer are applied to the box to a thickness of 5.18 mm. After the lacquer has dried, it is carved, in relief or fretwork, by hand, and landscapes, figures, flowers, birds, animals or other patterns are carved onto the lacquer ware. Beijing lacquer ware is applied to a variety of objects, such as vases, plates, boxes, jars and decorated screens. They make nice decorative presents.

Silk Flowers

With fine, coarse, satin and silk fabric as raw materials, the silk flowers are all delicately hand-made. In the natural hues of fresh flowers, they look very genuine and are almost indistinguishable from real ones. In addition to flowers, any kind of plant can now be made of silk or nylon. Silk flowers keep their color for longer if they are not placed in direct sunlight. Because of their fame, the silk flowers made in Beijing are also known as "Capital Flowers".

You can buy silk flowers in department stores, arts and crafts shops and souvenir shops. They are easy to pack in your luggage as they can be twisted or squeezed flat and pulled back into shape after unpacking.

Painted Snuff Bottles

These are mainly made of glass, though jade, crystal agate and jadeite are also used to make the more valuable ones. They are pretty in shape, but their unique feature is that the paintings are done from the inside of the bottle.

First, small flat bottles are made. Then iron sands are put into the bottle and shaken to make the inside of the bottle a smooth milky white. After cleaning, a tip-bent bamboo painting brush is used to paint the inside of the bottle.

Since the bottle is small and its neck narrow, the painting requires extreme skill. The paintings are normally of flowers, birds, landscape, calligraphy, beauties, or scenes from historical or legendary stories.

Dough Figurines

Dough figurines, also known as dough modeling, are another typical Beijing handicraft. Wheat flour and glutinous rice flour are the main ingredients, plus paint, paraffin wax and honey, to make soft and shiny dough following a crack and mould-proof treatment.

Artisans then knead the dough and cut it with bamboo knives to form bodies, heads, hands, legs, etc. These figurines are then decorated with hair, clothes and other accessories (also made of dough).

Cloisonné

Cloisonné is an enamel handicraft made with roughcast brass and copper wire inlay. It is one of the traditional arts and crafts in Beijing. First appearing in the Yuan Dynasty, it rapidly developed during the Jingtai reign of the Ming.

Jingtailan was the name of the dazzling color of one of the most frequently used cloisonné enamels which appeared at that time. It is now used to refer to cloisonné enamels in general.

The cloisonné process begins with the casting of bronze into different shapes - vases, bowls, boxes, and even bracelets - to which flat copper wire is then affixed in decorative patterns. Enamels of different colors are applied to fill the "cloisonné" or hollows. Each cloisonné piece is fired three times with a fresh coat of enamel each time. After firing, the pieces are ground and polished to look like gold. This requires sophisticated techniques and artistic flair. Chinese cloisonné received first prize at the Chicago World Fair in 1904.

Bargaining

Prices are usually higher in the morning and lower before the market closes in the afternoon. So long as there are profits, the sellers are willing to make more sales before packing up for the day. It is often easier to bargain with non-Beijing traders who usually do not really know much about antiques; most of the Beijing traders are semi-professional though.

Whether you get a better price sometimes depends on the buyer. If the buyer is a foreigner, he/she may not be able to bargain the price down. If the buyer speaks in pure Beijing dialect, whether he/she really knows about antiques or not, he/she may be able to hoodwink the seller, so you will always get a better deal if you have a Beijing friend go with you to the market.

JIANGUO SWEET HOME

Jianguo Sweet Home an oasis in Beijing's Central District

History

Built in 1982, the Jianguo Hotel Beijing was the first joint venture hotel in China and it proved to be an instant success. Occupying 11,000 square meters and with total building area of 30,000 square meters, Jianguo's unique structure and classic interior décor creates an elegant and lively atmosphere.

Location

Jianguo Hotel Beijing is located right in the Beijing Central Business District (CBD), in the heart of Beijing's business and administrative center, and within walking distance of government offices and trade missions.

Jianguo Hotel's tastefully-refurbished function rooms combine comfort and practicality, and provide comprehensive amenities for business people.

Jianguo Hotel is a mere 20 minutes from Beijing Capital Airport, 10 minutes from Tiananmen Square and a stone's throw from Beijing's numerous historical sights.

Conveniently located, many bus routes serve Jianguo Hotel, such as No. 120, No. 9, No. 403, No. 43, 48, 52, 1,4, 120 branch, 938, 728,729, 848, 808, and 37. Or hop onto Subway Line 1 to visit us.

Address

5 Jianguomenwai Dajie, Chaoyang District

Beijing 100020, People's Republic of China

Telephone: (8610) 6500 2233 Fax: (8610) 6500 2871/ 6501 0539

Website: www.hoteljianguo.com Email: exec@hotelJianguo.com

Rooms and Facilities

The Best Choice in Beijing for Business Travelers

Jianguo Hotel Beijing is an upscale 4-star business hotel. It has 467 suites and rooms which are oases of comfort and yet meet all business requirements.

The hotel is divided into the East and West Wings. The reception counter, which handles all administrative matters, is in the four-storey tall East Wing. Linked to the East Wing at ground level, the West Wing is a nine-storey building offering a variety of restaurants. Its lobby is affectionately known as "the favorite meeting place in Beijing".

To further enhance the hotel's reputation as the premier business address in Beijing, and with a focus on the needs of business travelers, newly-renovated Superior and Business Levels, as well as Jianguo Club rooms and suites were introduced, adding a new dimension of comfort. Amenities such as IDD lines, coffee/tea making facilities, air-conditioning, and multi-channel satellite TV and radios, mini bar, refrigerator have been upgraded. Furniture in the hotel is new and elegant.

High-speed broadband has been installed in every room and guests are entitled free use. Personalized voice mail is a plus. The new 25-inch TV enables one to watch his or her favorite satellite programs in greater comfort. The bathroom has been fully renovated and extended. Larger closet space is now available. From the deluxe guestrooms and duplex suites you can look over the Jianguo garden or you can choose a unit that faces the city. The bathrooms offer a separate shower area. Deluxe suites have two separate bathrooms and the living rooms are enhanced with new fireplaces.

On the Jianguo Club Executive floor, business and leisure travelers experience a higher standard of accommodation and a more personalized service as well as a host of privileges including:

- Deluxe guestrooms and duplex suites overlooking the Jianguo garden or facing the city. The bathroom offers a separate shower area. Deluxe suites have two separate bathrooms and the living rooms are enhanced with new fireplaces.
- The Jianguo Club lounge provides a wide selection of international newspapers, magazines and books.

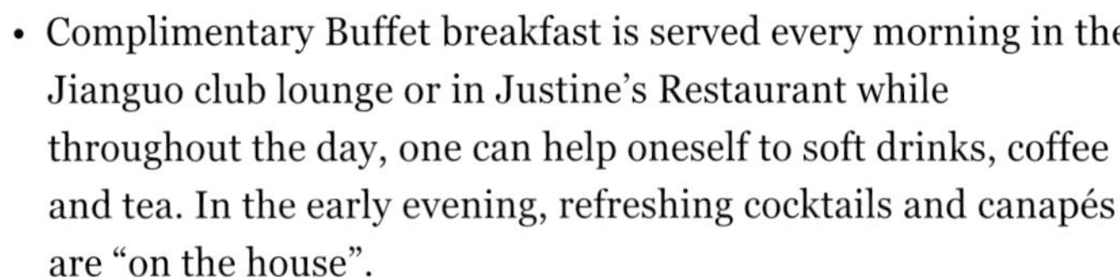

- Complimentary Buffet breakfast is served every morning in the Jianguo club lounge or in Justine's Restaurant while throughout the day, one can help oneself to soft drinks, coffee and tea. In the early evening, refreshing cocktails and canapés are "on the house".
- Newspapers and fresh fruit are provided on a daily basis.
- Incoming faxes are free of charge for all guests.
- Happy hour cocktails are served daily with hot & cold hors d'oeuvres

The Business Center offers the busy executive peace of mind and total confidence when using its comprehensive facilities. Our services include secretarial, photocopying, facsimile, internet access, express mail, photo scans, safe-deposit boxes, typewriters and personal computers. Two conference rooms are also available. We have all kinds of modern facilities and amenities you would expect from a truly international hotel.

Jianguo Hotel guests have an excellent range of food and beverage outlets to choose from:

- Justine's Restaurant is Beijing's most famous French a-la-carte fine dining venue. It has an intimate and elegant setting and unobtrusive service. Justine's has a firmly established tradition of excellence and promises a superb dining experience. Dedicated to French cuisine, the excellent menu reflects the varieties and richness of French tradition. Your meal will be complemented by the finest French wines.
- The Café is an all-day dining restaurant featuring Western and Asian specialties, as well as superb evening buffets.
- Four Seasons serves Cantonese cuisine and some local and regional dishes as well as dim sum specialties daily.
- Charlie's Bar has a lively atmosphere enhanced in the evening with performances by a Filipino band. Daily lunch and dinner buffets are popular with local residents and foreign guests alike.
- Lobby Lounge is the perfect meeting place after work for cocktails. Enjoy a unique "Old World" afternoon tea while listening to traditional concerts and piano recitals.

Our exquisite home-baked pastries and a fine range of international gourmet delicacies have been highly praised by both locals and foreigners alike.

The Banqueting Centre hosts many kinds of meetings: cocktails, weddings, exhibitions and banquets. The brightness of the lights in every meeting room can easily be adjusted. In the big and superior rooms, we supply Barco System Projector, a podium and banner shelves. We also supply the stereo component system for guests to play background music during their events. Internet and microphone access and basic audio equipment are also available.

As a first class member of the SRS World Hotels Collection of Hotels and Resorts, we are partners of United Airlines, Delta Airlines, Asian Club, Lufthansa Miles & More, ANA mileage and Thai Royal Orchid Plus frequent flyer programs.

As the first joint-venture hotel in China, Jianguo is also a hotel with a splendid history which has witnessed the whole development process and the internationalization of the city. Having an inspiration to deliver the highest standards of service to you, we promise that Jianguo Hotel will always be your Sweet Home in Beijing!

北京建国门外大街5号　邮政编码：100020　No.5 Jianguomenwai Da Jie,Beijing 100020, P.R.China
电话TEL: + 86 (10) 6500 2233　传真FAX: + 86 (10) 6500 2871
电子邮件E-mail: jianguo@hoteljianguo.com　网址http://www.hoteljianguo.com

FORMS OF INVESTMENT

Main types of foreign direct investment

China is relatively restrictive when it comes to setting up business although this is changing. The government is keen to attract foreign investment, and Foreign Direct Investment (FDI) is still the predominant form of investment. In 2003, FDI accounted for 95.3% of total foreign investments.

There are three main types of foreign direct investment in China, namely, the equity joint venture (EJV), the cooperative joint venture (CJV) and wholly-owned foreign enterprise (WOFE). Collectively, they are referred to as "foreign invested enterprises (FIEs)".

By definition, joint ventures (including both EJV and CJV) are jointly invested and established by one or more Chinese business entities or individuals together with one or more foreign business entities or individuals in accordance with the Equity Joint Venture Law and Regulations or the Cooperative Joint Venture Law and Regulations. The fundamental feature of a joint venture in China is that the foreign party or parties hold 25% or more in the ownership of the joint venture.

In contrast, a WOFE refers to a separate legal entity with limited liability status set up in China based on the Wholly Owned Foreign Enterprise Law and Regulations. In such an entity, the foreign investors hold 100% ownership.

Telecommunications equipment makers are usually all joint ventures. Some sectors, such as that of telecommunications service providers cannot even permit foreigners as minority shareholders.

However, there are more and more companies being given special approvals. Even smaller foreign companies have succeeded in setting up wholly-owned foreign enterprises.

> It is increasingly common for a foreign investor to begin with a JV partner to facilitate setting up a business and dealing with government officials. Eventually, these foreign investors simply buy out the JV partner and start on their own.

The best rule of thumb is to investigate thoroughly any business opportunity before talking to any prospective partner. Chinese partners are often invaluable for navigating the murky depths of business in China and facilitating the setting up of a business.

Equity joint venture (EJV) and cooperative joint venture (CJV)

EJVs are legal persons under Chinese law and may own assets, sue and be sued. In other words, equity joint ventures operate in the form of a limited liability company, which means that the personal wealth and property of the shareholding partners are shielded from corporate loss.

In comparison, CJVs can choose to acquire or not to acquire a legal person status. In other words, a CJV with non-legal person status is allowed. It is legally equivalent to a partnership establishment. It does not enjoy limited liability protection. In practice, the majority of CJVs are set up as limited liability companies.

The most significant difference between EJV and CJV is the allocation of profits and liabilities. In an EJV, profits and liabilities are allocated according to the ratio of the capital contributions made by the partners. It simply means that if one party contributes 30% of the capital investment, they will be rewarded 30% of the total profits and required to take up 30% of the liabilities.

CJV allows for greater flexibility in the agreement between the joint venture parties. In a CJV, profit sharing is generally prescribed by the joint venture agreement between the parties. In practice, the foreign party generally receives a higher percentage of profit in the early years of the CJV while their Chinese partner will become the owner of the fixed assets of the CJV at no cost after termination of the joint venture.

Some areas in the *encouraged* category are reserved exclusively for joint ventures. These are considered strategic or of great importance to the nation's social and economic development and security:

- Construction and operation of municipal light railways;
- Construction and operation of civic airports;
- Construction and operation of nuclear power plants;
- Exploitation and mining of copper, lead, zinc and aluminum;
- Repairing, designing and manufacturing of special type or high quality ships;
- Manufacturing of nuclear power units (more than 600 megawatts);
- Construction and operation of comprehensive water irrigation systems;
- Construction and operation of trunk railway line networks;
- Airlines;
- Postgraduate-level education institutions;
- Manufacturing of air transportation control network equipment;
- Designing and manufacturing of civilian airplanes and airplane engines;
- Designing and manufacturing of satellites for civilian use; and,
- Designing and manufacturing of rocket launchers for civil purposes.

The areas in the *restricted* category exclusive to joint ventures are:

- Development and production of grain, cotton and oil seeds;
- Processing of wood from precious trees;
- Exploration and mining of special and rare types of coal;
- Printing of publications;
- Smelting and separation of rare earth;
- Manufacturing of automobile cranes with capacity under 50 tons;
- General services (used in areas such as photography, mineral exploration and industries);
- Development of large tracts of land;
- Medical facilities;
- Senior high schools; and,
- Construction and operation of cinemas.

Wholly-owned foreign enterprise (WOFEs)

To promote more foreign investment, greater flexibility was introduced more than three years ago for foreigners to set up wholly-owned enterprises. WOFEs are now an alternative to joint ventures in some specific sectors.

Industrial restrictions on WOFEs have been lifted gradually. According to the Catalog for Guiding Foreign Investment in Industry, wholly-owned foreign enterprises can be set up in all the *encouraged* and *restricted* sectors except those specified as “exclusive for joint ventures”.

Due to a more liberalized and transparent regulation system, WOFEs have already overtaken JVs in recent years to become the most popular form of foreign investment. The restrictions imposed on WOFEs in areas such as foreign exchange balance, export obligation, priority of domestic sourcing, and the reporting requirements for production and operation plans have all been removed.

Export obligation

Under the revised law, WOFEs no longer have to export all or the majority of their products. According to the original law, enterprises with foreign capital "shall" be established in such a manner to help promote the development of China's national economy and they "shall" adopt advanced technology and equipment, and market all or most of their products outside China.

But the amended laws state that foreign enterprises are "encouraged" to market their products outside China and use advanced technology. This change gives a greater degree of autonomy to WOFEs to sell their products in China's domestic markets.

Sourcing

According to previous regulations, WOFEs should purchase their production equipment and raw materials in domestic markets. The revised law now stipulates that when purchasing raw materials within the permitted scope of its operation, an FIE "may purchase the goods in China and may also buy them in the international markets". With these new amendments, WOFEs in China can enjoy greater freedom in purchasing.

Foreign exchange

The original regulation on WOFEs required a WOFE to achieve the balance of foreign exchange income and expenditure. If a WOFE is unable to achieve the balance of its foreign exchange income and expenditures on its own, it may, in accordance with State provisions, apply to relevant authorities for assistance. In the current amendments, the provisions on "foreign exchange balance" requirement for WOFEs have been removed.

Production and operations

WOFEs were also previously required to submit their production and operation plans to the authorities for filing. This requirement has, to a certain extent, impeded the daily operation and management of WOFEs. The revised laws on Foreign Capital Enterprises and Sino-foreign Equity Joint Ventures have deleted this item. WOFEs now have greater autonomy in operation.

Other types of foreign direct investment

In addition to setting up EJV, CJV or WOFE, other forms of investment are now available for foreign investors. Foreign investors can set up holding companies and foreign-invested joint stock limited companies in China. These two new forms of investment are expected to become more and more popular as China relaxes its laws and regulations in accordance with the WTO entry agreements.

Foreign-Invested Holding Companies (FIHCs)

Foreign-invested holding companies (FIHCs) refer to those EJVs or wholly-owned subsidiaries engaging in direct investment activities set up in China by foreign investors. They are set up as separate legal entities with limited liability status and independent from enterprises in which they invest (i.e. their subsidiaries).

In terms of business activities, FIHCs are restricted to only direct investment activities. Since 2001, FIHCs can also act as a promoter or shareholder of a joint stock company in China.

Unlike foreign manufacturing and trading enterprises, which are restricted to carrying out business only in the location specified in its business registration, FIHCs are able to invest in projects all over China.

However, there is a minimum registered capital requirement for FIHCs. For FIHCs, the minimum registered capital varies with business nature. For example, for production enterprises, the minimum registered capital is RMB 500,000 (USD 60,000); for commodity retailing, on the other hand, it is RMB 300,000 (USD 36,000).

The total loan amount that a foreign-invested holding company can borrow should not be more than four times its actual paid-up registered capital unless approved by MOFTEC. This is clearly different from the case of the other forms of FIE, where the debt financing limit is determined by the total investment of the relevant foreign-invested enterprise.

Foreign-invested joint stock companies

A foreign-invested joint stock company refers to an enterprise or a legal person that meets the following conditions:

- its capital consists of shares of equal denomination;
- the liabilities of its shareholders are limited to the respective subscription of shares by such shareholders;
- its liabilities are limited to the value of all its assets; and,
- the shares are held by Chinese as well as foreign shareholders and the foreign investors together hold more than 25% of total shares.

A foreign-invested joint stock company is considered a type of foreign investment enterprise. With regards to foreign investment in China, all laws and regulations are applicable. In other words, it would be legally impossible to set up a foreign-invested joint stock company in the industrial sectors that prohibit foreign investment.

Like FIHCs, foreign-invested joint stock companies also face a minimum registered capital requirement. The amount varies with business nature, but is not lower than RMB 10 million (USD 1.2 million).

Build-operate-transfer (BOT)

BOT (Build-Operate-Transfer) refers to the cooperative arrangement in which the government signs a contract with a project company, which will, according to the contract, collect funds and construct infrastructure projects. Over an agreed period of time, the project company will own, operate and maintain the project while reclaiming investment and making reasonable profits by charging fees.

When the contract period is over, the ownership of the project will be transferred to the government. BOT is mainly adopted in developing infrastructure projects such as toll roads, power plants, railways, wastewater processing facilities and subways etc.

Types of indirect foreign investment

International leasing

Primarily, there are three kinds of leasing trade, namely, financial lease, operating lease and comprehensive lease. Under financial lease, long-term credit is extended by a leasing company to its client, that is, the leasing company will first pay for the purchase of the equipment selected by the client and then lease it to the client.

For the duration of the use of the equipment, both parties shall not arbitrarily terminate the contract; the lender shall retain ownership of the equipment while the client shall possess the right to use it. The client is responsible for the maintenance of the equipment and the leasing company shall collect rents from the client. Upon expiry of the lease, the client may require an extension of the lease or purchase the leased equipment at a negotiated price.

With this method, the leasing company provides equipment needed by the client and is responsible for the maintenance and repair of such equipment while the client pays rents according to the lease contract and returns the equipment upon termination of the lease.

Operating lease is limited to the period the equipment is used. It is usually applicable to short-term projects. The lease expires when the project is completed.

The comprehensive lease is a method whereby lease is combined with equity or contractual joint ventures, or lease is combined with inward processing and compensation trade. However, the method of combining lease with equity or contractual joint ventures shall be the portion outside the registered capital of the joint venture.

Compensation trade

On the basis of credit, the foreign party provides the Chinese party with capital or equipment, technology and raw material, and undertakes to buy a certain quantity of products from the Chinese party.

The Chinese partner compensates by installments to the foreign party directly or indirectly by using the products manufactured and the equipment and technology provided by the foreign party, or other products agreed upon with the foreign party. Inward Processing and Compensation Trade has been very popular since the beginning of China's economic reforms.

Processing and assembling

The foreign investors provide raw material, auxiliary material, parts, components or drawings, while the Chinese partner processes them or assembles them into finished products which are then returned to the foreign party for marketing. The Chinese party charges a fee for the processing.

Alternatively, the foreign party provides production equipment with or without a price and funds for building the plant premises where the Chinese party collects a processing fee. The cost of production equipment purchased by the foreign partner shall be transferred to the Chinese party in installments using the processing fee.

PROCEDURES AND GUIDELINES FOR INVESTMENT

Foreigners intending to invest in Beijing may first inquire at the China embassy or consulate in their home country for the correct procedure to follow before proceeding to China (Beijing), or you may directly contact the Beijing Chapter of China Council for the Promotion of International Trade (CCPIT) or the Beijing Foreign Investment Service Center (BFISC), stating your purpose of coming to Beijing, proposed dates of stay and some details of your investment projects.

The above-mentioned Chinese government organs may apply on your behalf to the China embassy or consulate in your country for an entry visa for you. Upon receiving a letter of invitation, you can call at China's diplomatic organ stationed in your country with the letter of invitation to apply for the issue of entry visas.

Project examination and approval authorities

Before establishing their business in China, foreign investors need to prepare the requisite documents and go through the approval and registration process. Projects should be submitted to the specific governing authorities for examination.

Foreign-funded investment projects with a total input of USD 30 million or greater will be submitted by the Beijing Development & Planning Commission to the Municipal Government for initial examination. This will then be submitted to the State Planning Commission for examination and approval. Foreign-funded production investment projects with total cash input exceeding USD 5 million, along with certain non-production projects with capital investment more than USD 3 million should submit to the Municipal Planning Commission for examination and approval.

Beijing municipal economic & trade commission

If the project is relevant to industrial upgrading and meets the required capital bottom-line, the initial examination will be done by the Beijing Municipal Economic & Trade Commission, before being submitted to the State Economic & Trade Commission for examination and approval. If the total investment capital exceeds USD 100 million, the projects must go through a final examination by, and meet the approval of, the State Council.

District or county governments

For examination and approval, proposals or feasibility study reports on foreign-invested production projects that call for capital input of USD 5 million or less should be submitted to the relevant district or county governments or municipal bureaus or the relevant group corporations that are authorized for the work. The same rule applies to foreign-invested non-production projects that call for capital input of USD 3 million or less.

Authorities of development zones

The administrative authorities of the Beijing Economic & Technological Development Area (BDA) may independently examine and approve any foreign-funded investment project to be implemented within BDA. That is, the administrative authorities of the BDA may approve projects independently of the municipal authorities.

The administrative authorities of the Beijing New High-tech Pilot Development Zone examines and approves proposals and feasibility study reports on projects to be carried out within its Zone that call for USD 30 million or less in capital input, provided the projects are for development of high-tech products. This rule applies to any foreign-funded project, be they Chinese-foreign joint ventures or Chinese-foreign cooperative projects.

Other authorities

The following foreign-funded projects require examination and approval by the relevant state organs:

- Those projects that fall into Category B listed in the Directory of Industries for Foreign Investment (revised in 1997) as projects in which foreign investment is restricted;
- Real estate development projects undertaken in the city by corporations affiliated to central government departments (including departments of the People's Liberation Army) and are partners in joint or cooperative ventures with foreign enterprises;
- Projects undertaken by local real estate development corporations that involve a floor space of more than 100,000 m^2 or Chinese-foreign joint ventures or cooperative projects for development of high-class property that call for a capital input of USD 30 million or greater;
- Foreign-funded hotels and restaurants of four-star or higher standards;
- Condominiums, villas and vacation resorts;
- Apartment buildings with development cost at least double the average cost of residential buildings in the capital (RMB 2,000 per m^2);
- Office and business buildings and other multi-purpose structures with a construction cost at least double the average cost for construction of non-residential buildings (RMB 4,000 per m^2).

Setting up foreign-invested enterprises (FIEs) in Beijing

The required procedures and documents are different for Joint Ventures (JVs) and Wholly Owned Foreign Enterprises (WOFEs), but in general,

there are some basic stages that FIEs have to go through.

Stage 1: Letter of intent (LOI)/ memo of understanding (MOU) (For JV only)

This stage is only for foreign investors who want to establish a joint venture in Beijing. They need to reach a preliminary understanding (LOI/ MOU) with their Chinese partners. These documents provide a basic description of the project contemplated, planned equity distribution between the partners, the amount of planned capitalization (which will determine the government level to which the project approval application will be directed) etc. Although LOI/ MOU does not have any legal binding effect on the parties, it should nevertheless expressly provide that provisions concerning exclusivity and confidentiality are legally binding on the parties.

The preliminary agreement is attached to a project proposal that the Chinese partner is required to submit to the appropriate authorities mentioned above for examination and approval before proceeding to the next stage.

Stage 2: Preliminary approval – project proposal (For both JV and WOFE)

For JVs, the next stage is to submit a project proposal to the appropriate authority. The project proposal is prepared and submitted by the Chinese partner and will include the LOI/ MOU as an attachment. This step in the approval process is entirely the responsibility of the Chinese partner.

Foreign investors monitoring this process have, at times, found "errors" in the translation of the preliminary agreement attached to the project proposal (all of which are in Chinese); this would, of course, alter the terms of the project. In addition, Chinese partners have sometimes drafted the project proposals to facilitate speedy approval and included export requirements, which were not part of the original agreement.

For WOFEs, drafting a project proposal is the first step. The project proposal is prepared and submitted by the foreign investor directly to the appropriate authorities. The foreign investor sometimes contracts a designated agent to serve as a liaison with local authorities. The foreign investor will sign an agreement with the agent stipulating the agent's scope of authority, areas of responsibility, and fees.

Generally, the examination and approval authority shall give a reply (approval or disapproval) within 20 days of receipt of the proposal. An approval document will be issued to the investor, if a WOFE, or directly to the Chinese partner, if a JV. The foreign investor in a JV should request a copy of this document from the Chinese partner to confirm that the approval is consistent with the agreed terms of the project.

The Chinese partner in a JV or the foreign investor in a WOFE should apply to Beijing Industrial & Commercial Administration (BICA) to register the name of the enterprise upon receiving a positive reply from the governing authority.

Stage 3: Submission of feasibility study report (For both JV and WOFE)

Upon the preliminary approval of the project proposal, a feasibility study is to be prepared by the WOFE foreign investor or, for a JV, jointly by the joint venture partners. A feasibility study is in essence a more detailed and expanded version of a project proposal. Specifically, the feasibility study must include:

- A general description of the project and the parties involved in the venture;
- Production plans and a simple market study;
- Location of the project and reasons for the selection;
- Description and explanation of purposes of equipment and technology to be utilized;
- Organizational structure of the enterprise;

- Environmental protection, labor arrangements, construction plans and timetable;
- Capital sourcing and the calculation thereof;
- Plus a number of attachments such as certificate of incorporation and business license, certificates of legal representation, and power of attorney and financial reports of the investors.

One important issue in the drafting of the feasibility study is the "scope of business" for the enterprise. The scope of business should be carefully defined as it will likely be repeated in the JV contract, articles of association, and on the enterprise's business license. The "scope of business" field on a Chinese business license delineates activities the company is authorized to conduct, and the language is usually narrowly construed. Thus, investors must be sure to state all categories of business activities planned for the enterprise.

However, Chinese authorities will reject overly broad or vague language, so the business scope must be described in precise terms. In addition, Chinese authorities will usually interpret broad or ambiguous wording in the scope of business narrowly. This is to prevent the enterprise from engaging in business activities that the investor did not seek approval for.

Another key issue to be addressed in the feasibility study is capital contributions. Chinese authorities have a series of guidelines that must be followed with respect to the minimum amount of capitalization for each type of FIE. There is also a timetable, based on the size of investment, for foreign partners to fulfill commitments for capital contributions. In addition, depending on the size of investment, there is a maximum ratio of debt and equity allowed for a JV. There are also regulations requiring audits in order to confirm the valuation of state-owned assets when used as the Chinese partners' contributions to capital. Finally, foreign investors' contributions of equipment or other kinds of contributions also require appraisals by Chinese import & export authorities.

Stage 4: Formal approval – Contracts, articles of association (For JVs and WOFEs)

For JVs, the next step is the completion of contract, articles of association and the formal application for approval. While the feasibility study is under review, JV partners can work to complete negotiations on the actual contract and articles of association. The contract incorporates all understandings and terms from the preliminary agreement, project proposal and feasibility study, though there may be some modifications by mutual agreement between the parties.

Chinese law views the joint venture contract as the fundamental document for the establishment of joint ventures. The contract must meet the requirements spelt out in China's joint venture law (for equity JVs) or cooperative enterprise law (for cooperative JVs). The feasibility study and preliminary project approval document are included as attachments when the contract is submitted for formal approval.

For WOFEs, the contract is not needed. The relevant documents include a written application for the establishment of WOFE, a feasibility study report, the articles of association, a list of board members and the legal representatives, the foreign investor's incorporation documents and evidence of credit standing, the written approval of the project proposal, and other necessary documents.

For both JVs and WOFEs, articles of association must be drawn up and submitted as part of the formal application process. Under Chinese law, the articles of association are viewed as the code of company governance – similar to the company by-laws or memorandum of association in other legal jurisdictions. Chinese law (JV regulations) contains detailed provisions regarding issues that must be addressed in the joint venture contract and articles of association. The articles of association include basic information about the enterprise: the enterprise's name and address, scope of business, total capital and organizational framework.

JV regulations require that the JV contract and articles of association be written in Chinese. However, a foreign language version of the documents is frequently prepared together with the Chinese version, and the parties may agree that both language versions have equal validity.

Generally, the examination and approval authority will give a reply (approval or disapproval) within 30 days on receipt of the feasibility study report, contract and articles of association. If approval is granted, the Chinese party of the JV or the foreign investor in the WOFE may apply for the approval certificate.

Stage 5: Apply for business license and others

Within 30 days of receiving the approval certificate, the WOFE or JV may register with Beijing Industrial & Commercial Administration (BICA) and apply for the business license. BICA will issue the business license within 10 working days to successful projects. The enterprise is deemed as established on the date that the business license is issued.

After the issuance of the business license, the enterprise is to continue with the following registrations with relevant authorities:

- Registration for Taxation Authorities within 30 days after getting the business license;
- Registration for Customs and Commodity Inspection at Beijing Customs House and Beijing Import & Export Commodity Inspection Bureau;
- Registration with Finance Administration within 30 days after getting the business license; and,
- Going through Capital Examination by a Certified Accountant.

Setting up a representative office in beijing

An overseas enterprise that wishes to establish a Representative Office (RO) in Beijing may entrust an agency authorized by Beijing Municipal Foreign Economic Relations & Trade Committee to submit an application on its behalf to the Beijing Municipal Trade & Economic Commission.

The Beijing Foreign Investment Service Center (BFISC), which is authorized by the MOFTEC and Beijing Foreign Economic Relations & Trade Commission, will accept applications and go through examination and approval procedures. The business activities of the established Representative Office are limited in business connection, product introduction, market survey, technology exchange and consulting services etc. Direct business activities are not allowed.

Application documents

The applicant shall complete "The Form for Establishing Residential Representative Office by Overseas Enterprises" and present the following documents:

- The original application letter;
- Certificate of Incorporation (original or copy);
- The original Capital Credit Standing Certificate. This is a letter from the company's bank regarding the company's capital and credit standing. The following information should be included: establishment date, authorized capital, business scope, and assessment of the company's financial standing by the bank;
- Authorization certificates of the representatives. It should be the original and issued by the chairman of the board of directors or the general manager of the headquarters. In the case that the chairman of the board is the chief representative, the other two directors should sign. In the case that the general manager is also the chief representative, the chairman of the board and the other two directors' signatures are necessary;
- Resume, photographs, and copy of ID card/passport of the Chief Representative;
- Lease contract of the office in Beijing & residential certificate. The leasing period should be more than a year, and it should be in the buildings granted the right, by the Beijing Economic & Trade Commission, to sell or lease apartments for use as foreign representative offices. This certificate may be obtained from the

management department of the building;
- Brief introduction of the company. This document should include registered capital, turnover, business scope, staff size, and business establishments in other parts of China, etc; and,
- The Chinese translation of all documents mentioned above shall be provided if the original documents are in foreign languages.

Provided that the foreign enterprise submits all documents needed for setting up the Representative Office, Beijing Foreign Investment Service Center (BFISC) will start primary examination and charge service fees of USD 800. The service center is responsible for verifying various documents, including the approval document of Beijing Economic Relations & Trade Commission, BICA registration certificate and representative certificate.

Other procedures

After the approval, the following procedures would have to be completed before the Representative Office can begin to operate officially:
- Registration with the BICA to obtain a registration certificate as well as a representative card;
- Registration with Public Security Bureau and preparation of company stamp;
- Registration with the Technical Supervision Bureau to obtain a coy ID number;
- Registration with the Authority for Foreign Exchange and opening a forex account with the Authority;
- Opening forex and local currency account with a local bank;
- Registration with Local Tax Bureau;
- Registration with State Tax Bureau;
- Registration with Beijing Municipal Customs House;
- Complete procedures for hiring of local employees;
- Application to the Labor Bureau for employment pass for foreign employees; and,
- Application to the Public Security Bureau for residential permit

and visa for foreign employees.

The entire Representative Office registration process may be completed within two months. The approval is valid for three years. The registration of the Representative Office is only valid for the duration of a year and has to be renewed annually.

Small- and medium-sized enterprises (SMEs): More room for growth

The Chinese government is improving the "operational environment" for small and medium-sized enterprises (SMEs). Challenges marring this bright spot of economic reform include insufficient access to capital and local corruption that saps SMEs' dynamism. Nonetheless, adaptable SMEs are generally well-positioned to take advantage of opportunities created by China's entry to the WTO.

The growing significance of SMEs in China's economy has gained recognition. Chinese and foreign experts estimate that SMEs are now responsible for about 60% of China's industrial output and employ about 75% of the workforce in China's cities and towns. SMEs are responsible for creating most new urban jobs, and they are the main employers of workers laid off from state-owned enterprises (SOEs) in the current economic restructuring.

The Chinese government is fully aware of the impact that SMEs as job-creators can have on forestalling potential social unrest. Chinese officials have said that SMEs would be more important for preserving social stability than the nascent social security system, particularly when increased foreign competition as a result of China's WTO entry forces more layoffs from uncompetitive state-owned firms.

Entrepreneurial start-ups

Many SMEs are private firms, started by enterprising individuals. In the early days of China's economic reforms, private firms faced an openly hostile political atmosphere and, as a result, were extremely limited in scale. The 14th Party Congress in 1992 saw the announcement of the socialist market economy, which implied that firms in the non-state sector would play an important role in national economic development. The 15th Party Congress in 1997 made this position official, openly acknowledging that the private sector was an important component of the economy. The revision of the constitution two years later equating the state and non-state sectors further improved the political environment for private entrepreneurs.

In addition to private firms, some SMEs were "collectives" (i.e. operated by authorities below the county level) rented by individuals who offered to manage them and use their semi-public ownership status as protection from official harassment. These SMEs expanded considerably throughout the 1990s in the second half of the landmark "grasp the large, release the small" policy for state-owned firms. Under this policy 80% of the hundreds of thousands of state-owned SMEs changed their ownership status through corporatization, shareholding, or private management through leasing the enterprise. The State Council's Commission to Reform the Economic System managed the process until the 1998 government restructuring, when responsibility was shifted to the State Economic and Trade Commission's (SETC) new SME office.

Limited funding

SMEs still lack access to the resources lavished on larger state-owned firms, according to investment statistics. Widespread caution on the part of both borrowers and lenders of the higher risks accompanying private projects is a key cause of the slower growth in private sector investment. The central government is concerned about this imbalance in bank lending. The State Development Planning Commission is attempting to address the slow growth in private investment by announcing incentives to "guide" private investment towards public works and high-technology projects.

Chinese officials have said that banks are "too conservative" in lending money to SMEs. Loan officers in state-owned commercial banks are not rewarded for making good loans but are penalized when they approve loans that are not repaid. Other officials are more candid, expressing the view that state-owned commercial banks will continue giving priority to large state-owned enterprises because of their implicit government guarantees.

Some SMEs, typically former collectives, do in fact turn to the banking system for at least a small portion of their lending needs. In these cases, SME managers typically use their housing as collateral. As a result of the banking system's continuing preference for lending to large state-owned firms, SMEs usually raise money through indirect financing, primarily from family members or from their local communities. Retained earnings are another key source of financing.

Chinese officials recognize that vibrant SMEs are an essential part of sustained economic development and are trying to promote a more favorable environment to encourage their growth. At the national level, the focus is on the SME Promotion Law, which aims to codify the official definition of SMEs and clarify what government financial support will be made available to them. The law should help to protect SMEs, particularly former township and village enterprises (TVEs) that had become share-issuing firms.

Credit guarantee agencies

Recognizing the limited financial opportunities available to SMEs, the central government created a network of credit guarantee agencies in the late 1990s and tasked the SETC's SME bureau to oversee them.

The bureau maintains a catalog listing what kinds of firms can apply for a guarantee. After checking on a given firm's financial background (using data provided by the State Administration for Industry and Commerce) and reviewing the proposed project, the credit guarantee agency uses the SETC's money to guarantee that the SME in question will repay its bank loan. The bureau presently manages guarantees worth about USD 120 million a year.

Lack of modern management

Another factor limiting SME development is the mindset of their managers. Some SME proprietors respond to China's uncertain regulatory environment by not fully expanding their businesses. They know that being "too successful" could draw the attention of local government officials who might then impose high levies and fees.

In this context, the long tradition of family-based businesses also works to limit the development of SMEs. Many of these firms are unwilling to transform themselves into larger corporate entities because that would require entrusting non-family members with the firm's valuable information and resources.

Not surprisingly, SMEs are not eager to shoulder more of the national tax burden, which is still primarily carried by the state-owned sector. In most cities and towns, small and medium-sized firms pay a disproportionately small share of taxes.

Impact of WTO accession

All is not bleak though. SMEs look set to take advantage of China's WTO entry. Officials at the Ministry of Foreign Trade and Economic Cooperation (MOFTEC) have said that SMEs can further integrate themselves into multinational companies' supply chains, so China's "small giants" can one day become "big giants" in their own right.

The principle of "national treatment" in WTO is often cited as an additional benefit for SMEs because it creates new opportunities to launch businesses in industries once dominated by state companies. MOFTEC officials have said that SMEs were better positioned to adapt to the WTO economy because they are not burdened by the social, managerial, and financial baggage of most large state-owned firms.

While SMEs are better positioned than most of the state sector to adapt to the new environment, WTO membership will not immediately or conveniently improve most SMEs' future as SMEs themselves still need time to improve their competitiveness and product quality.

Supporting foreign companies

The most remarkable aspect of China's small and medium enterprises is their rapid growth despite their inability to tap the official financial system. Two factors suggest even faster development in the near term. The first, suitability for the post-WTO accession economy. SMEs in China will continue to thrive as they are the more responsive partners of foreign companies than large state firms. They will also have the opportunity to move into market segments once dominated by state firms.

The other factor is that the policy environment for SMEs appears to be steadily improving. The SME Promotion Law will help, especially if it means better access to bank lending, as would improvement in, and expansion of, the credit guarantee system.

Top Ten Tips on Doing Business in China

1. Do your due diligence twice

The scouts are right: be prepared. Some firms believe that China is so different and so opaque that they cannot obtain the information they would usually require, so they enter the market without it. This is foolish. It is difficult to perform due diligence in China, but not impossible.

2. Choose the right partners

Before you settle into a long-term relationship, take time to get to know your potential partners. Visit their facilities. Talk to their employees, clients and competitors. And remember that your partners are not just the firms you want to joint-venture with, but everyone you do business with: your distributors, your customers, your suppliers and your advisors.

3. Pay attention to "*guanxi* "

A lot is said about Chinese "*guanxi* " (relationships). Most of it is garbage. Relationships are important everywhere, not just in China. The key things to remember are that good *"guanxi"* is a network of relationships with people at various levels across a broad range of organizations and that *"guanxi"* is created and cultivated. A partner whose "*guanxi*" consists of a single relationship to a key government official is usually not a good partner—you want to be supported by a complex web, not a single string. With manners, diligence, courtesy and goodwill, you can construct your own web of supporting relationships.

4. Don't be afraid of the short-term

Many U.S. firms are attracted to China by its long-term potential. Long-term plans are great, but the rapidly changing Chinese market often presents excellent short-term opportunities. American firms should not be afraid to avail themselves of an opportunity that may disappear in a year or two.

5. Be flexible . . .

China is unique. Where else can you find "a socialist market economy with Chinese characteristics"? The Chinese legal and regulatory regime can force firms to find creative solutions to business problems, but China is large enough and growing rapidly enough to be worth some flexibility.

6. But don't be afraid to say "no"

The Chinese market may not be right for you. Your products may be too advanced, subject to prohibitive tariffs, banned from import or otherwise unsuitable for this market. Know what your bottom line is.

China is changing so rapidly that the idea that you must be in China today to compete in fifteen years is rubbish. Being out of the market is better than losing money in the market.

7. China is not a single market

From Harbin to Haikou, from Guangzhou to Kashgar, China encompasses diverse topographies, climates, cultures and peoples. There are five languages on the Chinese currency and Chinese "dialects" (such as Shanghainese or Cantonese) are actually mutually unintelligible languages. Provinces and cities compete fiercely for investment and trade, and regional protectionism is a big problem for Chinese firms – let alone foreign firms.

8. Get professional help

Don't sign a contract or agreement that hasn't been reviewed by a qualified local attorney. If you need office space, hire a professional realtor. Reputable, reliable, professional service providers are increasingly available in China, so use them.

9. Hire an interpreter

Interpretation and translation are professional skills that firms neglect at their peril. Being bilingual does not qualify one to interpret and having your professionally written, carefully conceived product literature translated by a graduate student from a local Chinese university will not impress your clients. If communication is important to your business, hire a professional interpreter.

10. Be polite

Be tough, be firm, but be polite. The two most important words in Chinese are "*xie xie*," which mean "thank you." Learn them and use them. Often.

(by Mr Alan Turley, Minister Counselor for Commercial Affairs at the U.S. Embassy in Beijing, China)

HUMAN RESOURCES

Local talent

Talent in Beijing

Engaging capable and competent staff is a fundamental factor for the development of enterprises. Currently, there are 62 universities and colleges in Beijing, including the following:

- Peking University,
- Tsinghua University,
- People's University of China,
- Peking Union Medical College,
- Beijing University of International Studies,
- Beijing University of International Business & Economics,
- Beijing Normal University,
- Beijing University of Aeronautics & Astronautics,
- Beijing Institute of Technology,
- Beijing Language and Culture University,
- Northern Jiaotong University,
- China Agricultural University, Central University of Finance & Economics,
- Beijing Forestry University,
- Beijing University of Traditional Chinese Medicines, and,
- Beijing Polytechnic University etc.

In all, there are 1,348 universities and colleges in China. 21 of the 71 universities and colleges under the direct leadership of China Education Ministry are located in Beijing. In contrast, there are only eight such institutions in Shanghai, seven in Wuhan, four in Chengdu, four in Xi'an, two in Guangzhou and two in Tianjin.

Peking University was established in 1898 and is recognized as one of the most prestigious Chinese universities. It is known particularly for its departments of natural science and social science. It has very strong R&D resources including 46 Chinese Academy of Science (CAS) fellows, 7 Chinese Academy of Engineering (CAE) fellows, and over 1,600 professors and associate professors.

Tsinghua University is also widely recognized as the most prestigious polytechnic university in China, and is strong particularly in natural science, engineering and advanced technology. It has 26 CAS fellows, 25 CAE fellows, 1,035 professors, 1,740 associate professors and 446 postdoctoral fellows.

People's University of China is particularly strong in social science, business, economics and law.

In 2001, universities in Beijing admitted 116,000 new students in all. The number of students enrolled at universities and colleges reached 340,000, representing an increase of 20.4% over the previous year. There were around 32,000 postgraduate students in all institutions, representing an increase of 20.7% over the previous year. Over 15,000 postgraduate students graduated with master and doctoral degrees, representing an increase of 15.1% over the previous year.

Along with the increasing number of MNCs in Beijing comes the dramatic increase in the number of local talent flocking into the city. Local enterprises in Beijing are also keen on attracting talent from around the country.

Beijing has attracted skilled workers and experienced managers from all over the country and even overseas. Beijing, as well as Shanghai, Guangzhou and Shenzhen, is setting the trend for human resources in China. Interestingly, in addition to local executives, growing businesses are creating strong demand for qualified foreign professionals.

Beijing has over 14 million residents. A large part of its population are non-local Beijing residents who have moved to the city from other parts of China in the past few decades. To enhance its human resource advantage, Beijing has announced a plan to direct talent to the city – the "Implementation Measures on Attracting Domestic Outstanding Professionals to Beijing".

With a strong inflow of professionals, human resource in Beijing has been further enriched. In accordance with the development strategy, the municipal government makes a special effort to attract talent from fields such as information technology, microelectronics, finance and insurance, venture capitalism, biomedicine, urban agriculture and international legal practice.

Advantages in human resources

Beijing has very impressive advantages in terms of human resources as compared to other Chinese cities. It has a well-developed education system that covers elementary education, occupational skills education, higher education and adult education. Beijing also has a mature human resource market and a complete regulation system to attract international and domestic talent. It is also one of the regions where most returned Chinese students settle in.

Returning chinese talent

According to the vice-dean of the Guanghua Management School at Peking University, Beijing is a city with tremendous competitive strength and many talent assets.

Experts say that the returning talent tide is the best symbol of Beijing's dynamic development. The improvement in China's national power, robust economic growth, stable social environment and globalization tendency are all key factors in attracting more and more talent.

In the 1930s, the Chinese government encouraged and sent students to study abroad. In the 1950s and 1960s, many of these Chinese students came back, mostly after completing studies under government sponsorship and scholarship support in the United States and European nations.

To date, about 200,000 Chinese students have returned to China to pursue employment opportunities or set up their own businesses. The number grows by more than 10% a year, so much so that the newly-concocted phrase of "Hai Gui Pai" (returned overseas generation) is now included in the latest published Chinese language lexicons.

Official statistics show that in the past two decades, approximately 400,000 Chinese students have gone to study in 103 countries and regions worldwide, making China the world's largest source of students studying overseas.

Three years ago, a total of 42 leading scientists from the Chinese Academy of Sciences and the Chinese Academy of Engineering, all of whom are returned overseas Chinese, in a written proposal, called for overseas Chinese talent to contribute more actively to the country's scientific and technological development.

To welcome this tide of returning talent, Beijing, as well as Shanghai and Guangzhou, have gone to countries where many Chinese students are pursuing their education and held recruitment fairs.

Meanwhile, Beijing Municipal Government and other agencies have stepped up the pace in drafting relevant policies and regulations conducive to attracting overseas Chinese students to return and launch businesses. Specialized business zones and incubation centers have been set up for returned overseas Chinese talents.

Take Zhongguancun Science Park in Beijing for example. It has attracted more than 8,000 returned overseas Chinese scholars and students, five times more than a decade ago.

Along with the returning flow of talent, large numbers of Hong Kong and Taiwan residents have also settled down and launched many business establishments in mainland China, including Beijing. It is estimated that at least 300,000 to 400,000 residents of Hong Kong have been working long-term in mainland China.

Staff recruitment

Under China's Labor Law, foreign enterprises can decide for themselves the timing and means of recruiting staff as well as the terms and conditions of employment and the number to be engaged. At present, enterprises may hire staff through the following channels:

Employment agencies

At present, the majority of employment agencies in China are organizations within the labor and social security and personnel departments.

There are also agencies run by enterprises, organizations and individuals. These agencies are usually called "employment centers", "human resources market" and the like. In recent years, head-hunting companies have also emerged.

Employment agencies operated by labor and social security departments and personnel departments usually offer standard services such as staff recruitment, personal files management and matters related to social insurance. They also maintain huge human resources databases in order to meet the requirements of enterprises in hiring staff at all levels and head-hunt qualified senior executives for them.

Before using the services of an employment agency, an enterprise may request that the agency provides proof of its legal status, and ask to see the approval certificate issued by the labor department.

When appointing an employment agency, the enterprise should present a letter of introduction of the enterprise itself, its business license (copy) or other proof of registration as a legal entity, a profile of recruitment requirements, and identification documents of the person in charge of the recruitment exercise.

Profiles of recruitment requirements should contain information such as an introduction to the enterprise, number of staff to be recruited, job types, job requirements, terms of employment, remunerations, fringe benefits and labor protection etc.

Headhunting firms

Similar to other parts of China, headhunting firms are increasing in number in Beijing, with more and more firms placing young, well-educated and highly-experienced professionals in Chinese companies.

Among the 120 human resources intermediary agencies now registered in Beijing, several dozen are headhunting firms. Most of these firms call themselves *human resource consultation service companies.* At present, headhunting firms serve many foreign-invested enterprises (FIEs) and joint ventures, which constitute 80% to 90% of their clients. Non-government Chinese organizations have a smaller share, while state-owned enterprises (SOEs) make up only 1% to 2% of the firms' clients.

The most sought-after talent are management-level individuals in such industries as communications, computers, chemical engineering, medicine, consumer products and food products. Basic prerequisites include excellent educational background, professional experience, fluency in English or other foreign languages and strong computer skills.

According to the executive director of a major headhunting firm in Beijing, two main types of talent are in great need now. The first is short-term, technical talent, usually sought when a certain department in the company is not performing well and the company wishes to engage external help in order to implement reorganization and improvement measures. The second type is long-term, or strategic talent.

More agencies for international talent exchange

At the 2004 China International Talent Exchange Conference held in Nanjing, more foreign talent agencies have been accredited to carry out international talent exchange. This is a significant milestone – the Chinese government will standardize its international talent market according to international practice.

So far, China's State Administration of Foreign Experts Affairs (SAFEA) has accredited 332 foreign talent agencies to operate in China, including 96 foreign experts' organizations and 236 foreign talent-training agencies. In addition, it has accredited 390 local Chinese units to employ qualified foreign educational experts.

Source: China Business

Mass media

With the prior approval of the local labor and social security department, an enterprise may place recruitment advertisements in the mass media such as newspapers, magazines, and radio/TV stations. Without such approval, recruitment advertisements are not permitted in the news media.

Human resources fairs

Human resources fairs are a popular way to recruit employees in China. These events are specifically organized for enterprises to recruit staff, and there are events such as senior executives recruitment fairs, FIE staff recruitment fairs, and interview sessions with university graduates. Usually organized by employment agencies, enterprises rent a space and set up recruitment booths, and job-seekers are admitted for a fee.

Employment procedures

Signing of labor contract

Under the Labor Law, a labor contract must be signed between an individual worker and an enterprise, or workers may sign a collective contract with the enterprise. The contract forms the basis of labor relations between the enterprise and the employee.

In recruiting staff, an enterprise should obtain the relevant particulars of the candidates and check the validity of their documents before signing labor contracts with them.

The Labor Law and other relevant regulations clearly state the mandatory terms and conditions to be included in a labor contract, such as the term of the contract, conditions for changing, dissolving or terminating the contract, as well as compensations in the event of dissolving the contract. The Labor Handbook provided by the local labor department should be used as reference by enterprises in formulating their labor contracts.

Contract authentication

Contract authentication is a legal process whereby the labor administrative department conducts full-scale examination, verification and validation of all labor contracts signed between an enterprise and its employees. Hence, the process confirms the legality of a labor contract. At present, it is compulsory for all labor contracts signed between enterprises and their staff to be authenticated.

The enterprise should submit the labor contract to the local labor administrative department for authentication within 30 days of the commencement of service of an employee. In the case of collective labor contracts, they should be filed with the local labor administrative department for record keeping purposes. Collective contracts automatically enter into force 15 days after the date of receipt by the labor department, if no objection is raised during that period.

The following documents are required for contract authentication (the list may vary in different localities, so enquiry at relevant local departments may be necessary):

- Labor contract and its copy;
- Business license or its copy;
- Proof of identity of legal representative or authorized person;
- Identity card or proof of domicile registration of the employee; and,

- Proof of education attainment, medical report, Labor Handbook, and other relevant information regarding the employee.

Staff management

An enterprise or its resident representative office may entrust a service agency which specializes in human resources employment to manage the personal files of its mainland staff. Such agencies should be located at the place of domicile registration or current workplace of the staff concerned. The services they offer include verification of the staff's identity, track record, previously-drawn salaries and travel reports. Other services such as assessment of technical qualifications, contract authentication and social insurance may also be provided.

Salary

Under the "Temporary Regulation of Salary and Income in the Foreign-Funded Enterprise" regulation, the enterprise decides the salary system, salary level, bonus and stipends in line with the national and local minimum salary standards. The increase of average salary of the employees is usually based on the performance of the enterprise. The company's annual returns, productive rate and the price index of local consumer goods are some of the factors to take into consideration for the payroll.

Insurance

As required by law, foreign-funded enterprises are expected to participate in the social insurance system of pension, unemployment, medical care, injury and childbirth through regular and adequate payment to the insurance agencies. Employees too, are expected to pay the required amount for their pension, medical care and unemployment insurances.

Working hours

Foreign-funded enterprises generally adopt China's current working-hour system – eight hours per day and 40 hours per week. With permission from the labor bureau, enterprises can operate on a non-standard working-hour system, e.g. irregular working hours, if the enterprises, for practical reasons, cannot follow the standard working hours.

THE OFFICE MARKET

Latest market trends

After the slump in demand for office space in recent years, Beijing's office market slowly recovered at the beginning of 2004. During the first quarter, demand came mainly from domestic and foreign companies, with the majority of the deals concluded for space located in East Beijing and Zhongguancun. As the municipal government accelerates building works in preparation for the Olympic Games, market demand is expected to grow even further.

According to a DTZ Debenham Tie Leung Research Report, Grade A office vacancy dropped slightly, from 14.8% to 12.4% over the previous quarter. However, average Grade A office rental rates remained stable at USD 24.57 per m^2 per month, reversing the downward trend in the last three years.

Ideal Plaza, the first Grade A office property in Zhongguancun West Zone entered the market and boosted total supply to approximately 1.97 million m^2. For the rest of 2004, few Grade A office buildings are expected to be completed, especially in eastern Beijing.

Market analysts believe that China's economic development and favorable policies will continue to attract more investment into Beijing, further boosting market demand for office space. Rentals, however, are not expected to escalate significantly in other areas of the city, especially in Zhongguancun which has approximately 140,000 m^2 of new office space available to meet demand.

New Generation Business Approach

Office Outsourcing

> "By using flexible space we have an immediate and **cost-effective exit strategy**."
>
> **Joe Howard, *Manhattan Associates***
> ***Area Development*, Feb. 2004**

More and more businesses are turning to companies combining property and services to deliver flexibility. Regus' aim is to provide to a client anything that they would use in the normal course of a working day.

Regus, the global leader in outsourced offices, provides companies with cost-effective workspace on flexible terms.

Regus already has seven locations in China, two in Beijing, two in Shanghai and three in Hong Kong. In China the Regus solution eliminates the substantial investment, restrictive lease terms and drain on management time normally involved in sourcing office accommodation, fitting it out and finding staff to run it. With Regus you can select a location ready to go.

Regus' flexible terms enable companies to craft the appropriate mix of long and short-term property commitments. With over 90,000 workstations, Regus' worldwide portfolio enables companies to match their workforce to exactly the workspace they need, when and where they need it, for as long as they need it. This dynamic approach to property allows companies to match their office needs to their business needs.

As well, with Regus there is a choice of 3,000 meeting rooms across 50 countries worldwide. Each of its 400 centres features a variety of private meeting, interview, conference and training rooms, all in a professional business environment. Regus can help clients plan every detail from audio-visual equipment to catering. Simply book and turn up.

Regus' complete menu of business support services includes telecommunications and IT services, videoconferencing, desktop publishing, administrative and concierge services provided by a multi-lingual team.

Regus also gives business travellers access to its global network. The Regus Global Membership Card gives business travellers complimentary access to Regus' business centres worldwide, where they can work and relax in a professional business environment with soft seating, reading material and refreshing facilities. All centres are in prime locations, close to communications networks, airports or in city centres. Global members can also access Regus offices, meeting facilities and business support services on a pay-as-you-use basis. The Regus infrastructure is perfectly suited to the needs of the business traveller.

Regus Centres in China

Beijing:	*Pacific Century Place* *Lufthansa Centre*
Shanghai:	*Jin Mao Building* *One Corporate Avenue*
Hong Kong:	*One International Finance Centre* *Pacific Place* *Shui On Centre*
Phone:	(8610) 6539 1020
Web:	www.regus.com

For the first quarter of 2003, the market stayed generally active, with demand largely driven by new representative offices being set up in the city, as well as expansions in sectors which expect to benefit from China's WTO membership. This increased activity did not however translate into higher volume of actual transactions in the subsequent quarters. A wait-and-see attitude prevailed, as reflected in the lower net take-up rates for the whole year, and remained until early 2004. Office take-up rate still appeared to lag behind corporate hiring rate as companies keep back-filling previously underused space or simply making do with overcrowded accommodation.

Despite the weak demand and the substantial vacancy rate of about 16% (coupled with a projected high supply over the next 24 months), landlords remained firm on rents of USD 27.22 per m^2 per month or a decrease of only 3.7 % from the previous year.

The most significant source of growth came from insurance, banking, oil exploration and manufacturing sectors although some companies in the IT, software, telecommunications and bio-technology industries seemed to have revived their interest in Haidian, which offers proximity to Beijing's universities, tax incentives, comparatively lower rents and an improved infrastructure network.

While the flow of new entrants to the city are small-space users, requiring only between 40 m^2 and 150 m^2, established multinationals are looking to consolidate their scattered operations and often require space of between 2,000 m^2 and 5,000m^2. Small-space users and new entrants have outnumbered big-space users and have contributed to the current growth of business center operators, such as Business Plaza, Far Glory and Regus Business Center.

Supply review

At the end of 2003, total stock of office space had reached 5.72 million m^2, of which Prime and Grade A office space comprised 2.87 million m^2.

The remainder of this existing supply or approximately 2.83 million m² is of Grade B standard. 48% of the existing stock is in Chaoyang District, followed by Xicheng and Haidian Districts.

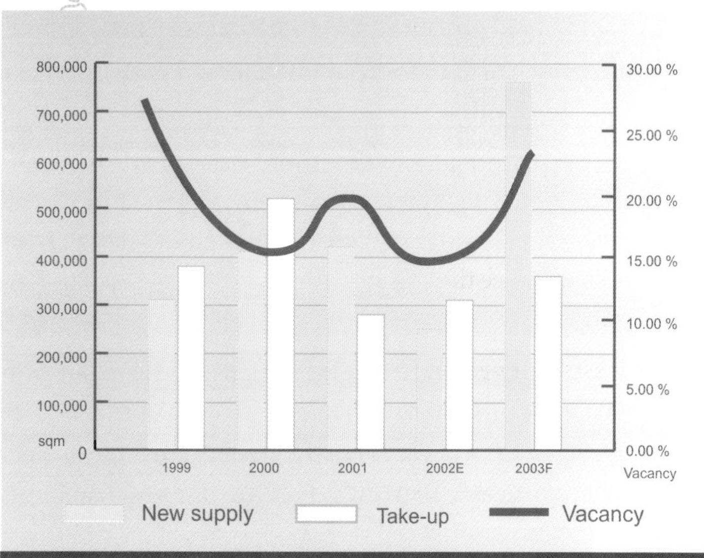

Residential sales market

Beijing's residential market demand stems mainly from lower-priced home ownership and the government's intention to permit private ownership of properties. On the other hand, the government's recent cancellation of the distinction that existed between properties for sale to foreign nationals and local buyers has enlarged the demand pool for Beijing's residential properties.

China's successful entry into the World Trade Organization (WTO) has attracted a flood of fresh investments into its capital, creating more jobs

and increasing household incomes which will in turn result in stronger demand for better housing. This, coupled with the presence of a large number of Taiwanese, Hongkongers and Singaporean nationals currently living in Beijing, is likely to keep the residential property market in Beijing buoyant.

Already the government is said to be considering various ways to improve and develop the secondary market for residential housing projects in Beijing which will in turn enhance the liquidity in the market and the desirability of owning a unit.

Last but not least, Beijing is in the process of urbanization, with more people migrating from rural areas to the city. It is projected that with the current rate of urbanization, well-developed areas will increase from around 34% today, to 45% by 2010. Migrant workers and the expatriate community will push demand for residential space in the cities. In addition, the expatriate community, estimated to be around 80,000 individuals but projected to reach 500,000 people by year 2008, will certainly boost the demand for residential units.

Following the cancellation of the distinction between foreign sales and domestic sales, residential projects can now be clearly defined in terms of location, quality and overall market perception. The above attributes, together with the prevailing more or less balanced supply-demand situation in most segments of the market, are expected to cause prices to move moderately upwards.

北京科技园置业股份有限公司
Beijing Science Park Development Co.,Ltd.

The article is contributed by Beijing Science Park Development Co., Ltd.

Zhongguancun is a fertile land that fosters and drives Chinese entrepreneurship. Since the 1980s, Zhongguancun has been growing rapidly, at a 30%-plus rate annually. Today, more than ever, Zhongguancun stands out as the Mecca for creating wealth and for shaping the future. Thanks to the concern and support of the Central Party Committee and the State Council, a monumental project, the Zhongguancun Square, is now being developed in the birthplace of Zhongguancun, the Haidian Township. Zhongguancun Square, which occupies an area of 51.44 hectares and has gross floor area of 1 million-plus m^2, can be likened to an air carrier that navigates across the oceans of the world economy. Zhongguancun Financial Center is the very mast of this air carrier.

Zhongguancun first started out as an electronic street. In 1988, a new and high technology pilot zone was set up in the area. In 1999, Zhongguancun became part of a national level science park. The development of Zhongguancun is now mainly driven by high and new technology innovation. Still, finance and venture capital support is indispensable to the sustainable development of the new and high technology industry. The Zhongguancun Financial Center is set to create an excellent business environment for financial enterprises to establish their presence in Zhongguancun, and will suitably start a fresh chapter of financing for the Zhongguancun Area. Zhongguancun Financial Center has not only attracted the attention of the communities of Zhongguancun, but has also drawn the focus of stakeholders worldwide. Beijing Science Park Development Co. Ltd. is a young enterprise that was born against the backdrop of the historic opportunity to build and develop the Zhongguancun Science Park. BSPD was jointly founded in December 1999 by seven notable shareholders, including Beijing Science and Technology Park Construction Co. Ltd., H.K.I. Development Co. Ltd., and Beijing Haikai Real Estate Group. BSPD is now undertaking the development and construction of 3 projects with a floor area of 400,000 square meters, including Zhongguancun Financial Center. BSPD boasts a large, professional real estate development team, which is also a learning team, a specialist team and an innovative team. Moreover, BSPD has partnered world-leading firms in developing and constructing Zhongguancun Financial Center and other projects. Our professional development team and our world-leading partners guarantee the delivery of comfortable and satisfactory office space. Located in Zhongguancun Central Business District, namely, Zhongguancun Square, in Beijing's Haidian District, Zhongguancun Financial Center is positioned as a top-level international office building. It is designed by world-leading architectural firm, Kohn Pedersen Fox Associates (KPF). It is the first such architecture in China, where the outer plane surfaces of the structure are curved in some places, yet flat in others. The Project covers an area of 17,600 m^2, with a gross floor area of 112,031 m^2. The building comprises a 34-storey office tower A, an 8-storey office tower B, and a tower C that links the two. With its 150m-high main tower, Zhongguancun Financial Center will emerge as the tallest building in the Zhongguancun area and in Western Beijing.The project was set in motion on October 30th, 2002 and is planned for completion by the end of 2004. As the tallest and most centrally located structure in the Zhongguancun Area, and with its unique architectural quality and fully self-contained functions, Zhongguancun Financial Center will come to stand as a symbolic landmark in the Zhongguancun area and more, all of Western Beijing.

Environment

ZGC Financial Center is located in the center of ZGC Square, and surrounded by a 1.74-ha central garden with excellent visibility and scenery. The ZGC Square is planned as a comprehensive business zone. The Financial Center is an international high-quality office building and provides comprehensive business services for clients. Other facilities include Grade A office buildings, five-star hotels, service apartments, exhibition centers, health clubs and a retailing zone.

The ZGC Square has a 200,000-m^2 developed underground area for a large shopping mall, which carries well-known brand-name goods from all over the world. Within the mall, there are a host of retailing, entertainment and food & beverage outlets.

Traffic

The biggest underground solid transportation system and underground ring roads in Asia. Buildings within the district are all linked underground. Pedestrian and vehicle traffic enjoy separate carriageways. Adjacent to the ZGC Avenue in the east, Haidian South Road in the south, connected to the CaiHeFang Road in the west, and joined to the North Fourth Ring Road in the north. More than 40 bus lines, as well as, the No.4 and No.10 subway lines traverse the area. It is only 1 km from the urban light rail station and only 25 km from Beijing International Airport.

Innovation in Construction

The construction of ZGC Financial Center breaks all traditional construction patterns, embraces innovation in geometry, and embodies the technology development principle:

Tower A curves horizontally and vertically, reflecting the Financial Center's forceful striking style. The uniquely hyperbolic structure demonstrates its unique form as a landmark tower. Tower B is an 8-storey, 40-meter-high independent office building, while Tower C is like a rainbow, like Exhibition Bridge. The three components, and their unique designs, are combined into a perfect and contemporary composition.

Equipment and Establishment

The design of the ZGC Financial Center pursues the application of high technology, makes good use of precious resources, and meets the requirements of clients. The Center adopts advanced designs and equipment, making great improvements to the elevators, as well as, air-conditioning and automation systems, ensuring fresh air and smooth traffic, to ultimately achieve the pursuit of efficiency and to adequately meet human needs. Column Free Floor Plate 2,000-m^2 standard floor area on average. Standard floor-to-floor height of 4 m, floor to finished ceiling height of 2.7 m.

2. VAV Air Conditioning VAV gives flexibility for adjusting temperature to comfortable levels. Fresh air volume achieves the US standard of 36 cubic metres per person per hour. Super-efficient air circulation maintains a fresh comfortable atmosphere. Sterilized air pumped into workspaces guarantees a healthy working environment.

3. Deluxe Elevators42 elevators—24 in Tower A, 12 in Tower B, 6 in the Connecting Bridge. 1600kg service elevator. And a high-speed elevator in Tower A, with a top speed of 5m/sec.

4. Communications SystemAccess through ZGC Square's public telecom platform, multiple service providers, high speed connection. Utilize the most advanced technology, CAT 6 and fibre optic cable. Complete broadcast TV reception. Receive Chinese and overseas news. Raised floor for free and easy cabling satisfies the most demanding needs.

As the tallest and most centrally located structure in the Zhongguancun Area, and with its unique architectural quality and fully self-contained functions, Zhongguancun Financial Center will come to stand as a symbolic landmark in the Zhongguancun area and more, all of Western Beijing.Zhongguancun Financial Center is positioned as a top-end office building in Zhongguancun CBD. Its architecture and business environment are the finest in the Zhongguancun Area. Zhongguancun Financial Center is surely your ultimate business office solution—a good place for you to open up new horizons and achieve ever greater ambitions.

Beijing Science Park Development Co., Ltd.

Add: No. 1 Nanjie of Haidian Town, 8798#, Beijing, China, 10080

Tel: (8610) 8287 2288, (8610) 8262 6622 Fax: (8610) 6252 5466

URL: www.sciencepark.com.cn

E-mail: "mailto:marketing@sciencepark.com.cn"
marketing@sciencepark.com.cn

Architect Kohn Pedersen Fox Associates PC

China Architecture Design & Research GroupMarketing consultant and Sales Agency CB Richard EllisRealty consultant Cushman & Wakefield Premas

Beijing's housing prices can be segmented as follows:

High-end Projects

Above USD 2,400 per m^2

USD 1,200—USD 2,400

Semi-high-end Projects

USD 960—USD 1,200

Mid-range Projects

USD 700—USD 950

USD 480—USD 720

Low-end Projects

USD 240—USD 480

Below USD 240

Beijing's Average Housing Prices by District

Source: DTZ Research 2003

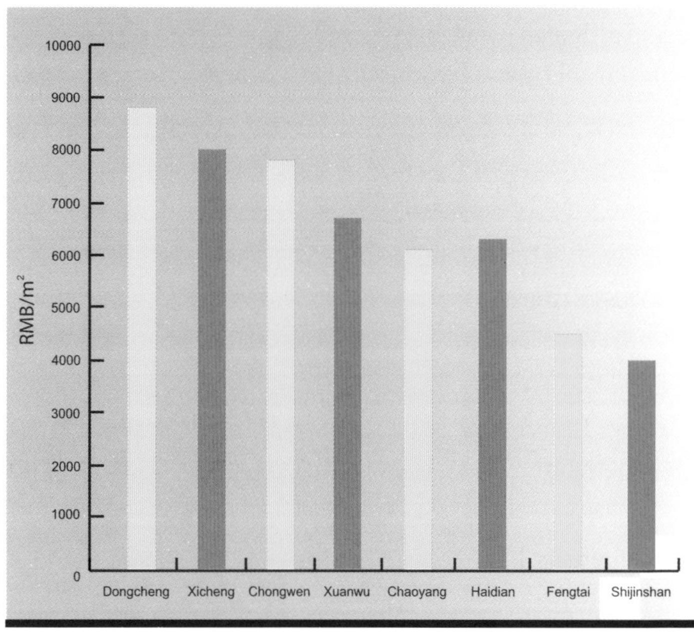

Land market and land use rights

The property market in China is a relatively recent institution. From the 1950s, when private ownership of property was abolished, the State was the sole land-owner, and all allocations and use of land were centrally planned. In the 1970s, China began slowly to shift to a market-based economy, and in the 1980s, the PRC government started to experiment with land reforms. Amendments to the PRC constitution and the Land Administration Law in 1998 allowed the acquisition of long-term rights to use land and created a formal legal system for the transfer of long-term rights to use State or collectively-owned land.

Thus, the PRC managed to avoid the ideologically prickly question of ownership; the underlying property was still owned by the State or collectives, and land may only be used if permission was granted for its use. Theoretically, this resulted in the emergence of a secondary market. However the secondary market took longer than previously planned to materialize and although some progress has been made towards this end, there is bound to still be a number of obstacles to overcome.

China's land-lease policy rather than land-ownership policy means that all land belongs to the country. Investors can however obtain a "land use right," which indicates the legal right to use the land for a stipulated period of time.

Land use tenures vary according to the type of land use.

Market outlook

First-time buyers (the majority being educated individuals with stable income) and their purchases are anticipated to be the major growth drivers.

Urban resettlement is likely to contribute to some growth although resettlement fees may not be sufficient without any additional source of income.

There is strong demand for local housing, and increased requirement for high quality/ high value.

Additional improvements in legal and property ownership regulations will be needed for a sustainable secondary market.

Construction of new residential units will remain high in Beijing in the next few years, especially as part of the urban resettlement and renewal campaign in preparation for the Beijing Olympics in 2008.

Suburbanisation will become a major trend in Beijing, as the average white-collar worker is not able to afford homes in the city proper. Development of residential communities will focus on the planned communities designated by the Beijing government. The new public transport roads and rail lines will play a critical role in defining Beijing's new residential developments.

FINANCIAL SERVICES

Most of China's national financial institutions have their headquarters in Beijing. For example, People's Bank of China, the central bank, is based in the capital. So are the state-owned policy banks and commercial banks, as well as many non-banking financial institutions like insurance companies and trust & investment companies. Of the top 10 commercial banks in China, six have their headquarters in Beijing.

China's banking system consists of the central bank, namely, the People's Bank of China (PBC), three wholly state-owned policy banks, 104 commercial banks, and a large number of urban and rural credit cooperatives.

The three policy banks are the China Development Bank (CDB), Export-Import Bank of China (EIBC) and Agricultural Development Bank of China (ADBC).

The wholly state-owned commercial banks include Industrial & Commercial Bank of China (ICBC), Agricultural Bank of China (ABC), China Construction Bank (CCB) and Bank of China (BOC).

China's Top 10 Banks, 2002 (unit: USD million)

Institution	Headquarters	Assets	Profits	Profit as % of	
				Assets	Equity
Industrial & Commercial Bank Of China	Beijing	480,071	614.6	0.1%	2.7%
Bank Of China	Beijing	382,730	553.3	0.1%	2.8%
China Construction Bank	Beijing	305,856	910.9	0.3%	6.6%
Agricultural Bank of China	Beijing	263,958	35.9	0.0%	0.2%
Bank Of Communications	Shanghai	75,891	244.7	0.3%	6.6%
Citic Industrial Bank	Beijing	28,347	111.6	0.4%	10.8%

China Merchants Bank	Shenzhen	26,156	134.8	0.5%	10.7%
China Everbright Bank	Beijing	25,061	72.4	0.3%	4.8%
Guangdong Development Bank	Guangzhou	18,215	23.9	0.1%	4.4%
Shanghai Pudong Devt. Bank	Shanghai	15,793	115.7	0.7%	12.9%

Source: Asia Week, May 2003

Beijing has a relatively advanced urban financial system. The financial industry has become the largest sector in Beijing's tertiary industry. In 2003, there were more than 2,000 banking service outlets, and the volume of bank deposits handled that year was 55 times as large as 20 years ago. At present, Beijing boasts over 30 listed companies, nearly 100 securities brokerages and more than 1 million investors.

Foreign exchange certificate

Within 30 days of being issued the business license, the foreign-invested enterprise should apply for the Foreign Exchange Certificate from Beijing's branch of the State Administration of Foreign Exchange (SAFE) and at the same time submit the documents issued by the Administration of Industry and Commerce.

Enterprises with the certificate may open a foreign currency account in the designated banks. With the approval of the SAFE, the foreign-funded enterprises can also open foreign currency accounts at financial organs within or beyond the Chinese territory.

Opening accounts in Beijing

Opening a foreign currency account

Foreign-funded enterprises may choose any bank allowed to operate foreign currency business to open a foreign currency account. In applying for the opening of account, the following documents have to be submitted:

- Business license ratified and issued by the Administration of Industry and Commerce,
- Approval certificate for establishment of the enterprise, and,
- Foreign Exchange Certificate of Foreign-funded Enterprises issued by SAFE.

Opening a RMB account

Foreign-funded enterprises may choose any bank that has been permitted to do RMB operations to open a RMB account. For the application, the following documents are to be submitted:

- Business license ratified and issued by the administration of industry and commerce, and,
- Approval certificate for establishment of the enterprise.

Payment and remittance of foreign exchange

With relevant certificates and documents, payment of foreign exchange within the business scope of the foreign-funded enterprise can be directly remitted through the bank of deposit.

Foreign-funded enterprises can make repayment of foreign capital and interest with the bank of deposit by using the Examined Paper of Foreign Loan issued by the Administration of Foreign Exchange. Profits of foreign investors, salary income of foreign employees and employees from Hong Kong, Macau and Taiwan can be remitted through the bank of deposit.

The remittance of foreign exchange under the items of the enterprise's capital, such as the capital transfer of foreign-funded enterprises, recovery of investment, and the remittance of outlay of the enterprise's branches outside China, must be approved by the Administration of Foreign Exchange.

Profits in RMB obtained by foreign investors

Approved by the Administration of Foreign Exchange, the foreign investor of the foreign-funded enterprise can invest its profits in RMB in Chinese enterprises that can create foreign exchange or increase foreign exchange income. Besides the preferential treatment in the form of partial refund of the paid income tax, the investor can also get the same treatment for foreign exchange earnings obtained from abroad.

Foreign currency exchange

Examined and approved by the Administration of Foreign Exchange, foreign-funded enterprises can sell their revenue in foreign currencies, foreign investment, etc. on the swap market. Also on the swap market, they can buy foreign currencies needed for activities within their business scope, foreign loan repayment, and for remittance of the foreign investors' profits, etc.

Annual examination on use of foreign currency

Foreign-funded enterprises should entrust accountant firms appointed by the Administration of Foreign Exchange to conduct annual checks on their use of foreign exchange and present an annual report on the results of the inspection before 30 April each year.

The enterprises should go to the Administration of Foreign Exchange with the annual report and their Foreign Exchange Certificates of Foreign-funded Enterprises to renew the certificates before 31 May each year.

Preferential policies for foreign investment

Foreign-funded enterprises may open foreign currency accounts in the local designated banks with the Foreign Exchange Certificate of Foreign-funded Enterprises. Foreign-funded enterprises may adjust their foreign currency surplus or shortage on the swap market.

Authorized by the relevant departments, foreign-funded enterprises may export products bought with RMB from domestic producers in order to achieve comprehensive compensation of foreign currency. Foreign investors may reinvest their RMB profits in other enterprises within China which can generate new and additional foreign currency earnings. Meanwhile, they can enjoy the same preferential treatment as that for investment in foreign currencies.

Financing facilities

By June 2004, 192 operations have been set up by 64 foreign banks from 19 nations and regions, and 88 of them have been approved for RMB business. Total assets of these foreign-funded banks in China had reached USD 49.5 billion. In addition, foreign-funded banks have opened 209 representative offices in China.

From December 2003, qualified foreign banks are allowed to offer RMB services to Chinese enterprises. Foreign financial institutions' ratio of equity in Chinese-funded commercial banks has also increased.

China implements a highly regulated system of Foreign Exchange and strictly monitors foreign debt levels. FIEs are free to take foreign currency loans from foreign banks under certain conditions. However, when borrowing from overseas parties (including offshore branches of foreign banks and other parties such as foreign shareholders) or from foreign banks in China (such as mainland branches of foreign banks or joint venture banks), FIEs are required to undertake foreign debt registration at the State Administration for Foreign Exchange (SAFE). Failure to do so may mean penalties for the borrower and the inability to remit money or to repay the debt.

FIEs can also seek Chinese currency financing. Chinese currency financing is available from Chinese banks and, subject to some geographical and other restrictions, from licensed foreign banks in China.

When lending to FIEs, banks usually require some credit support. The most common forms include guarantees from foreign shareholders, bank guarantees with standby letters of credit (particularly in RMB loans), and mortgages over real estate and equipment. Securities given by FIEs in favor of foreign banks (including mainland branches of foreign and joint venture banks) must be registered at SAFE.

Foreign-funded enterprises in China are permitted to apply for loans from Chinese domestic banks with overseas assets of the foreign partners as mortgages. Inter-company loans (i.e. loans between Chinese domestic companies) are not permitted except through a financial intermediary. Foreign-funded enterprises are permitted to apply for A- or B- stock issues.

IMPORT AND EXPORT

As for import and export, several procedures are expected to be followed. For enterprises applying to qualify for conducting import & export-oriented business, they are required to submit a list of related documents, which include the national certificate, the official application letter and the approval letter issued by the provincial-level Foreign Trade and Economic Cooperation Commission, providing basic information on the enterprise, reasons for the application and specific plans related to the import and export business involved.

In addition, they are to submit an official letter issued by the local customs house, local taxation administration, local foreign exchange administration and local banks with which the companies have opened their corporate accounts, indicating how the enterprises had been performing in the last three years.

The application process is as follows. First, the entreprise applies for the certificate and approval from the provincial-level Foreign Trade and Economic Cooperation Commission. Then, the application will be passed to the Ministry of Foreign Trade and Economic Cooperation (MOFTEC) and then the State Economic Trade Committee (SETC).

On the other hand, enterprises authorized by the central government apply directly to MOFTEC. The related application materials would then be forwarded to the SETC. Third, the approved enterprise will be notified after the relevant examinations.

Conducting import and export trade

For Beijing-registered enterprises that wish to obtain import and export authorization, there are certain adjustments related to application procedures and terms and regulations which should be followed.

There will no longer be a one-year-limitation for the registration period of the enterprise. For enterprises categorized as engaging in commerce and trade, the required condition is that the enterprises should have a certain amount of registered capital, usually no less than RMB 1 million (USD 120,000) and have approved juridical person authorization. For enterprises categorized as engaging in manufacturing and scientific research, the registered capital required will be no less than half a million RMB.

The enterprise may choose business channels that it thinks suitable to conduct its import and export business, provided those channels are in accordance with MOFTEC regulations. Importing and exporting of products and technology of all kinds are allowed, except for those specified by MOFTEC as "prohibited" categories. Manufacturing enterprises applying for import and export business may, upon approval, export their own products and import machinery, components or materials as needed, except those which are prohibited.

Administrative procedures

For enterprises that have been examined and approved to conduct import and export business, they are to follow a few procedures. They should register with the local industrial & commercial administration, local customs houses, local quality supervision, inspection and quarantine administration, local taxation administration, local foreign exchange administration. These procedures are compulsory for initiating their import and export business.

As for enterprises approved to hold import and export operation rights, they are required to arrange for certain professionals to acquire the relevant knowledge on the latest regulations on foreign trade and economic cooperation.

For enterprises which have been approved to conduct the import and export business, they are under the supervision of local authorities. From January 1 to April 30 every year, these enterprises submit their national

certificate and related documents to local authorities for annual routine examination. Those who fail to participate in the examination will be disqualified from continuing their import and export business in the following year.

Beijing Municipal Foreign Economic Relations and Trade Commission

Address: 190 Chaonei Avenue, Dongcheng District , Beijing 100010

Tel: (8610) 6523 6688

Email: wjmw@bjfetc.gov.cn

Website: www.bjfetc.gov.cn

Annual examination of import/export-oriented enterprises

In accordance with related regulations and schedules, the annual examination of import and export-oriented enterprises in Beijing is carried out between the period of January 1 to April 30. The Beijing Municipal Foreign Economic Relations and Trade Commission is the major government agency in charge of the annual examination.

All enterprises categorized as import and export-oriented, and have been registered before 31 December 2001 must participate in the examination process. All enterprises have to submit the application form for the annual examination, certifying that they have never been fined in the past year by the local customs house, foreign exchange administration, taxation administration and other related authorities. For enterprises that had made certain changes in the name of the enterprise, juridical person's name, registered capital amount and the like, they have to clearly indicate the changes and apply to have their certificates renewed.

In order to enhance efficiency and to simplify related procedures, the annual examination also adopted an e-registration mode. Eligible enterprises may choose to go through the application by visiting the relevant website. For those not eligible for direct Internet application, they may authorize the Beijing Foreign Trade Enterprises Association to process the Internet application on their behalf.

For enterprises failing to go through the annual examination within the specified period, they would be treated as giving up the authorization for conducting import and export business. The commission will then cancel their certificates; the enterprises in question will subsequently no longer be permitted to apply for the new certificate to operate import and export business in that year.

Export processing zones in Beijing

The central government established 15 state-level export processing zones to augment infrastructure facilities for export-oriented production and create favorable investment conditions. Tianzhu Export Processing Zone in Beijing was approved in April 2000 and was officially put into operation in June 2001.

Like EPZs in other countries, the Chinese government hopes that the establishment of EPZs would help attract foreign investment to China, boost the country's manufacturing capacity and bring in the latest technologies.

In fact, the import and export business in Beijing has been developing rapidly. In 2003, total import and export volume was USD 68.46 billion, representing an increase of 30.4% over the previous year. The total import volume was USD 51.61 billion, while exports volume was USD 16.85 billion, an increase of 29.4% and 33.6% respectively.

The import and export volume of local enterprises reached USD 18.93 billion, representing an increase of 34.8% over the previous year. The import volume was USD 11.57 billion, an increase of 42.1% over the previous year; and the export volume was USD 7.37 billion, an increase of 24.9% over the previous year. As much as 59.8% of the export volume was constituted by high-tech products. Other major export products were telecommunication equipment and electronic products.

Overall, 814 enterprises in Beijing have been authorized to conduct import and export business. Based on the classification categories, there are 118 comprehensive foreign trade enterprises, 416 manufacturing enterprises, 154 high-tech enterprises, 17 small-scale export enterprises, 30 commercial enterprises, 34 research institutes and 45 private enterprises.

Beijing Import/ Export Performance, 2003 (unit: USD billion)

	Import	YoY increase (%)	Export	YoY increase (%)	Total	YoY increase (%)
Overall	51.61	29.4	16.85	33	68.46	30.4
Local Enterprise	11.57	42.1	7.37	24.9	18.93	34.8

Import/ Export Enterprises in Beijing

Comprehensive foreign trade enterprises	118
High-tech enterprises	154
Manufacturing enterprises	416
Small-scale export enterprises	17
Commercial enterprises	30
Research institutes (authorized to conduct import/export business)	34
Private enterprises	45
Total number authorized	**814**

Source: Ministry of Commerce, China

TAXATION

Tax incentives serve as one of the most important factors to be considered by foreign investors when making decisions to invest in China. Currently, the major taxes applicable to foreign invested enterprises (FIEs) include enterprise income tax, value-added tax, consumption tax, business tax, personal income tax, resource tax, land appreciation tax, stamp tax, tax on urban real estate, tax for vehicle usage and license, resources tax, customs duty and vessel tonnage tax. Various tax concessions or breaks are available to foreign invested enterprises (FIEs) under certain circumstances.

It is worth noting that all state preferential tax policies for encouraging foreign investment, though currently pursued, are progressively being phased out upon China's WTO membership. This is in line with WTO agreements that all enterprises, no matter Chinese or foreign, should enjoy the same "national treatment". In the future, tax incentives will be focused on encouraging investment in specific industries (e.g. high-tech industries) and specific locations (e.g. Western China).

Taxes applicable to foreign invested enterprises

Over the past 20 years, China has made significant progress and has gained more experience in its tax legislation, in particular those related to foreign invested enterprises. The main theme of such changes has been that while it continues to use preferential tax treatment as an important means to attract foreign investment, it has shifted its emphasis from mere *quantity* of foreign investment to the *quality* of foreign investment, i.e. encouraging foreign investment in sectors that will help promote the overall and sustainable economic development of China.

Major Taxes Applicable to Foreign Invested Enterprises

Levied By Tax Bureau

- On Business Transactions
- On Income
- On Property & Behavior
- On Natural Resources
- Value-added tax
- Consumption tax
- Business tax
- Enterprise income tax
- Individual income tax
- Urban real estate tax
- Vehicle usage and license tax
- Stamp duty
- Land appreciation tax

Levied by Customs

- Resources tax
- Customs duty
- Vessel tonnage tax

Enterprise income tax (EIT)

So far, China maintains two sets of EIT laws, one for domestic enterprises and the other for FIEs. For domestic enterprises, the EIT is 33%, while for FIEs, the EIT is 30% plus 3% local surtax where no preferential tax treatment is applicable. In fact, there are quite a lot of tax incentives available to FIEs tailored to specific industries and locations.

For those foreign enterprises that do not have an establishment in China but derives profit, interest, rent, royalties or other income from sources in China, or those that have an establishment or a few establishments in China but the income is not effectively connected with those establishments, a withholding tax of 20% on such income is taxable.

If an FIE is terminated before the prescribed 10-year period, the amount of income tax exempted or reduced shall be re-paid to the tax authorities.

Those who re-invest their profits to set up or extend export enterprises or technologically advanced enterprises with a business period no less than five years will get a full refund of EIT paid on the re-invested amount.

Individual income tax (IIT)

Individual income tax shall be levied on the following:

- Income from wages and salaries;
- Income from production or business operation derived by individual industrial and commercial households;
- Income from contracted or leased operation of enterprises or institutions;
- Income from remuneration for personal service;
- Income from author remuneration; income from royalties;
- Income from interest, dividends and bonuses;
- Income from lease of property;
- Income from transfer of property; and,
- Contingent income and other income specified as taxable

Income from wages and salaries is taxed at nine progressive rates, ranging from 5% to 45%. For foreign taxpayers, the monthly deduction is RMB 4,000 (RMB 840 for domestic employees). Income from compensation for personal services, royalties, interest, dividends, bonus, lease of property, transfer of property, contingent income and other kinds of income shall be taxed at a proportional rate of 20%.

Individual Income Tax Rates (applicable to monthly salaries)

Grade	Monthly Income Taxable (RMB)	Tax Rates (%)
1	The part less than 500	5
2	The part from 500 to 2,000	10
3	The part from 2,000 plus to 5,000	15
4	The part from 5,000 plus to 20,000	20
5	The part from 20,000 plus to 40,000	25
6	The part from 40,000 plus to 60,000	30
7	The part from 60,000 plus to 80,000	35
8	The part from 80,000 plus to 100,000	40
9	The part exceeding 100,000	45

Note: The Monthly Income Taxable refers to the remaining sum of an individual's monthly income after RMB 800 or an extra deductible sum is deducted as stipulated by Article 6 of the Law on Individual Income Tax. With regard to foreigners, it refers to the remaining sum of his monthly income after RMB 4,000 is deducted.

Value added tax (VAT)

There are three kinds of rates for VAT:

- For taxpayers selling or importing goods, or providing services of processing, replacement and repairs, the tax rate is 17%.
- For taxpayers selling or importing grains, edible vegetable oil, coal gas, natural gas, coal or charcoal products for household use, books, newspapers, magazines, chemical fertilizers, agricultural chemicals and agricultural machineries etc., the tax rate is 13%.
- For taxpayers exporting goods, except otherwise stipulated by the State Council, the tax rate is 0%.

For enterprises and individuals engaged in production or providing taxable labor service with annual sales volume under RMB 1 million (USD 120,000), those engaged in wholesale and retailing with annual sales volume under RMB 1.8 million (USD 700,000), and those designated by the tax authority as small VAT payers, the tax rate is 6% on a tax-in price basis.

Business tax

Business tax shall be levied on the organizations and individuals supplying taxable labor, transfer of intangible assets and sale of real estate. The rate of business tax is 3% for communications and transportation, civil construction, post and telecommunications, culture and sports industries, 5% for banking and insurance, service, transfer of intangible assets, real estate sales industries. The business tax rate for entertainment industries is 5% - 20%.

Resources tax

Foreign enterprises that exploit mineral and natural resources within the territory of China are subject to resources tax.

Resources Tax

Description	Unit	Tax quantum
Crude Oil	Ton	RMB 8 - 30
Natural Gas	Per thousand cum	RMB 2 - 15
Coal	Ton	RMB 0.3 - 5
Other non-metallic mine crude ore	Ton	RMB 0.5 - 20
Ferrous-metal mine crude ores	Ton	RMB 2 - 30
Solid salt	Ton	RMB 10 - 60
Liquid salt	Ton	RMB 2 - 10

Source: Beijing Local Taxation Bureau

Land appreciation tax

Land appreciation tax is levied on the income from the transfer of state-owned land-use rights, buildings and their attached facilities. The appreciation amount shall be the balance of proceeds received by the taxpayer on the transfer of real estate after deducting the following items:

- The sum paid for the acquisition of land use rights;
- Cost and expenses for land development;
- Cost and expense for the construction of new building and facilities, or the assessed value for used properties and buildings;

- The taxes related to real estate transfer;
- Other items as stipulated by the Ministry of Finance.

Land Appreciation Tax

The portion of the appreciation amount	Tax Rate %
• Not exceeding 50% of the deductible amount	30
• Between 50% to 100% of the deductible amount	40
• Between 100% to 200% of the deductible amount	50
• Exceeding 200% of the deductible amount	60

Source: Beijing Local Taxation Bureau

Stamp duty

Activities involving purchases and sales, processing, contracting, leasing, transportation, storage, loan lending, property insurance, technology contract and property transfer vouchers, business account books and licenses are subject to stamp tax. The minimum rate of a stamp tax is 0.005% and the maximum is 0.1%.

Stamp Duty in detail

Item	Taxable amount	Tax rate (%)
Purchasing and sales contract	Purchasing and sales amount	0.03
Processing and contracting	Income from processing	0.05
Construction project, exploration and survey and design contract	Fee collected	0.05
Building and installation project contract preparation	Sum from the lease	0.03
Property leasing contract	Sum from the lease	0.1
Goods transportation contract	Transportation fee	0.05
Storage and preservation contract	Fee collected	0.1
Money lending contract	Sum lent	0.005
Property insurance contract	Income from insurance fee	0.1
Technology contract	Sum specified	0.03
Property rights transfer contract	Sum specified	0.05
Business account book	each account book	RMB 5

Source: Beijing Local Taxation Bureau

Consumption tax

Consumption Tax is levied on the sale of goods and covers 11 taxable items and 25 tax rates (for details refer to the rules for the Implementation of Interim Regulations of the People's Republic of China on consumption tax), with 3% as the minimum and 45% as the maximum.

The tax on goods used in the production process is levied on the basis of the price of the goods, whereas the tax levied on yellow rice wine, gasoline and diesel is the value per unit quantity basis. Consumption Tax is exempted for the taxable consumer goods exported by the taxpayers, except those taxable consumer goods subject to export restrictions imposed by the Government.

Vehicle usage and license tax

The rate for vessels and vehicles is assessed on the basis of weight capacity and vehicle type or number of seats if they are passenger vehicles. The tax payable for passenger vehicles with no more than 10 seats is RMB 55 per six months; for those with 11-30 seats, the tax payable is RMB 65 per six months; for those with 31 seats or more, the tax payable is RMB 75 per six months. The tax payable for vehicles is RMB 24 per net ton per six months; for small motorcycles, it is RMB 10 per six months; for general motorcycles, it is RMB 18 per six months; and for motor tricycles, tax payable is RMB 24 per six months.

Customs duty

Imported goods are taxed on its normal C.I.F. (Cost, Insurance and Freight). Customs has the authority to determine the taxable price if the goods' C.I.F. is not quotable. The tariff rates are set in a detailed name list. For some special imported goods, tariff is exempted.

Export commodities produced by the FIE itself, except those prohibited from export by the State and those subject to other State regulations, shall be exempted from export tariff.

The necessary import goods, such as raw materials, fuel, parts and components, accessories or packaging materials for FIEs to produce export products, are regarded as bonded commodities and are supervised by customs.

Tax administration

The Law of China on Taxation Administration is the basic law on taxation administration and is also a procedural law. All enterprises, domestic and foreign, are treated equally under this law.

Taxation authorities

Beijing Municipal Finance Administration is the department of the municipal government in charge of fiscal revenue and expenditure, financial and tax policies and state-owned capital funds of the municipality.

Beijing Municipal State Taxation Administration is the administrative organ in charge of the taxation of the municipality.

Beijing Municipal Local Taxation Administration is the organ in charge of local taxation in this municipality under the direct supervision of the municipal government.

Beijing Municipal Finance Administration provides operational guidance to district and county bureaus of finance in conjunction with district and county governments. Beijing Municipal State Taxation Administration and Beijing Municipal Local Taxation Administration exercise vertical administration over all taxation establishments within the municipality.

Tax registration

Joint ventures, wholly-owned foreign enterprises (WOFEs), representative offices and other similar organizations in China are required to register with the tax authorities within the time limit prescribed in the relevant regulations. In general, this has to be completed within 30 days after the business license is issued. Registrations are to be filed with both the State Tax Administration and Local Tax Administration. The two bureaus have their own tax jurisdictions. To qualify as an ordinary VAT payer and be able to issue VAT invoices, a taxpayer has to undertake VAT registration as well.

Upon completion of the tax registration, the tax authorities will issue the applicant a tax registration certificate that must be renewed every year. During the registration process, the enterprise concerned should discuss with the tax officers and confirm the basis for tax calculation and filing. The consequence of late registration is a maximum penalty of RMB 10,000 or even the repeal of your business license. Any changes in business license or operating office require re-registration with the tax authorities.

Taxation control

The tax year is the calendar year, i.e., from 1 January to 31 December. If a foreign enterprise experiences difficulties in computing its taxable income on the calendar-year basis, it may apply to the tax authorities to adopt its own financial year as the tax year. For an enterprise that commences business within a calendar year or has operated for less than 12 months in a calendar year, the actual operating period will be treated as the tax year.

An FIE is required to file its annual tax returns, audited financial statements and the auditor's report to the tax administrations within four months after the end of the year. The application for deferring the filing of the above documents should also be submitted within this period of time. The penalty for failure to file the above documents within the prescribed time limit is 0.2% per day on the tax amount overdue.

Any taxpayer or withholding agent who fails to perform tax registration procedures, fails to set up an accounting system and fails to keep its business records for a prescribed time period is required to redress these within a prescribed time limit. Any failure to comply with this will be subject to a fine of up to RMB 2,000; if the violation is serious, a fine up to RMB 10,000 will be imposed.

The fine for tax evasion which involves such unlawful activities as forgery, falsifying or concealing relevant information, fraud, or failure again to pay tax within the prescribed time period, the fine is up to but not more than 500% of the tax due. In most of the above cases, serious offenders will be prosecuted by law.

Tax audit

The tax authorities have the power to carry out tax audits to examine taxpayer records and relevant documents. Refusal of tax examination will be subject to a maximum penalty of RMB 50,000. In general, tax authorities shall provide an enterprise a written notice about the impending tax audit.

One should adopt a cooperative attitude, but do not forget to check with the tax officers on the exact scope of audit and ensure that they show you their staff identity cards.

Tax reporting and payment

Different taxes have different reporting periods and payment due dates. In general, Foreign Enterprise Income Tax (EIT) is paid on a quarterly basis, VAT and Business Tax are usually on a monthly basis, and Individual Income Tax (IIT) is on a monthly basis too. Tax authorities will not send you tax returns. Instead, you should collect blank tax returns from tax offices, complete them and file accordingly.

Acceptable ways of submission differ from place to place and depends on the nature of the tax. For some locations, reporting via mail is acceptable, while at some other locations, submission must be made in person.

Late payment of tax will involve a fine of 0.05% a day on the tax owing. Withholding agents who fail to observe these obligations will be subject to a maximum penalty of 500% of the tax involved. Under the tax regulations, you may apply to the tax authorities for deferred tax filing and payment.

Preferential tax policies for foreign-funded high-tech enterprises in Beijing

The "Act on Foreign Investment Enterprises and Foreign Enterprises' Income Tax" outlines concessionary policies that foreign-investor companies can enjoy, but this is a complicated area because policies vary from region to region and have different structures.

There are many concessions for FIEs operating in industrial parks. Provided that FIEs have operating terms of more than 10 years, they may enjoy a five-year concessionary tax term. After their first profit-making year, these enterprises may enjoy a two-year tax holiday, where they are exempted from paying corporate income taxes. In the following three years, FIEs pay only half the corporate income tax rate (the corporate income tax rate for FIEs in industrial parks is 15%). When this five-year concessionary tax term expires, FIEs start paying the full corporate income tax rate, which is 15%. Two types of FIEs, however, may continue to enjoy tax concessions.

High-tech enterprises may enjoy a further three years of tax concessions, paying only 10% of corporate income tax for the three-year period, and reverting to paying the 15% corporate income tax rate when this period expires. Export-oriented enterprises – defined as enterprises which export more than 70% of its total production value –, on the other hand, pay a tax rate of 10% from the conclusion of the concessionary five-year period onwards.

China's tax policies encourage foreign investors to reinvest profits. Foreign investors that have been operating for at least five years and have reinvested profits in their enterprises may enjoy a 40% tax refund. For high-tech and export-oriented enterprises, they may receive 100% tax refund.

Tax exemption and reduction

The following are some of the major preferential policies for foreign enterprises.

Concessions on business tax, VAT and customs duty

(a) Incomes derived by research and development centers established by FIEs and foreign wholly-owned enterprises, and incomes derived by foreign enterprises and foreign individuals from technology transfer, technology development and related consultancy and technical services are exempt from business tax.

(b) The raw materials, auxiliary materials, parts, components, accessories and packaging materials imported by FIEs for the outward processing or assembly of products and for the production of goods for export are exempt from import tariffs based on the quantity of finished products actually processed and exported. Alternatively, import tariffs are levied on the imported materials and parts first and rebates are made later based on the quantity of finished products actually processed and exported.

(c) FIEs are entitled to full VAT rebate on the purchase of domestically-produced equipment within their investment amount if such equipment is listed in the catalogue of duty-free imports.

(d) Imports of equipment and supporting technologies, accessories and parts for own use by FIEs under the "encouraged category" or "restricted category II", foreign-invested R&D centers, FIEs with advanced technologies and export-oriented FIEs, are exempt from import tariffs and import-related taxes in accordance with the Circular of the State Council on the Adjustment of Tax Policy on Equipment Imports.

(e) Imports of equipment for own use by foreign investment projects encouraged and supported by the state, their total investment amount are exempt from tariffs and VAT (unless otherwise stipulated by the state). Imports of equipment and supporting technologies, accessories and spare parts for own use by foreign-invested R&D centers within their total investment are exempt from tariffs and import-related taxes in accordance with the Circular of the State Council on the Adjustment of Tax Policy on Equipment Imports if the import items cannot be produced in China or if the performance of the like domestic products or technologies cannot meet their demand.

Concessions on corporate income tax

(a) Preferential Tax Rate

Enterprises in the following regions (sectors) are subject to corporate income tax at the reduced rate of 15%:

- FIEs in the Shenzhen, Zhuhai, Shantou, Xiamen and Hainan special economic zones;
- Foreign enterprises with establishments or venues in special economic zones and engaged in production and business operations;
- Production FIEs established in economic and technological development zones approved by the State Council and in the Pudong New District in Shanghai;
- Technology- and knowledge-intensive projects launched by FIEs in old urban districts of special economic zones, economic and technological development zones and coastal economic open areas approved by the State Council with long investment recovery periods and foreign investment exceeding USD30 million;
- Production FIEs engaged in energy, transportation and port construction projects;
- Production FIEs engaged in export processing in bonded areas;
- High-tech FIEs in state new- and high-technology industrial development zones approved by the State Council.

Production FIEs in the following regions are subject to corporate income tax at 24%:

- Other types of production FIEs in old urban districts of coastal economic open areas, special economic zones, and economic and technological development zones where the 15% preferential tax rate is not applicable;
- Open coastal cities, open cities along the Yangtze River and in inland and border regions, as well as other areas designated by the State Council to enjoy the same concessions;
- State-class tourist resorts.

(b) Exemption and Reduction of Corporate Income Tax

Production FIEs with an operation period of over 10 years (excluding projects for the exploration of petroleum, natural gas, rare metals and precious metals) are eligible for corporate income tax exemption in the first two profit-making years and for reduction by half in the following three years.

With the approval of the State Administration of Taxation (SAT), FIEs engaged in agriculture, forestry and animal husbandry and FIEs established in the economically-backward remote and border areas may be levied corporate income tax at the reduced rate of 15%-30% for another 10 years after the expiration of the above said tax exemption and reduction period.

Sino-foreign joint ventures engaged in port and wharf construction and with an operation period of over 15 years are eligible for corporate income tax exemption in the first five profit-making years and for reduction by half in the following five years.

Infrastructure projects related to airports, ports, wharfs, railways, highways, power stations, coal mines and water conservancy facilities as well as agricultural development in the Hainan Special Economic Zone with an operation period of over 15 years are eligible for corporate income tax exemption in the first five years and reduction by half in the following five years.

The following types of enterprises are eligible for corporate income tax exemption in the first profit-making year and for reduction by half in the second and third years with the approval of the local tax authorities:

- FIEs engaged in services in special economic zones with foreign investment exceeding USD 5 million and with an operation period of over 10 years;
- Foreign-invested banks, Sino-foreign joint-venture banks and other financial institutions in special economic zones and other areas designated by the State Council with foreign capital investment exceeding USD 10 million and with an operation period of over 10 years;
- Recognised high-tech Sino-foreign joint venture enterprises in state-level high-technology development zones with an operation period of over 10 years are exempt from corporate income tax in their first two profit-making years with the approval of the tax authorities.

Foreign-invested export-oriented enterprises are entitled to pay corporate income tax at the reduced rate of 15% or 10% following the expiration of the corporate income tax exemption and reduction by half concession if their export value amounts to over 70% of their total output value in the current year.

- Foreign-invested high-tech enterprises are entitled to pay corporate income tax at the reduced rate of 15%or 10% for three years following the expiration of the corporate income tax exemption and reduction by half concession if their status of high-tech enterprises remains unchanged.
- The income of foreign banks from interest on loans at preferential interest rates to China's state banks is exempt from corporate income tax.
- Foreign leasing companies that lease equipment to Chinese enterprises and are paid leasing fees by products or in the form of product buy-back are exempt from corporate income tax.

- FIEs that undergo restructuring or merge with other enterprises to form joint-stock companies are eligible for a two-year corporate income tax exemption and three-year reduction by half concession.

(c) Tax Rebate on Re-investment by FIEs

Any foreign investor of an FIE re-investing its profit obtained from the enterprise directly into that enterprise or using the profit as capital investment to establish other FIEs with an operation period of at least five years is, upon approval granted by the relevant tax authorities, eligible for a 40% refund of the corporate income tax already paid on the re-invested amount.

If the foreign investor re-invests its profit directly in establishing or expanding an export-oriented or high-tech enterprise in China, 100% of the corporate income tax already paid on the re-invested amount will be refunded.

(d) Other Exemptions and Reductions of Income Tax

- The profits of foreign investors derived from FIEs are exempt from income tax.
- The interest revenue of international financial institutions derived from loans to the Chinese government or state banks and the interest revenue of foreign banks derived from loans to Chinese state banks at preferential rates are exempt from income tax.
- Royalties paid to foreign enterprises for their provision of special technologies to China for scientific research, exploitation of energy resources, development of transportation, production of agriculture, forestry and animal husbandry, and development of important technologies, are eligible for income tax at the reduced rate of 10%, with the approval of SAT. For those enterprises that involve advanced technologies or offer favorable terms, income tax will be exempted.
- In the case of FIEs or foreign enterprises with establishments

engaged in production or business operations within the territory of China, 40% of their investment in the purchase of domestically-produced equipment is exempt from income tax.

- With the approval of the tax authorities, FIEs that have increased their technological development expenses by more than 10% over the previous year are allowed to offset their taxable income in the current year by 50% of the amount of technological development expenses. The details are laid down in SAT's Procedures for the Administration of Pre-Tax Deductions of Enterprise Technological Development Expenses.
- The governments of various provinces, autonomous regions and municipalities have also introduced local income tax exemptions or reductions for those sectors or projects where foreign investment is encouraged.

Individual income tax concession for foreigners

The following incomes of foreigners are eligible for individual income tax concession:

(a) Housing allowance, food allowance, removal expenses and laundry fees received in non-cash forms or in the form of cash reimbursement;

(b) Travel allowance at reasonable levels;

(c) The portion of home visit allowance, language course fees and children's education expenses deemed reasonable by the tax authorities;

(d) Dividends and bonuses received from FIEs;

(e) Any foreign individual who resides in China consecutively for not more than 90 days (or 183 days for those from countries that have signed tax agreements with China) in a tax year is exempt from individual income tax if his wage or salary is not paid or borne by his employer in China and is not borne by a resident establishment or permanent venue of his employer in China.

(f) Any foreign individual who resides in China for more than a year but less than five years is required to declare and pay individual income tax on his wage or salary paid by his employer both inside and outside China during his duration of work in China. With the approval of the tax authorities, he may be allowed to pay tax only on that part of his wage or salary paid by his employer inside China.

Tax concessions for Central and Western Regions

Fees under the "encouraged" category in the Western Region that enjoy the "two-year exemption and three-year reduction by half" tax concession are eligible for corporate income tax at the reduced rate of 15% for three more years following the expiration of the said concession. FIEs recognized as high-tech or export-oriented enterprises with an export value amounting to over 70% of their annual output value in the current year are eligible for a 50% reduction of corporate income tax during the three-year period.

Foreign exchange receipts and payments

China's foreign exchange receipts and payments come under the current account and capital account. The current account covers trade and labor service receipts and payments as well as one-way transfers in foreign exchange. No restrictions are imposed on international settlements and transfers under the current account. The capital account covers foreign exchange receipts and payments in respect of direct investment, loans of all kinds, securities investment etc. Strict control is maintained over the capital account.

(a) Current account

- Receipts under the current account

Upon approval by SAFE, an FIE can open a foreign exchange settlement account with a designated bank by presenting its Foreign Exchange Registration Certificate and other supporting materials. For foreign exchange received under the current account, the FIE may retain a certain amount of it within the limit prescribed by SAFE. Any excess portion has to be sold to designated banks.

- Payments under the current account

When an FIE has to make external payments within its business scope, it may draw the required amount from its foreign exchange settlement account and any shortage can be made up for by purchasing foreign exchange with RMB at designated banks. Details are as follows:

(1) repatriation of after-tax profits and dividends to the foreign party of an FIE can be made from the foreign exchange account or at designated banks by presenting the board of directors' profit distribution resolution;

(2) the after-tax wages and other legitimate incomes in RMB of an FIE's foreign, overseas Chinese, may be converted into foreign currency and remitted at designated banks upon presentation of relevant supporting documents;

(3) after-tax share dividends payable in foreign exchange may be remitted from the foreign exchange account or at designated banks upon presentation of the board of directors' profit distribution resolution.

- Verification and cancellation of foreign exchange receipts and payments

The procedure of submitting all relevant documents to SAFE prior to receiving remittances has been cancelled. FIEs are now allowed to go through the procedures for verification and cancellation of foreign exchange receipts on exports in one go on a monthly basis, and can submit the documents online via the e-port system after export declaration instead of going to SAFE in person to do so.

Upon receipt of foreign exchange, the FIE can go to SAFE and complete the verification and cancellation procedures all at once by presenting the foreign exchange receipts on export verification/cancellation forms and counterfoil, export declarations, invoices, and foreign exchange.

(b) Capital account

- Receipts under the capital account

These are investment capital in foreign exchange contributed by the foreign and Chinese parties to the FIE; external debts, external debts-turned loans, and foreign exchange loans extended by domestic financial institutions in the mainland to an FIE; foreign exchange revenues derived from an FIE's share issue and other foreign exchange receipts under the capital account; and management of receipts under the capital account.

For foreign exchange receipts under the capital account, FIEs should comply with the relevant regulations and open foreign exchange accounts at designated banks. Any sale of foreign exchange to the bank must be approved by SAFE.

For investment capital in foreign exchange contributed by the foreign and Chinese parties to an FIE, a capital fund account should be opened. The foreign exchange deposits in the account can be used to pay for current account expenditures as well as SAFE-approved capital account expenditures.

For external debts, external debts-turned loans, and foreign exchange loans extended by domestic financial institutions in the mainland to an FIE, a loan account can be opened. Foreign exchange deposited into this account must be the contracted amount of the external debts, external debts-turned loans and foreign exchange loans concerned and the amount must be the same as that stipulated in the loan agreements registered with SAFE. By the same token, any withdrawals from this account must be used for the purposes stipulated in the loan agreements, but approval by SAFE is not required.

For foreign exchange revenues generated from issuing shares by FIEs, a securities account should be opened. Deposits in this account must be incomes from issuance of shares in foreign currency and payments from this account must be those for the purposes stipulated in the prospectus approved by the securities regulatory departments.

- Payments under the capital account

These include repayment of loan principal, and payment of external guarantee; increase, assignment or other forms of disposal of investment capital in foreign exchange of FIEs; remittances of capital upon liquidation of FIEs in accordance with relevant regulations; increased investment or reinvestment within the Chinese mainland by the foreign party to an FIE; and increased investment within the Chinese mainland by investment companies with foreign exchange capital.

- Management of payments under the capital account

In accordance with the Regulations for Foreign Exchange Control of the People's Republic of China, all foreign exchange receipts and payments under the capital account have to be approved by SAFE. Payments from the capital account of FIEs cover the following:

Repayment of loans
China adopts an approval system in managing external debts. SAFE will not approve any repayment of external debt unless it has been properly registered. When applying to SAFE for approval to make repayment of external debt principal, interest and related fees, an FIE should present proof of external debt registration, the external debt contract, and notice by creditor on repayment of principal and interest (the notice should state the respective amounts of principal and interest, interest rate, method of interest computation, and number of interest-bearing days, etc).

Upon approval by SAFE, the FIE may make payment through its foreign exchange account or at designated banks. For repayment of foreign exchange loan principal, interest and related fees to domestic financial institutions in the mainland, the FIE may, upon approval by SAFE, proceed to the financial institution where it has an account with to complete the necessary procedures by presenting the required documents such as the foreign exchange-turned-loan registration certificate, notice by creditor on repayment of principal and interest, and loan agreement.

External guarantee
The provision of external guarantee has to be approved by SAFE, with the relevant registration procedures completed at the local foreign exchange administration. As for external guarantee in relation to contract compliance, approval by SAFE is required.

Offshore investment
For investment abroad, the source of funds has to be examined by SAFE before an application is filed with the competent approval authority. Upon approval granted, the funds may be remitted out of the country.

Termination of enterprise
When an FIE is liquidated and after all taxes have been paid in accordance with the relevant regulations, the amount to be returned to the foreign party may, with approval from SAFE, be remitted through designated banks or carried in person out of the country. Foreign exchange belonging to the Chinese party should be sold to designated banks in full.

Reinvestment
Should the foreign party to an FIE wish to reinvest its profits in

RMB or foreign exchange in China, it has to apply to the local foreign exchange administration by submitting the relevant documents. Upon verification, the local foreign exchange administration will issue a certifying document with which the reinvested enterprise can apply for business registration and for credit checking by certified public accountants. Upon presentation of valid proofs from SAFE, the reinvesting enterprise can make payment from its foreign exchange account or capital fund account with the bank.

Increased investment
Should the foreign party to an FIE wish to increase its investment in China, it has to apply to the local foreign exchange administration by submitting the relevant approval documents from the competent departments and other materials.

Foreign-funded investment companies
Should these companies invest their foreign exchange funds in China, approval has to be sought from SAFE.

Increase, assignment or other forms of disposal of registered capital
Should an FIE wish to increase, assign or dispose of its registered capital in other ways, approval by SAFE is required. By presenting the "FIE foreign exchange investment capital domestic transfer approval letter" issued by SAFE, the FIE can transfer its foreign exchange at designated banks.

Foreign exchange incomes and expenditures

Foreign embassies, consulates, international organizations and other resident foreign organizations with legal entity status in China may keep their foreign exchange. The same applies to resident foreign personnel. They may open foreign exchange accounts at designated banks in accordance with the relevant regulations.

All legitimate RMB incomes of these resident foreign organizations and personnel may be converted into foreign currency and remitted out of China at SAFE-designated banks upon presentation of valid proofs and invoices. Foreign exchange remitted from abroad by such organizations or carried into China by such personnel may be kept by them or deposited into or sold to designated banks. Such exchange may also be remitted or carried in person out of China upon presentation of valid proof.

Should resident foreign organizations and personnel sell their personal items, equipment or appliances brought into China or purchased in China, they may convert the RMB proceeds into foreign currency and remit it out of the country through SAFE-designated banks by presenting their business registration certificate or personal identification document and the sales proof concerned.

Foreign nationals, overseas Chinese, and other Chinese from Hong Kong, Macau and Taiwan on short stays in China may convert their unused RMB back into foreign currency by presenting their passport and original RMB sales receipt (valid for six months).

Repatriation of profits

China allows FIEs and enterprises issuing shares offshore to remit their profits, dividends and bonuses out of the country. Such remittances do not require the prior approval of SAFE. By presenting the necessary documents, the enterprises can make the remittance direct through the bank, which will report details of the remittance to the local foreign exchange administration.

Documents to be submitted to the bank include:

- Tax payment statement and tax return (enterprises eligible for tax exemption and reduction should also submit proofs issued by local tax office);

- Audited report prepared by accounting firm on profits, dividends and bonuses of the current year;
- Resolution of the board of directors on dividend and bonus distribution;
- Foreign exchange registration certificate of foreign-invested enterprise;
- Credit report prepared by accounting firm;
- Other information as requested by SAFE; and,
- For remittance of profits, dividends and bonuses from previous years, an audited report on the FIE's financial situation during the year in question should also be submitted to the bank.

Remittance procedure

The banks will mark "profits, dividends and bonuses remitted" on the foreign exchange registration certificate and tax payment statement respectively, and endorse these documents with an official seal. When remittance is done, the bank will keep photocopies of these two documents for record.

The banks will then report to the local foreign exchange administration. Within the first five working days of each month, the bank will submit the reports (in the form of spreadsheet) on profits, dividends and bonuses remitted by FIEs during the previous month to the local foreign exchange administration department.

In accordance with the Notice on Issues Concerning the Remittance of Profits, Dividends and Bonuses by Designated Banks, SAFE is authorized to carry out random checks of remittances amounting to an equivalent value of USD 100,000 or more, or remittances deemed suspicious, in order to ascertain their authenticity.

*Source for this chapter: Beijing Local Taxation Bureau

INTELLECTUAL PROPERTY

Meeting WTO requirements

The year 2003 was an important year for China in further strengthening the protection of intellectual property rights (IPR) and implementing more measures to comply with the legal requirements of the World Trade Organization (WTO).

To provide effective protection to foreign investors, the Chinese intellectual property system was substantially improved, with the total number of applications of three kinds of patents exceeding 300,000, and the number of applications for trademark registration exceeding 450,000. Significant achievement was gained in the area of copyright protection. The fight against intellectual property infringement was further intensified.

To adapt to the new situation after China's entry into WTO, the Chinese government further improved the legal framework of intellectual property by amending and enforcing regulations related to intellectual property. In 2003, various regulations and rules were enacted, namely, the Regulation on Customs Protection of Intellectual Property Rights of the People's Republic of China, the Implementation Rule of Copyright Administrative Punishment, the Rule on Compulsory Licensing of Patents and the Rule on Patent Agent Administration.

Besides that, a number of regulations and rules, which were not in line with the agreements with the WTO, were revised or annulled. WTO has approved and passed the review of Chinese Intellectual Property Laws and its transitional review.

Protection of Intellectual Property Rights (IPRs)

In 2003, customs offices across China continued to fortify protection for IPRs. Cooperating closely with judicial organs, authorities in charge of IP work and other IP-related agencies, customs officers nationwide sought

to eradicate illegal acts of IP infringement.

In 2003, cultural administrations at all levels across China continued rectifying and regulating the audio-video market, fighting against massive illegal actions, such as smuggling and piracy. According to statistics, in the whole year, cultural administrations confiscated 120 million pieces of illegal audio-video products, revoked 3,984 operative permits. 1,583 cases were handed over to the public security authorities or judicial organs, among which 134 were charged with criminal liabilities.

Adherence to international practices

China has promulgated a vast array of laws and regulations and has joined major international organizations and conventions to protect intellectual property rights, including the *World Intellectual Property Organization, Paris Convention for the Protection of Industrial Property, Madrid Agreement Concerning the International Registration of Marks, Berne Convention for the Protection of Literary and Artistic Works, Universal Copyright Convention, Patent Cooperation Treaty, Nice Agreement and Budapest Treaty.*

Generally, trademarks, service marks and copyrights of Internet operators and users are protected by China intellectual property law. However, intellectual property rights protection afforded by existing Chinese laws on certain Internet sites is not sufficient.

For example, the China copyright law which was enacted before the introduction of the Internet in China, listed nine kinds of literary, artistic or scientific works to be protected by the law, but did not include Internet Web page design. Another example is related to the protection of integrated circuit (IC) design under the current copyright and patent laws. Although these laws contain provisions that afford both copyright and patent protection to original IC designs, the procedures for registration, which are necessary to obtain legal protection, are often cumbersome and time-consuming.

Fortunately, Chinese authorities have realized this problem and the National Copyright Administration has, in consultation with experts, created a framework for adopting a national law that protects online copyright. Newly amended laws are likely to contain provisions to the following effect.

First, copyright protection will be given to "information network-based publication rights," which will apply to the rights of writers whose works are provided to the public via wired systems and wireless systems. Second, such "information network-based publication rights" will be extended to artistic performers and audio and video recorders. Third, copyright-management organizations will authorize the website operators, on behalf of the writers, the right to use specific works of these writers.

Patents

In 2003, the State Intellectual Property Office (SIPO) received a total of 308,487 patent applications, an increase of 22.1% over the 252,631 of the previous year. A total of 1,171, international applications were received, 220 more than that of the previous year. A total of 182,226 patents were granted in 2003, an increase of 37.6% over 132,399 in the same period the previous year.

Out of this total, 149,588 domestic applications were granted, an increase of 33.4% over 112,103 in the same period the previous year, while 32,638 were granted to foreign applications, an increase of 60.8% over 20,296 in the same period the previous year.

	Number of patents		Increase
	2002	2003	
Domestic applications	252, 631	308, 487	22.1%
International applications	951	1, 171	23.1%
Total patents granted	132, 399	182, 226	37.6%
Domestic patents granted	112,103	149, 588	33.4%
Foreign patents granted	20, 296	32, 638	60.8%

Source: State Intellectual Property Office (www.sipo.gov.cn)

Each of the three categories of patents – inventions, utility models and industrial designs, accounted for about one-third of the total in quantity. The number of patent applications for inventions had caught up with that of utility models for the first time in 16 years. In 2003, invention patents increased by 31.3% over the previous year, far more than the other two categories.

Domestic invention patents exceeded foreign ones for the first time in the past eight years. Since China agreed to the Patent Cooperation Treaty (PCT) in 1994, patent applications for inventions from abroad went up sharply, while patent applications for domestic inventions fell behind. This situation was reversed in 2003 – applications for domestic inventions amounted to 57,000, while those for foreign ones were 49,000.

Service inventions have exceeded non-service inventions since the implementation of the Chinese Patent Law, which had resulted in a significant increase in domestic service patent applications (an increase of 26.1% over the previous year). Patent applications for domestic service inventions went up to 34,371 (an increase of 53.2% over the previous year), with a higher increasing rate than those of utility models and industrial designs (23.3% and 8.8% respectively). Patent applications for domestic service inventions had accounted for more than 40% of total domestic patent applications.

Since China embraced the open policy in 1978, nearly 2 million patent applications had been received by SIPO, of which, more than 1.60 million (82.6% of total patent applications) were domestic and 335,703 (17.4% of total patent applications) were foreign. More than 1.07 million applications were successful – 941,940 domestic and 123,321 foreign, accounting for 88.4%and 11.6% of the total respectively.

By 31 December 2003, a total of 438 applications for the registration of layout designs of integrated circuits were received, 366 of which were published, registered and issued with certificates.

In the same year, 125 countries and regions had filed their patent applications in China. The SIPO received applications from 90 countries and regions. The top 10 countries in terms of the number of patent applications were Japan, USA, the Republic of Korea, Germany, France, Netherlands, Switzerland, United Kingdom, Italy and Sweden.

How to apply for a Chinese patent

According to the Chinese Patent Law, any foreigner, foreign enterprise or other foreign organization not residing or having a business office in China, and wishing to apply for a patent, or to extend patent rights to China, should appoint a patent agency designated by the Patent Administration Department under the State Council to act as his or its agent.

China Intellectual Property Office

Location and mailing address: 6 Xi Tu Cheng Road, Ji Men Bridge, Haidian District, Beijing, China 100088

Telephone:	(8610) 6201 3288 (general) (8610) 6209 3905 (PCT matters) (8610) 6209 3637 (PCT matters)
Fax:	(8610) 6201 9615 (general) (8610) 6201 9451 (PCT matters)

In terms of patent rights enforcement, the local intellectual property offices handled the patent disputes far more efficiently than previously. These offices now took speedy action against counterfeiting patents and passing-off patents through various enforcement procedures and various administrative measures.

In 2003, it handled 1,517 patent dispute cases, of which 1,237 were resolved. A total of 1,873 cases were settled as passing-off patents and 164 cases were settled as counterfeiting patents.

Amendments to the Patent Law

The Decision of the Standing Committee of the National People's Congress Concerning Amendments of the Patent Law was promulgated on 25 August 2000, and came into force on 1 July 2001.

One of the main amendments was making judicial review available. This was to bring China's patent law in line with the Agreement on Trade-Related Aspects of Intellectual Property, which requires that parties be given the opportunity for judicial review of final administrative decisions. Decisions of the Patent Re-examination Board regarding utility models and industrial designs as well as other administrative acts may now be subjected to review.

Other amendments include authorizing patent holders to apply for injunctive relief before commencing court procedures in certain circumstances, the introduction of a provision that gives guidance on calculating the amount of damages where there has been an infringement and clarifying what constitutes a job-related creation or invention.

Also on 1 July 2001, the State Council promulgated the Detailed Implementing Rules for the Law of the People's Republic of China on Patents. Together with the Amendments (mentioned above), they repeal and replace the implementing rules adopted almost a decade ago.

These new Implementing Rules introduced many changes, including issues concerning the preliminary examination. Provisions on utility model searches by utility model patent-holders were introduced. The patent revocation procedure was removed. Other changes included changes to the rules governing fees, procedural rules governing patent application documents and a special rule on compulsory licenses for semiconductor technology.

Trademarks

In 2003, the Trademark Office (TMO) received the highest number of trademark applications ever, a total of 452,095 applications covering both goods and services, an increase of more than 80,000 or 21.6% over that of 2002.

Of this total number, 405,620 were domestic applications, an increase of more than 26.3% over the previous year, accounting for 89.7% of the total; 33,912 were from abroad, accounting for 7.5% of the total; 12,563 (or 2.8% of the total) were related to the territorial extension of international trademark registrations in accordance with the Madrid Agreement Concerning the International Registration of Marks.

In 2003, the Trademark Office reviewed 245,737 trademarks and approved 242,511 trademarks for registration. 34,378 were related to the changes of registered trademarks, 41,366 related to assignment, 23,184 related to renewal, 32,653 related to revocation and cancellation, 12,886 related to the records of trademark licensing.

	Number of trademark applications		Increase
	2002	2003	
Total number of applications	372,095	452,095	21.6%
Domestic applications	298,941	405,620	26.3%
Foreign applications	30,419	33,912	10.3%

Source: State Intellectual Property Office (www.sipo.gov.cn)

The State Administration for Industry and Commerce (SAIC) had issued The Notice Concerning Several Issues on Applying for Recognition of Well-Known Trademarks on 28 April 2000. This Notice was issued to further standardize well-known trademark application procedures and to address the problem of overcharging by agencies and individuals for helping enterprises process such applications. The Notice provides that applicants must refer to SAIC offices at the province level where the enterprise is located. The province-level office will carry out an examination and then submit the relevant application documents to the SAIC. The Notice also specifies the application procedures.

In 2003, the Administration for Industry and Commerce (AIC) at all levels across the nation continued intensifying legal enforcement efforts in trademark cases, and cracked down on trademark counterfeiting and infringement. The legitimate rights of trademark registrants and the interests of consumers are largely protected.

According to statistics, 37,489 trademark law-breaking cases of various kinds were investigated and handled across the country in 2003 (of which 11,001 were ordinary law-breaking cases and 26,488 were related to trademark-infringement and counterfeiting).

A total of 84,755,000 pieces/ sets of illegal marks were seized and removed. 15,597 molds, printing plates and other tools directly used in trademark infringement were confiscated. 5,754.92 tons of infringed products were destroyed. The fine imposed amounted to RMB 242 million (USD 29 million). 45 cases were referred to the court for criminal prosecution.

Since the Regulations on Protection of the Olympic Symbols were promulgated and implemented, protection of Olympic symbols has been enforced by AIC at all levels to tackle infringement of the exclusive right of using Olympic symbols.

Trademark Law

On 3 August 2002, the State Council promulgated The Implementing Regulations for the Trademark Law of the People's Republic of China, which came into force on 15 September 2002. The Implementing Regulations repeal the Detailed Implementing Rules for the Trademark Law of the People's Republic of China and the Official Reply of the State Council on Issues Concerning the Attachment of Documents in Connection with the Handling of Trademark Registration.

The primary reason for introducing Implementing Regulations was to overhaul the rules set forth in the Detailed Implementing Rules for the Trademark Law of China so as to bring the subsidiary legislation of the Trademark Law in line with the amended Trademark Law and WTO commitment.

The Implementing Regulations defined terms applied in the amended Trademark Law. They also provide rules on well-known trademark petitions, applications for registration of "geographical indication" as certification trademarks or collective trademarks, appointment of trademark agencies, language requirements, submission and service of documents, international registration of trademarks, application procedures, trademark examinations, oppositions, licenses, assignments, other transfers of trademark rights, licenses, renewals, review and adjudication, revocation of marks that should not have been registered, revocation for non-use, partial revocation, amounts of fines, infringement of well-known trademark rights and the cancellation of trademarks and other issues.

Preserving registered trademark assets

On 22 November 2000, the Judicial Committee of the Supreme People's Court adopted The Interpretation of the Supreme People's Court Concerning Implementing Preservation of Assets by People's Courts with regard to Registered Trademark Rights. It was issued on 2 January 2001 and came into effect on 21 January 2001.

The Interpretation provides guidance on the enforcement mechanism of the China Civil Procedure Law on the preservation of assets in cases where people seek to preserve registered trademark assets. According to the Interpretation, when the court takes such action, it would issue a notice to assist with enforcement at the Trademark Office. The notice specifies the type of assistance requested such as prohibiting assignment or cancellation of the registered trademark, prohibiting changes in the matters registered and prohibiting registration of trademark rights hypothecations. The term for a single period of registered trademark rights preservation may not exceed six months. The period may be extended if necessary.

Copyright issues

In 2003, copyright administrations at various levels made remarkable achievements in encouraging innovation, promoting industrial development, regulating market order, and further developing the opening-up policy.

Protection of copyright has also been greatly enhanced. In 2003, the National Copyright Administration of China coordinated a series of moves for fighting against piracy and infringement across the country, dispatching a total of 150,000 enforcement personnel to check more than 20,000 markets, 67,000 booths, 500 enterprises, and 8,000 schools. As a result, 12.9 million pieces/ sets of pirated products were seized, 2,542 infringing units received fines amounting to RMB 2.81 million (USD 340,000), and 1,981 illegal businesses were shut down.

In 2003, local copyright administrations across the country handled 23,013 cases, nearly 2.6 times that of 2002, and resolved 22,429 cases. Of the total number of cases, 21,032 cases received fines, 1,173 were mediated and 224 were referred to the courts. The top five regions, where the most cases were handled, resolved and fined, were Guangdong, Guangxi, Henan, Jiangsu, and Fujian.

Copyright Law

On 2 August 2002, the State Council promulgated The Implementing Regulations for the Copyright Law of China, which came into force on 15 September 2002. The Implementing Regulations repeal the regulations of the same name issued by the National Copyright Administration on 30 May 1991.

The Implementing Regulations provides definitions for terms used in the Copyright Law. They also provide rules addressing fines for infringement, protection of certain rights of foreigners, the time when copyright comes into existence, the exercise of copyright in works of joint authorship, alterations when a movie is made from written work, rules concerning works done in the course of employment, rules that apply when the author is unaware of, the status of the copyright after the author dies, remuneration for use of a piece of work when a license is not required, license contracts, recording of license contracts and assignment contracts, neighboring rights, copyright rules in book publishing and declarations prohibiting certain uses.

Business tax on assignment of copyright

The Notice of the State Administration of Taxation Concerning the Issue of Collecting Business Tax on the Assignment of Copyright was issued on 16 April 2001. It was issued to standardize Business Tax policies involving the assignment of copyright. The Notice indicates the potential of tax when an owner of intangible assets authorizes others to assign the intangible assets to a third party.

Royalty standards for use of copyrighted works in digital products

The Royalty Standards for Copyright in the Production of Digital Products (for Trial Implementation) came into force on 1 July 2000.

In accordance with the Regulations of the National Copyright Administration Concerning Copyright in the Production of Digital Products that was issued in December 1999, the Royalty Standards state that users must obtain licenses from the copyright holder and must pay copyright royalties when using works subject to copyright protection before producing digital products. The term Digital Products was defined as meaning tangible media with works protected by copyright law. Digital

Code refers to electronic products, including compact disks, laser disks, video compact disks, digital videodisks, floppy disks, CD-ROMs, CDs of all types and integrated circuit cards.

The Standards provide that, except for musical works, the user and copyright holder may negotiate and select one of the payment forms and the standards described for determining the amount of copyright royalties. Per unit standards are provided, such as between RMB 3 and RMB 30 for every 1,000 characters, and a formula using royalty percentage rates is also provided.

Rules for trial of internet copyright cases

On 22 November 2000, the Judicial Committee of the Supreme Court adopted The Interpretation of the Supreme Court Concerning Several Issues of the Applicable Law in the Trial of Copyright Dispute Cases Involving Computer Networks. The Interpretation clarifies copyright issues involving Internet cases that have not been specifically addressed by the Copyright Law or other related laws.

The Interpretation specifically provides that works protected by the Copyright Law include the digital form of the protected works. The Interpretation specifies detailed rules on when a service provider will be regarded as taking part in infringement activities and when copyright holders can demand action by service providers. It also addresses the question of the legal recourse available to parties wrongfully accused of copyright infringement. Rules are also provided for determining the amount of compensation to be awarded where there is infringement.

Regulations of copyright in computer software

On 20 February 2002 the National Copyright Administration issued The Measures for Registration of Copyright in Computer Software, which came into force on the same date. The Measures addressed the registration of copyright in software and the registration of exclusive license contracts and assignment contracts for copyright in software.

The National Copyright Administration is responsible for the nationwide administration of software copyright registration. The Copyright Protection Center of China is the software registration authority. Upon approval by the National Copyright Administration, the Copyright Protection Center of China may establish software registration offices at local levels. Software for which registration is applied are software that has been independently developed, or software bearing significant improvements in terms of function or performance over the existing software, with permission from the original copyright holder. The Measures also address the detailed requirements for applications for registration.

INDUSTRIAL PARKS AND DEVELOPMENT ZONES

National development areas

The Beijing municipal government is sparing no effort to improve the city's investment facilities and environment to promote industrial growth. It is going all out to build various urban functional districts, which will form a rational multi-level layout to attract foreign investment. By the end of 2003, there were 24,181 enterprises located in 26 development areas. 20,281 have started operations. Industrial production reached RMB 2,000 billion (USD 24 billion), generating a total profit of RMB 19.36 billion (USD 2.34 billion).

So far, a structure comprising Zhongguancun Science Park, Beijing Economic and Technological Development Zone, Beijing Tianzhu Export Processing Area, Central Business District, Financial Street and Industrial Development Areas, which are sophisticatedly designed, well-coordinated and closely connected, has taken shape in Beijing.

Zhongguancun Science Park is the earliest national high-tech industrial development area in China. Its focal point in promoting investment is to attract domestic and foreign investors to set up high-tech enterprises, R&D centers, incubators, and intermediary institutions in the Park, thereby making Zhongguancun Science Park an innovation and achievement transferring base.

Following years of development, **Beijing Economic and Technological Development Area** has become an important operational base for multinationals and world-renowned firms. It has an industrial structure characterized by pharmaceutical, IT, optical, mechanical & electronic integration and new-type materials industries. By attracting more multinational investment, the Development Area is expected to become a high-tech manufacturing-oriented industrial base.

Beijing Tianzhu Export Processing Area takes electronic communications, warehousing & free trade as well as aviation-related industries as its major industries, and encourages the development of pharmaceutical, machinery, fine chemical, biological engineering and new-type materials industries. As the first national free trade zone, the Area will further improve the investment environment and build itself into an international-level high-tech industrial area.

Financial Street in Xicheng District has become the most influential area in China's financial industry. It is now home to 530 domestic financial institutions and reputed companies which together manage assets worth RMB 1,300 billion (USD 157 billion).

Zhongguancun Science Park

Zhongguancun covers an area of 100 km^2, and the core district is located in the town of Haidian which is the seat of the District Party Committee and the District Government. In its vicinity are Peking University, Tsinghua University, the Science Town of the Chinese Academy of Sciences as well as many scenic historic spots. It is conveniently located next to the 4th Ring Expressway, Suzhou Street and Baiyi Road, all of which are main transport arteries of Beijing. The park is 25 km south of the Capitol Airport and 10 km north of the West Rail Station.

As the most famous and developed high-tech park in China, the core part of Zhongguancun Science Park (ZSP) is located in Haidian District, northwest Beijing, and has six additional subsidiary parks in other districts, namely, Changping Park, Fengtai Park, Yizhuang Science Park in Daxing, the Electronics City and Jianxiang Park in Chaoyang, and Desheng Park in Xicheng District.

The core part of ZSP is 75 km^2 and is often referred to as the "Silicon Valley" of China. It also consists of the 1.8-km^2 Shangdi Information Industrial Base and the 4-km^2 Yongfeng Experimental Base. In May 1988, the State Council of China formally endorsed the state-level status of ZSP.

Investment climate

In the past decade, ZSP has maintained a speedy growth trend, with total GDP revenue for 2003 increasing by 17% over 2002 to reach RMB 60.8 billion (USD 7.35 billion). In the same year, the turnover of all enterprises was RMB 285.25 billion (USD 34.5 billion), with total industrial output of RMB 128.7 billion (USD 15.6 billion) and total value added of RMB 45.57 billion (USD 5.5 billion). It is estimated that by the end of 2010, the GDP of ZSP will reach RMB 130 billion (USD 15.8 billion).

By end-2003, a total of 16,299 enterprises were established in ZSP, with the number of wholly-owned foreign enterprises (WOFEs) or Sino-foreign joint ventures having increased at an unprecedented rate. Utilized FDI had accumulated to more than USD 3.5 billion.

Many Fortune 500 companies have subsidiaries in ZSP and more than 30 have set up R&D institutions in the Park. Major foreign investors including Nokia, HP, UTStarcom, Matsushita, Mitsubishi, Microsoft, Oracle, Norvatis, SMC, Ericsson, Sun Microsystems, Schlumberger and Bell have bases in the Park. Some well-known domestic enterprises including Lenovo Group (formerly Legend), Stone, Founder, Datang Telecom, Tsinghua Unisplendor and Tsinghua Tongfang have also located their projects there. More than 120 companies have individual revenue of at least RMB 100 million (USD 12 million).

Various incubators (e.g. Fengtai Innovation Center, Haidian Innovation Center for Overseas Chinese Scholars and Tsinghua Innovation Center) have been fostered in the zone for the commercialization of scientific achievements and development of high-tech enterprises. Fueled by the Technological Innovation Fund, as many as 3,000 new enterprises have set up in the period 1999 – 2002. Over 20 venture capital firms are now co-operating with ZSP.

According to the master plan, the focus of ZSP is on the development of software, IT products and services, optical electron-mechanical integration technologies and products, bioengineering, pharmaceuticals, new materials, environment protection technologies, education and commerce.

One of ZSP's subsidiaries, the 5-km^2 Changping Park is located in a northern suburb of Beijing. It hosts over 1,000 high-tech enterprises with total industrial output of RMB 40 billion (USD 4.8 billion). Emphasis has been put on biotechnology, telecommunications, mechanical photoelectron technology and new material. Fengtai Park is located in the south of Beijing, covering an area of 5 km^2, and Yizhuang Science Park, with an area of 7 km^2, is located in Daxing. Electronics City, located in the Jiuxianqiao area in northeastern Chaoyang District, is a 0.5 km^2 area that aims to be the microelectronics production center in North China.

Local talent

ZSP enjoys great advantages in utilizing the top talents of China. Haidian District is home to 50 Chinese universities and 41 research institutes of the Chinese Academy of Science (CAS), Chinese Academy of Engineering (CAE) and others. Top Chinese universities such as Peking University and Tsinghua University both reside in this territory.

While Peking University has unparalleled strengths in the arts, humanities, sciences and social sciences, Tsinghua has the best graduates in engineering in China. People's University of China, a stone's throw away from the above two, has its forte in business, political science, economics and journalism. There are other famous universities nearby specializing in foreign languages, international trade, finance, telecommunications, aeronautics, tourism and even sports etc.

In recent years, more than 3,000 Chinese students or research scholars have returned to Beijing from overseas education to start their own ventures or join major companies in the Park, adding fresh vitality to the existing pool of local talent in ZSP.

The ZSP Administrative Committee
2nd Level, Haidian Technologies Building
Zhongguancun South Avenue
Haidian District, Beijing
P. R. China 100081
Tel: (8610) 6891 5118
Fax: (8610) 6891 5214
Email: zgc@zgc.gov.cn
Website: www.zgc.gov.cn

Location Map of Zhongguancun

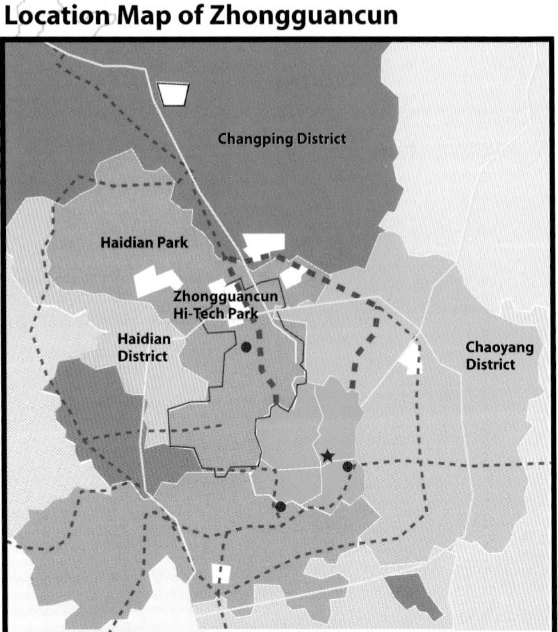

Beijing Economic and Technological Development Zone

Beijing Economic and Technological Development Zone (BETDZ) was approved by the State Council as a state-level Economic and Technological Development Zone (ETDZ) on 25 August 1994. The first phase is planned on a 15-km^2 area. BETDZ enjoys preferential policies allocated to both the coastal ETDZs and the national high-tech parks.

Located in Yizhuang in Daxing District, BETDZ is just next to the Beijing – Tianjin Expressway and near to the south 4th Ring Road of Beijing. Tiananmen Square, the heart of the capital city, lies 16.5 km north of BETDZ.

BETDZ has facilities for sewage treatment, natural gas and steam supply. It is connected to the North China Power Grid. 10,000 lines cabled with optical fibers provide cabled, wireless, microwave, digital telecommunications, IDD, facsimile, computerized data network, satellite and cable TV, video-phone system and Internet services.

In 2001, BETDZ achieved GDP of RMB 6.97 billion (USD 85 million) and total sales turnover of RMB 46.7 billion (USD 5.67 billion), up 139.2% and 375% respectively over the previous year.

At the end of 2001, 1,044 enterprises had registered in BETDZ, with total investment over RMB 3.6 billion (USD 44 million). Among them were 762 domestic enterprises, with total investment of RMB 7.7 billion (USD 93 million). According to the Customs department, annual import and export of BETDZ amounted to USD 3.58 billion in 2001, an astonishing increase of 495.4% over the previous year.

To date, BETDZ hosts 282 foreign-invested enterprises. Among others, Hong Kong, Macau and Taiwan enterprises have invested approximately USD 2.70 billion, with an average of USD 9.87 million per project. Major foreign investors in BETDZ include Bayer, Lucent, NCR, Lotte, Matsushita, Sanyo, Shiseido, Unilever, ABB, Coca Cola, Cummins, GE, Ronabranc, Nokia and BMW.

Major industries encouraged in the park are pharmaceuticals, information technology, optical electro-mechanics, new materials, light industries and services.

Economic Development Bureau of BDA Administrative Committee

Beijing Economic and Technological Development Area

Tel: (8610) 6788 1209

Foreign Investment Service Center of BDA Administrative Committee

Tel: (8610) 6788 1236, 6788 1126

Fax: (8610) 6788 0226

Website: www.bda.gov.cn

Peking University Science Park

Jointly established in 1992 by the Ministry of Science & Technology (MOST) and the Ministry of Education (MOE), Peking University Science Park (PKUSP) was designated as a National University Science Park in May 2001. Among its 22 counterparts nationwide, PKUSP has the largest corporate realm and highest amount of turnover, with 390 enterprises deriving a total of RMB 15 billion (USD 1.8 billion) in operating income.

Enterprises in PKUSP enjoy preferential policies given by the State Council, Beijing Municipal Government and Zhongguancun Science Park. Peking University and Huaxia Bank have jointly pooled together RMB 600 million (USD 72.5 billion) to co-develop PKUSP.

Located in Haidian, a northwest urban district of Beijing, PKUSP is about 35 minutes' drive from the downtown area. It comprises three parts – the Eastern Chengfu Zone, the South Street Belt and the Western Loudouqiao Zone. The Park faces the west of Zhongguancun and adjoins Shangdi Information Industrial Base in the north.

Among the existing enterprises, more than 80% are engaged in high-tech industries. These include Founder Group (www.founderpku.com), Jade Bird Group (www.jadebird.com.cn), PKU Weiming (www.weiming.com.cn), WBL PKU Biotech (www.wpu.com.cn), Pulead Technology Industry (www.pulead.com.cn) and PKU High-tech (www.pku-ht.com), Qinghua Tongzhou, Lianchuang Hangli, Royal Stone, PKU Pioneer, PKU Xifei, PKU Zoteq and PKU Resources. Their R&D and industrial sectors cover electronics, information technology, broadband and mobile communication, computer network, software, POS system, genetic engineering, biopharmaceuticals, new materials, new energy and environmental protection.

The Founder Group of PKU is a pioneer in China's high-tech development and commercialization of academic research. Once a publishing-related software developer, it now has a workforce of more than 5,000 employees and owns three listed companies – Founder Holdings, Founder Digital and Shanghai Founder Yanzhong Science & Technologies Group and 17 subsidiaries. The total assets of the whole group are over RMB 6 billion (USD 73 million).

The attraction of PKUSP lies in Peking University (www.pku.edu.cn) itself. Founded in 1898 in the late Qing Dynasty, the university consistently ranks among the top Chinese universities, leading advancements in natural science and social science. In April 2000, Peking University merged with Beijing Medical University.

Its R&D capabilities are shown in the credentials of its staff – 46 CAS fellows, 7 CAE (Chinese Academy of Engineering) fellows, and over 1,600 professors and associate professors. Their research subjects cover a wide range of areas, such as life sciences, physics, business administration, politics, economics, foreign languages, law, education, electronics, urban planning, psychology, sociology and medical science etc. The university also hosts 42 State Key Programs, 42 research institutes, 52 research centers and 15 State Laboratories. There are about 37,000 students in all the levels.

With registered capital of RMB 100 million (USD 12 million), PKUSP Development Corporation provides a one-stop service and continuous support through the various developmental stages of its member enterprises. Companies such as PKU Zhengyuan Science & Tech, PKU New Century, PKU Pioneer, PUK Royal Stone, PKU Xifei and Yunnan PKU Resources have been successfully incubated in the park.

Peking University Science Park Construction & Development Co. Ltd

17th F, PKU Pacific Technologies Plaza

52 Haidian Road, Haidian District. Beijing, China 100871

Tel: (8610) 8266 7188 Fax: (8610) 8266 7840

Email: info@pkusp.com.cn Website: www.pkusp.com.cn

Tsinghua Science Park

A joint venture between Tsinghua University and the Beijing Municipal Government, the Tsinghua Science Park (THSP) is also a member enterprise of the Tsinghua University Enterprise Group that has more than 30 affiliates such as Unisplendour, Tongfang, Tongli, Sunshine Energy, Venture Investment, Industrial Arts Corporation, Huayuan Electronics and Wanbo Internet Technologies. In 2001, the total assets and sales revenue of the whole group reached RMB 16 billion (USD 1.9 billion) and RMB 10 billion (USD 1.2 billion) respectively. The Group registers an average growth of more than 50% annually.

THSP Development Council and Tsinghua University's Planning Committee have been established to manage and supervise the development of the park. THSP Development Center is responsible for providing full-range services for member enterprises as well as the planning, construction, development and daily operation of the Park.

The THSP has long been recognized by the Beijing municipal government as an important R&D base for the capital's high-tech industries. The 22-ha park is located at the southeastern part of Tsinghua University campus.

The development of THSP started in 1993 and the start-up zone, or the Entrepreneur Sector, was opened in August 1998 as a key industrial base for high-tech development in Beijing. In May 2001, with authorization from MOST and MOE, THSP became one of the 22 National University Science Parks.

Tsinghua University and Haidian District have invested RMB 500 million (USD 60 million) to co-establish the Beijing THSP Development Corporation while Bank of China provided credit support of RMB 1 billion (USD 12 million).

Since its inauguration, many enterprises have joined the Park. Among them are prestigious high-tech enterprises and MNCs like Tsinghua Unisplendour (www.thunis.com), Schlumberger, SUN Microsystems,

NEC, Tsinghua Tongfang (www.thtf.com.cn) and Beijing P&G Technologies; there are also major research institutes such as Optical Memory National Engineering Research Center and National Engineering Research Center for CAD Supporting Software; and other organizations such as National University Science and Technology Collaboration Network, Beijing Tsinghua Industrial Development Research Institute, THSP Entrepreneur Service Center and Guochuang Venture Capital Fund.

Tsinghua University (www.tsinghua.edu.cn) is widely recognized as the leading Chinese institution in natural science, engineering and advanced technology. It has 26 CAS fellows, 25 CAE fellows, 1,035 professors, 1,740 associate professors and 446 postdoctoral fellows. Their research areas cover civil engineering, hydraulic engineering, hydropower, environmental science, mechanical, chemical and electrical engineering, architecture, physics, mathematics, computer science, biopharmaceutical and management.

At the university, there are more than 13,000 undergraduates, about 7,000 masters students and over 3,000 doctoral students. In fact, many contemporary Chinese leaders are alumni or have close ties with the university.

Currently, the university owns 29 State Key Programs, 39 research institutes and 15 State Key Laboratories. It has also formed strategic alliances with more than 128 top Chinese enterprises, such as Beijing Electronic Information Industry, Eastcom, Guangdong Nuclear Power, Haier, Hongta Group, Huawei Technologies, Jilin Chemicals, Shanghai Auto Industry, Shanghai Baosteel and Three Gorges Development Corporation; and 30 major MNCs, such as AT&T, General Motors, Hitachi, HP, IBM, Mitsubishi, Motorola, Rockwell, Shell and Sun Microsystems etc.

Tsinghua Science Park Development Center
Huaye Building, Tsinghua University, Haidian District,
Beijing, P. R. China 100084
Tel: (8610) 6278 5888 Fax: (8610) 6277 2777
Email: thsp@tsinghua.edu.cn Website: www.thsp.com.cn

Beijing Software Development Base

Established on 26 June 1998, Beijing Software Development Base (BJSDB) comprises three individual software parks in Zhongguancun, Beijing Polytechnic University and Changping district. The Zhongguancun part of BJSDB occupies a total area of 139 ha and is the most advanced national software park in China.

The development of BJSDB is closely related to Beijing's competitive advantages in R&D facilities, human resources, information supply and market.

Besides major MNCs such as IBM, Microsoft, Oracle, Sun Microsystems and Computer Associates, there are also many Chinese IT enterprises and their software divisions, including Lenovo (formerly Legend), Founder, Tsinghua Tongfang, UFSOFT, Tsinghua Unisplendor, PKU Jade Bird, Stone Group, Beijing Hope Computer, CASS, Sinosoft Group, Federal Software, Hunan Computers, Daheng Info Technologies and Great Wall Software System.

At the beginning of 2002, 723 software firms were operating in BJSDB. The population of software professionals is said to have reached 70,000. The annual growth rate of sales revenue of these enterprises has been above 35% for the past few years.

The BJSDB Administrative Committee
16 Xizhimen South Street, Beijing, P. R. China 100035
Tel: (8610) 6802 6999 Fax: (8610) 6615 3423
Website: www.bsw.gov.cn/rjjd/rjjd.jsp

ECONOMIC OVERVIEW

The outbreak of the Severe Acute Respiratory Syndrome (Sars) in the earlier part of 2003 was an unexpected interruption to Beijing's booming economy. Fortunately it was only a temporary setback. When it was over in a matter of two months, the city quickly regained its viability and continued to expand with dynamism, so much so that the government found it necessary in early 2004 to cool down the economy.

Overall, the year 2003 witnessed the beginning of an all-faceted development of the economy with major sectors moving rapidly towards higher levels of growth. The strategic target of "New Beijing, Great Olympics" was highlighted. Accelerated development was accorded top priority and improvement of the environment became the main task as the city strives to capitalize on the buoyant Olympic mood.

Beijing people had devoted every effort to eliminating the negative effects brought about by the Sars epidemic. The further opening up and reform effort together with the modernization drive made new headway. Science, technology, education, culture, health, sports and other social undertakings progressed in a substantial way. The income of urban and rural households increased steadily. Beijing residents' living standards further improved.

Economic strength

According to preliminary statistics, the gross domestic product (GDP) of Beijing was RMB 361.19 billion (USD 43.7 billion) in 2003, up by 10.5% over the previous year, maintaining an annual expansion of over 10% for a consecutive five years. Per capita GDP reached RMB 31,613 (USD 3,823), up by 9.2 % over the previous year. Economic performance reflected a roller coaster trend as shown in the chart below:

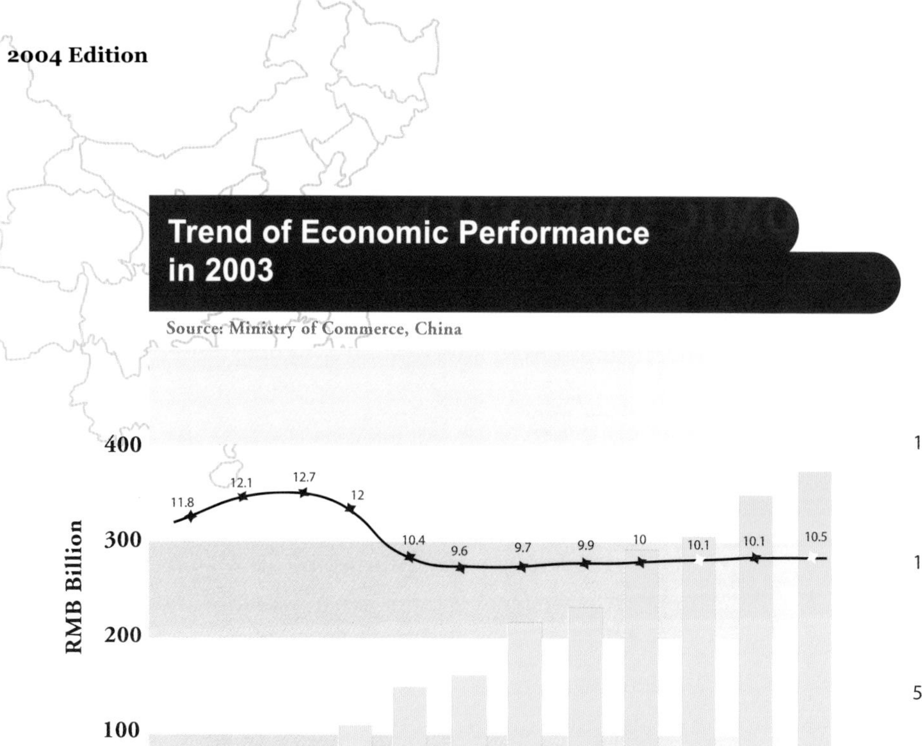

Industrial transformation

The overall structure of the tertiary, secondary and primary industries was stable. In 2003, the added value of the primary industry was RMB 9.53 billion (USD 1.15 billion), up by 3.3% over the previous year; that of the secondary industry, RMB 129.85 billion (USD 15.7 billion), up by 11.9%; and that of the tertiary industry, RMB 221.82 billion (USD 26.8 billion), up by 10% over the previous year. The proportions of the three industries were 2.6%, 36% and 61.4% respectively. The proportion of the secondary industry was 1.2 percentage points higher than that of the previous year. The three industries contributed 0.93%, 41.74% and 57.33% respectively to Beijing's economic growth.

Structure of GDP by Industries

Source: Ministry of Commerce, China

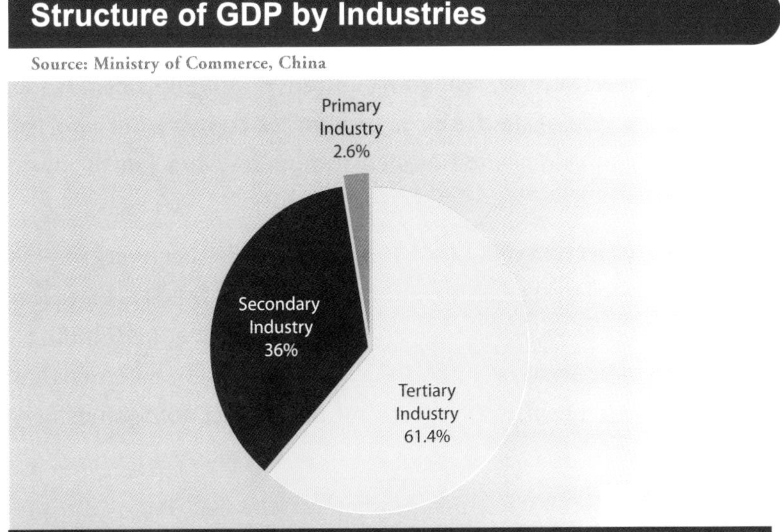

The financial sector maintained its momentum of growth, with the revenue of local governments of Beijing reaching RMB 59.25 billion (USD 7.16 billion), up by 18.2% over the previous year. Financial expenditure totaled RMB 73.72 billion (USD 8.9 billion), up by 17.3%.

Price indices rose slightly. The consumer price index of Beijing was 100.2%; the ex-factory price index of industrial products was 101.5%; the purchasing price index of raw material, fuel and power was 104.7% an increase of 2 percentage points, 4.9 percentage points and 7.6 percentage points respectively over the previous year. All in all, the economy was a picture of good health.

Effect of WTO accession

Since China's accession to the WTO, foreign investors in Beijing have been realigning their businesses in China while expanding their investments so as to adapt to a more open post-WTO China and fiercer global competition.

Such realignment efforts are manifested by the following: first, the creation of a complete industrial chain in the city by turning it into a global production base; second, realigning and integrating businesses into the global production system; third, promoting cooperation and healthy competition with domestic-invested companies; and fourth, positively reacting to import surges.

Progress achieved by foreign investors in Beijing has been very impressive. According to the latest government statistics, import and export of foreign-invested enterprises (FIEs) in 2003 totaled USD 472.26 billion – an increase of 43% over the same period in 2002, 5.89% higher than the national growth rate of 37% for the same period, and accounting for 55.5% of total import and export of FIEs in the whole country.

For the past eight years, China has been the second-largest recipient of foreign direct investment (FDI) in the world after the United States. Beijing, as the capital leading the country's overall economic transformation, had attracted foreign direct investment worth USD 2.15 billion in 2003, an increase of 19.8% over the previous year.

Economic restructuring

After more than 40 years of construction, Beijing has changed from a consumer city to a major city with advanced industries. Beijing ranks second among the top 50 cities in China in terms of comprehensive development, and is the first among the 40 best cities in China in terms of investment environment.

Beijing, as China's political, cultural and international exchange center, is a dynamic city with a wide range of industries. During the years after China embraced reforms and opened up its economy, and especially in the last five years, the Chinese Communist Party Beijing Committee and Beijing Municipal Government have made a series of adjustments to the city's economic planning and structure to ensure healthy and sustained economic growth.

In recent years, the Beijing government has managed to overcome the effects of a slowed-down world economy and has made active adjustments to the new economic environment after China's entry to WTO.

Beijing has a fully integrated industrial structure. It has to date nearly 23,800 industrial enterprises, covering fields of electronics, machinery, chemicals, light industry, textile and car manufacturing. High-tech and modern manufacturing industries have become the leading forces of Beijing's industrial growth. Of great significance has been the establishment of a modern agricultural structure highlighting cash crops and fruit tree plantations, livestock breeding and eco-tourism. Beijing has come a long way from the traditional practices of the olden days.

Changing way of life

Beijing has designed and developed its service facilities to meet the standards of a modern cosmopolitan city. It features many shopping malls with comfortable shopping environments. People are now able to enjoy Chinese delicacies of any kind and cuisines from any part of the world in Beijing . Gross retail sales revenue for Beijing's consumer goods amounted to USD 23 billion in 2003, which was an increase of 14.5% over the previous year.

In developing new and high technology industries, priority has been given to five major industries, namely the electronics and information, bio-engineering and new medicine, optical, mechanical and electrical integration, new materials, and environment protection and multi-purpose utilization of resources. New and high technology bases have been

built for the development of software, microelectronics, electronics and telecommunications, computer and networking, and new materials.

Efforts are currently being made to develop a series of high technology products while new technology and capital are being injected into domestic and foreign corporations and multinationals, so as to provide strong technological support for the Olympic Games. In the meantime, new and high technologies will also be introduced to improve the traditional enterprises and upgrade their production levels.

Gearing up for the Olympic Games

The tertiary industry constitutes the mainstay of Beijing's economy and will play a direct and important role with regard to services for the Olympic Games. The development of information and consultant services, agent services, tourism, convention and exhibition industry, science and technology, education, culture and sports will be highlighted.

Other elements of the services sector, including financing, commodity circulation, real estate services, transportation, post and telecommunications, will also be enhanced so as to further improve the city's overall service capacity. It is estimated that up to 2008, the added value of the tertiary industry will make up 65% of the city's GDP.

One of the important steps in optimizing the industry structure is to relocate some factories out of the urban area. By 2008, all factories that cause pollution will either be moved out of the Fourth Ring Road or shut down, while the rest will be upgraded to become high technology enterprises fit for the urban environment. Within the Fourth Ring Road, only knowledge-intensive services and other service industries, including financing, commodity circulation, post and telecommunications, culture and sports, will be encouraged.

The further development of the Zhongguancun Park and Beijing Central Business District will be accelerated. Together with the Olympic Green, they will form three key functional districts in the city of Beijing. In the meantime, other major business and commercial centers, including the Financial Street and Wangfujing Street shopping area, will also be developed, in addition to such functional areas as trading ports and commodity transaction bases. All the above new developments will considerably raise the service capacity of the city and contribute to the success of the Olympic Games.

Economic outlook

As China opens up its service sectors to foreign investment after joining WTO, there has been an increasing influx of overseas investment into the capital city. In fact, Beijing is the leading Chinese city in attracting representative offices of overseas financial organizations. The investment fever will continue in view of the upcoming Olympic Games in 2008. With a planned investment of around USD 34 billion for infrastructure development, Beijing's hosting of 2008 Olympics would present immense business opportunities for domestic as well as foreign investors.

AGRICULTURE

Of Beijing's 16,800-km^2 land, approximately 65% is utilized for agricultural purposes. A breakdown shows that dry cultivated land and forest account for most of the municipality's agricultural land. To promote agriculture and improve the livelihood of farmers, Beijing decided to abolish agricultural tax in February 2004.

With the abolition, the city accomplished zero tax in the agriculture sector. It is estimated that the move would provide over RMB 80 million (USD 9.7 million) annually for the benefit of the local farmers. It is expected to boost agricultural production in the years to come.

The important decision is also expected to promote wider use of modern technology to raise productivity, particularly in view of decreasing land area available for agricultural production.

Agricultural industry of Beijing, 2003

Description	Unit	YoY (%)
Total value-added of production	USD 1.15 billion	+ 3.3
Cultivated land	195,600 ha	- 21.5
Food cultivation	2,120,000 ha	- 16.3
Animal husbandry	USD 1.64 billion	+ 9.6
Food production	580,000 ton	-29.5
Total production of modern agriculture	USD 14.83 billion	+133.6

Source: Beijing Statistics Bureau

In 2003, total agricultural value-added of Beijing rose to RMB 9.53 billion (USD 1.15 billion). Animal husbandry and fishery, though taking up a smaller proportion of land area, accounted for 7.7% of total output, followed by plantation of crops and non-staple produce, which contributed RMB 10.23 billion (USD 1.23 billion), an increase of 5.2%. Together with other industries like geological exploration, the primary sector accounted for 3.1% of the GDP of Beijing, down 2.6% over the previous year.

By the end of 2003, there were 3.42 million workers engaged in agricultural activities, constituting 25% of Beijing's total population.

Composition of Beijing's Agricultural Output in 2003

Item	Quantity (ton)	YoY (%)
Grain	580,000	- 29.5
Vegetables	5,273,000	- 3.4
Meat	737,000	+ 0.3
Egg	162,000	+ 106.6
Milk	637,000	+ 15.6
Freshwater fish	72,000	+ 97.3
Pig	4,701,000 (unit)	+ 99

Source: Beijing Statistics Bureau

Agricultural development

As the secondary and tertiary industries rapidly develop, the importance of agriculture is gradually on the decline in Beijing. Even in the rural areas where township and village enterprises traditionally prospered, contributions made by agriculture to the total economic income had decreased from 23.2% in 1990 to about a mere 2.6% these days, compared to a level at more than 20% in neighboring Hebei Province and the average level in China.

Since the 1990s, due to the sufficient and even over-supply of crops temporarily, the agricultural structure of Beijing had shifted its focus on plantation onto animal husbandry to cater to the growing urban demand for fish, meat, egg and milk. It is expected that animal husbandry will increase to a share of 60% in the next three to five years.

Agriculture in Beijing is currently in transition from traditional to highly efficient agriculture with metropolitan characteristics, concentrating on seed selection, deep processing, agricultural equipment, sightseeing and export etc.

Among the exports, fruits, oilseeds, flowers and processed agricultural products are newly added to the traditional export list of vegetables. Export destinations now extend from Southeast Asian countries to Europe and America. As Beijing is rich in natural scenic spots, sightseeing agriculture, a combination of farming and tourism, expands the source of income for suburban regions.

Market challenges

Rapid changes in the agricultural sector in Beijing in recent years have given rise to a new set of challenges – periods of macroeconomic instability stemming from partially complete reforms; increased insecurity in employment and incomes; mounting environmental pressures associated with population pressure, agricultural intensification and urbanization; rising costs; low income of the farming community and an occasionally hostile world trading environment.

China has demonstrated remarkable capability in meeting these challenges. Based on China's strengths, projected annual per capita income growth in China up to year 2020 stands between 4% and 8%, with a strong likelihood of 7% growth annually. A combination of rapid economic and income growth, coupled with population growth and urbanization, are likely to result in major increases in food consumption expenditures, in part as a result of shifts in the consumption of cereals, root crops and tubers to meats, poultry, chicken, marine products, fruits, vegetables, dairy products and oilseeds.

Investments in agriculture

It is clear that future development will depend on investments in agricultural research, fertilizer production and import policies, investment in irrigation and pricing and trade policies. As agricultural supplies have far exceeded population and income growth, consumer reliance on government-distributed grain has been reduced to a minimum in the last several years.

This suggests that the government could gradually liberalize the domestic grain market by 2020, while also liberalizing international trade in grain, in much the same way that it has liberalized industrial production and trade both domestically and internationally.

Fertilizer consumption

Fertilizer consumption in Beijing has quadrupled in the last two decades. But most farmers still use low quality fertilizers and there is much scope for improving the efficiency of fertilizer applications.

Policy reforms are being considered in the fertilizer sector involving, for instance, liberalizing trade in fertilizers – particularly in the types of fertilizers in which the country is not a producer –, rationalization of the domestic fertilizer industry to increase efficiency in production, and a more balanced application of fertilizers.

Environmental challenges

Environmental cleanup will pose a considerable challenge to investment in agriculture. Abundant use of coal to meet the burgeoning demands for energy and rapid growth of cities with associated growth of automobiles and increased municipal waste have been large sources of air pollution, causing high pollution levels in the Beijing region. Acid rain and pollution associated with industrialization and urbanization are other major sources of environment problems.

Integrating with the world market

China's integration with the rest of the world has been remarkably swift, and its trade patterns have been highly diversified. China wants to shift foreign investments towards its hinterland and towards infrastructure projects. Foreign investors are increasingly involved in power generation and the construction/development of railways, ports and highways as local governments begin selling shares to foreign investors. Agro-industries will benefit from these investments in the country.

China's accession to the World Trade Organization and the associated reduction in trade barriers will also benefit many of China's trading partners, particularly if it involves agricultural trade reforms where substantial adjustments in costs, reduced protection of state enterprises and more flexibility in the labor market are in store.

The future directions for agricultural development will stress on:

- Advanced technologies and high economic returns;
- Efficient utilization of water and land resources;
- Environment protection and ecological sustainability; and,
- Sightseeing and tourism.

To leverage on innovative technology and engineering, future development will focus on livestock embryo, new fertilizer, biological pesticide, domestic animal vaccine and agricultural equipment. High-tech agricultural parks will be the bases to host them.

Among others, these parks include Little Tangshan Modern Agricultural & Technological Exemplary Park in Changping, Jinxiu Dadi Agricultural Exemplary Park and Sang'ao Agricultural Exemplary Park in Shunyi.

In the face of globalization after China's entry into WTO, Beijing meets both opportunities and challenges. Foreign trade may encourage modernization and innovation in agriculture and promote exports of Beijing's agricultural products to the global market. However, fierce market competition and influx of cheaper produce will also harm the less competitive areas in Beijing.

Agriculture at the Forefront of Reforms

Agricultural reforms became the cornerstone of reforms in the entire economy and provided the basis for reform of the industrial structure. Increased rural household incomes drove demand up while increased rural savings and investments provided greater profitability for the rural industry.

The agricultural reforms involved increasing procurement prices for grains, allowing farmers to sell above quota production at market prices, lowering grain quotas, increasing grain exports, and expanding private inter-provincial trade.

But certainly the most important feature of the reforms has been the household responsibility system in which collective land was assigned to households for up to 15 years and local governments took the strong initiative of transferring production decisions and profits to households.

These changes were supported by new political philosophy and attitudes leading to reduced government controls, reduced production restrictions and lower taxes. The combination of reforms resulted in substantial expansion of the agricultural industry in Beijing and the industry is expected to continue to grow in the years to come.

Major agricultural sectors

Plantation

The total output of plantation increased by 5.2% to RMB 10.23 billion (USD 1.24 billion) in 2003. Within the plantation sector, in terms of area or turnover, the ratio of grains to economic crops drops constantly. In 2003, the ratio of total farming area of grains to economic crops stood at 43:57, down from 45:55 in 2002.

Wheat and rice have been replaced by economic crops with higher value added or cost effectiveness. The plantation area of vegetables, fruits, flowers and herbs had all increased by 18% and more. While the yields of rice, winter wheat and corn dropped remarkably in 2002, the yields of vegetables, cotton, oilseeds and herbs went up by 6.9%, 119.9%, 12.3% and 28.9% respectively.

Animal husbandry and fishery

Animal husbandry grew from only 25% in total agricultural output in 1995 to nearly 45% in 2003. Together with fishery, this sub-sector accounts for more than 52% in the city's agricultural sector. It has been the single largest sector in agriculture, surpassing plantation, and for the first time exceeded RMB 20 billion in output. In 2003, growth rates for animal husbandry and fishery reached 9.6% and 7.7%, respectively.

In particular, meat production went up by 0.3% in 2003, supplying the residents of Beijing a yearly average of 50 kg per capita. All suburban regions together produced 4.7 million pigs, 229,248 cows and 2.01 million

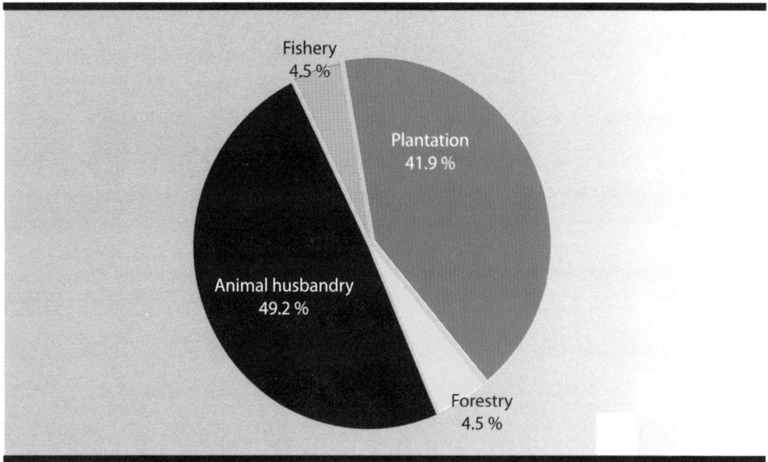

Source: Beijing Statistics Bureau

lambs, up 9%, 32.8% and 93.6% respectively.

By the end of 2003, there were more than 1,600 estates with 51,400 households engaged in the cultivation business, with the proportion of modern agricultural processing industry constituting 62.9% of total output. The total output value was USD 1.8 billion. Beijing now has 10 towns and 10 villages that are specialized in the raising of livestock and domestic birds.

AUTOMOBILE AND AUTOMOTIVE PARTS

Market overview

The automobile market in China in 2003 was extremely robust due to two major factors—increasing income of urban dwellers and falling prices of all types of vehicles. As liberalization of the market draws near under China's WTO commitments, foreign car manufacturers are rushing in to gain a bigger share of the fast growing market. Local manufacturers are bracing for competitive times ahead.

Beijing, being the fore-runner of automobile manufacturing in China, inevitably faces the brunt of the fierce foreign competition. With falling prices, the industry is suffering a profit squeeze and is poised for a shake-up in the near future.

To boost the competitiveness of local manufacturers, Chinese authorities are drafting a new policy on the future development of the country's automotive industry. The new policy is expected to give a much-needed impetus to the further restructuring of the industry.

Rapid expansion

In 2003, the country produced 4.43 million vehicles, an increase of 35.2% over the previous year. Of the total production, sedan cars constituted 2 million, an increase of 83.25%; goods vehicles constituted 1.23 million, an increase of 10%; and passenger vehicles reached 1.19 million, an increase of 11.9%.

According to statistics released by China Automotive Industry Association, the country had only slightly more than 9 million vehicles in 1994. The car population has swelled to 24 million in 2003, achieving an almost three-fold increase in a matter of 10 years.

> "The first quarter of 2004 saw an increase of 560,740 units produced and 542,600 units sold. Total market demand is expected to exceed that of Japan in 2005, making China the 2nd-largest automobile market in the world."

Under WTO agreements, import quotas for cars will be abolished by 2005 and import tariffs gradually reduced to 25% by 1 July 2006. However, imported cars will still be subject to 17% value-added tax and 3% to 5% consumption tax. This will make taxes for imported cars higher than

Tariff Reductions on Automotive Products

Items	Current Rates (%)	Reduced Rates (%)	Year Due
Luxury Vehicles	70 - 80	25	July 2006
Passenger Vehicles	45 - 60	20 - 25	1st January 2005
Commercial Vehicles	40 - 50	20 - 25	1st January 2005
Motorcycles	48 - 50	30 - 45	2004
Motorcycle Parts	30	-	-
Automobile Parts	25	10	1st July 2006

Source: Fudan University, School of Economics, China Center for Economic Studies

domestically-produced ones.

Nevertheless, in order to capture a bigger share of the market, foreign manufacturers have been drastically slashing prices for cars imported into the China market. Prices for many models have dropped to very low levels in the first quarter of 2004. Unbridled competition is putting great pressure on local manufacturers whose cost of production is higher and production technology is still lagging behind foreign car makers.

A recent market survey revealed that Beijing and Chengdu had the highest private car ownership rates among the five major cities in China. As neither of the cities place restrictions on the purchase of private cars, 25% of the people of the two cities have become car owners.

In Beijing, it is estimated that 18% of all families own two cars. The mini cars are becoming more popular with private buyers because the mini models have various advantages, particularly in terms of price, cost of maintenance and convenience in parking.

Diversified market

Car brands are more diversified in Beijing than in other cities. Santana, Jetta, Xiali and Audi, are the most favored car models in Beijing, making up half of all models in China's capital city. Santana, Accord and Fukang—the local brands from Shanghai, Guangzhou and Wuhan—dominate the private auto market in Beijing as well as other major cities.

As the demand for private cars is increasing rapidly in Beijing, the market potential is growing fast, with foreign and local car manufacturers competing fiercely for larger market shares. A recent survey indicates that with rising incomes, more than 40% of city residents nationwide are keen to buy cars, with the figures in Beijing topping the list. As for preferences, the majority of prospective buyers favored car models between 1.6 L to 2.0 L. A total of 42% of new owners chose car models in that range.

China to restructure auto industry

As WTO deadlines draw closer, Chinese authorities are worried about the profit squeeze that would affect many domestic manufacturers. It is hence drafting a new policy to expedite the development of the country's automotive industry. The new policy is expected to give an added impetus to the further restructuring of the industry.

In the past, huge profits had attracted a large number of manufacturers to set up in China. However, in terms of size, they are much smaller than their foreign counterparts. Chinese auto manufacturers bear enormous risks by churning out products of a low technological level. As competition grows in the Chinese market, some auto manufacturers are doomed to make huge losses.

A possible result of this will be rising numbers of non-performing loans in banks and unemployment of workers. Foreseeing that the profits of domestic car makers would plunge as imported products increase after 2005, the State Development and Reform Commission, which oversees China's overall economic restructuring, has quickened the formulation of a new policy to curb construction of redundant auto projects for the healthy development of the industry.

Under the new industrial policy, the government will discourage car production that involves the assembling of imported parts and components, in order to promote and develop the local auto industry. The new policy will also aim at raising the standards of new automobile factories, lifting levels of research, development and services of existing factories, examining the origin of new products, and encouraging technological progress, energy economy and sustainable development.

The government will also endorse the development of automobile-related industries, including metal melting, chemical, machine building, electronic and textile industries. The government will encourage relevant enterprises in these industries to increase their scale of operations and upgrade their technology so as to compete in the international market

Greater demand for auto parts

According to statistics provided by Beijing Customs, the city imported USD 157 million automotive parts in 2003, an increase of more than 400%.

North Korea, Japan, Germany and the US are four major automotive parts-exporting countries represented in Beijing, accounting for 59.2%, 26.5%, 6.05% and 6.5% respectively, of total import volume. Imports from North Korea, Japan and Germany increased substantially between January and July 2003. Import values of automotive parts from North Korea, Japan and Germany were USD 93.08 million, USD 41.68 million and USD 9.52 million respectively.

Beijing Jeep Corporation Ltd. and Beijing Hyundai Motor Company are two of the biggest importers of automotive parts. Between January and July 2003, Beijing Jeep Corporation Ltd. imported USD 44.01 million of automotive parts, accounting for 28% of Beijing's total import volume; while Beijing Hyundai Motor Company imported a total of USD 47 million, accounting for 30.5% of Beijing's total import volume.

Transmissions and automobile body parts are two major imported items. Transmission imports and auto body parts reached USD 21 million and USD 66.70 million, respectively in July 2003.

According to China Auto News, joint ventures and wholly foreign-owned automotive manufacturers dramatically increased their automotive parts imports in the first half of 2003. Import values of these two types of enterprises were USD 117 million and USD 23 million respectively, whopping increases of 600% for joint ventures and 240% for wholly foreign-owned automotive companies.

Value of Chinese Automotive Parts Industry

Source: China Knowledge Consulting

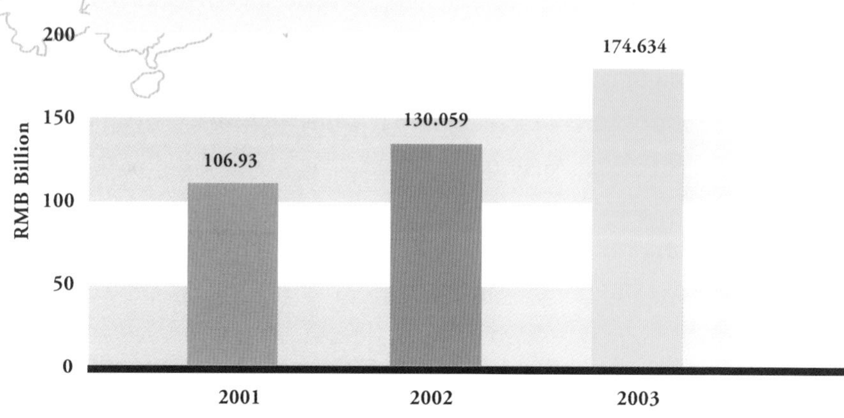

Chinese Automotive Parts Exported

Source: China Knowledge Consulting

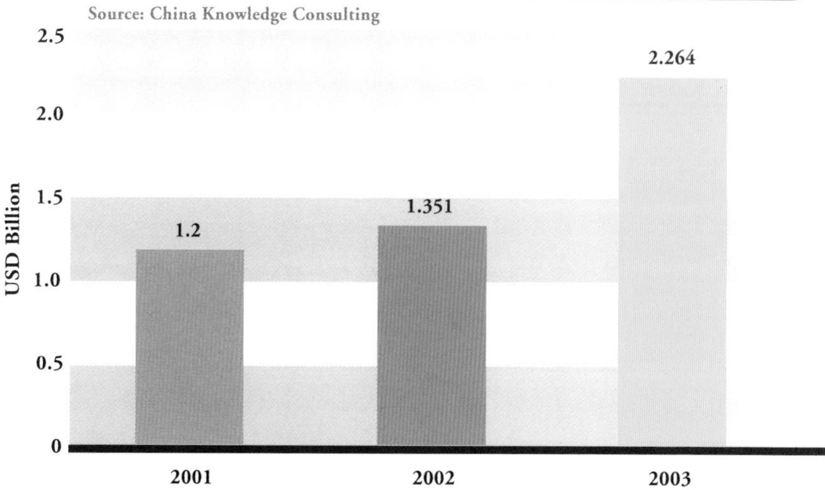

Future directions

In order to fulfill its goal to be a world leader in auto production, China is planning to develop an excellent auto parts industry. It hopes to make auto components less expensive while meeting international standards.

Once domestic auto parts companies reach a certain size and financial standing, China's policies encourage mergers and acquisitions in the industry. This would enlarge the size of local companies, making them more similar to MNCs like Delphi, Bosch, Visteon, and Denso.

Domestic companies are developing more sophisticated production techniques. For example, in an attempt to reduce their capital costs, Fulin and Fushi Machinery Groups plan to share engines and gearboxes in their new vehicles.

In line with new policies, Beijing auto makers are trying to shed their image as a low-tech assembler and to move into the production of high value-added auto components – ABS, GPS, and systems for electronic fuel injection, airbags, and central locking. They are also endeavoring to produce interchangeable auto components, so that for instance, parts manufactured for a Mercedes luxury car can also be used in a Citreon or Opel. This would facilitate mass production while reducing production costs. Non-polluting auto components are also in the works—solar and electric engines for example.

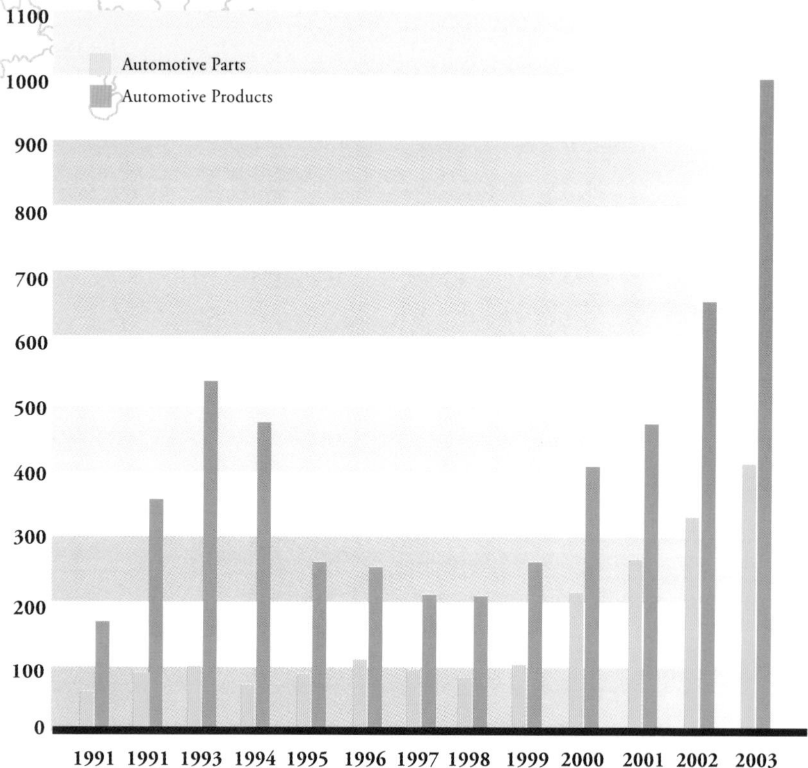

Meeting international standards

The industry is taking steps to ensure that domestic auto parts meet the rigorous standards of international accreditation bodies like the International Organization for Standardization (ISO). Currently only a handful of the larger companies have attained ISO 9000 or QS 9000 accreditation—Shanghai Automotive, Wanxiang Group, United

Automotive Electronic Systems, Shanghai Ek Chor General Machinery, and Fuyao Glass.

Some domestic auto parts companies are aiming at turning their products into well-known international brands along the lines of Delphi, Bosch, and others. Such a brand name helps to assure quality and reliability. China now has very few such brand names. Fuyao Glass may be the best-known brand in the auto parts industry, as it has substantial market shares in China, North America, Europe and Japan.

If Beijing's car makers succeed in making the necessary changes to its auto parts industry and can effectively harness new foreign technologies, they would be nearer to reaching the overall goal—developing a world-class auto components network. Only with an advanced auto parts industry would Beijing be able to compete with foreign manufacturers effectively and contribute substantially to making China a leading car producer in the world.

Foreign Investors in the Chinese Automotive Industry (2003)

Source: Fudan University, School of Economics, China Center for Economic Studies

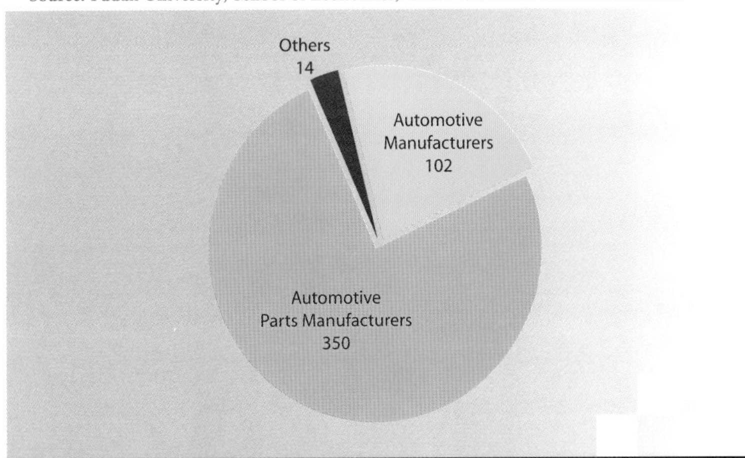

BANKING & FINANCE

Overview

The financial sector has become an important force behind Beijing's fast economic growth. In recent years particularly, Beijing's financial industry had developed consistently, and its proportion in the city's GDP had risen from 10.5% in 1996 to 14.2% in 2003. The value-added of banking and insurance services totaled RMB 51.38 billion (USD 6.2 billion) in the year, up by 8.5% over the previous year.

Beijing city has the largest number of foreign financial institutions in China. By the end of 2003, Beijing had seen 102 foreign financial institutions from over 30 countries and regions set up their Representative Offices within its city. In addition, there are 18 foreign banks from 11 countries and regions that have established operational branches in Beijing. The assets of foreign financial institutions rose almost 22-fold from RMB 3.9 billion (USD 47 million) in 1995 to over RMB 105.2 billion (USD 12.7 billion) in 2003.

Banks' Foreign/ Local Currency Deposits & Loans, China 2003
Unit: USD Billion

Deposit Item	Balance	Loan Item	Balance
A) Total Deposits	22,036.35	A) Total Loans	16,977.1
1. Corporate Deposits	7,679.48	1. Short-term loans	8,739.9
(1) Demand Deposits	5,358.59	2. mid-term Loans	6,725.2
(2) Fixed Deposits	2,319.9	3. Trust Loans	2,47.3
2. Savings Deposits	11,069.5	4. Bill Financing	923.4
(1) Demand Deposits	3,621.8	5. Other Loans	341.5
(2) Fixed Deposits	7,447.71	B) Securities & Investment	3,749
3. Nominees' Deposits	257.2	C) Gold/silver Assets	33.72
4. Other Deposits	3,031.1	D) Financial Borrowings	
B) Debts owed to foreign banks	48.26	E) Assets in Foreign Banks	87.34
C) Others	1,237.39		
Total Capital Resources	20,847.2	Total Operating Capital	20,847.22

Source: People's Bank of China

Banks RMB Deposits & Loans, China 2003

Unit: USD Billion

Deposit Item	Balance	Loan Item	Balance
A) Total Deposits	20,805.56	A) Total Loans	15,899.62
1. Corporate Deposits	7,248.71	1. Short-term Loans	8,366.12
2. Financial Deposits	512.7	(1) Industrial Loans	2,275.6
3. Institutional Deposits	672.77	(2) Commercial Loans	1,799.44
4. Rural Savings Deposits	10,361.77	(3) Construction Industry Loans	300.22
(1) Demand Deposits	3,511.9	(4) Agricultural Loans	841.14
(2) Fixed Savings	6,849.87	(5) Township Enterprise Loans	766.16
5. Agriculture Savings	489.84	(6) Joint-Venture Loans	256.94
6. Nominees' Deposits	245.81	(7) Private Enterprise/ Individual Loans	146.16
7. Other Deposits	1,273.99	(8) Other Short-term Loans	1,980.47
B) Financial Debts	222.63	2. Medium and Long-term Loans	6,340.14
C) Cash in Circulation	1,974.6	3. Trustees' Loans	228.13
D) Debts owed to Foreign Banks	48.26	4. Other Loans	965.24
E) Others	-519.72	B) Securities and Investment	3,025.95
		C) Gold/Silver Assets	33.72
		D) Foreign Exchange Assets	3,484.7
		E) Financial Borrowings	-
		F) Assets with foreign financial Institutions	8,7.34
Total Capital Resources	225,313.26	Total Operating Capital	225,313.26

Source: People's Bank of China

Banking

At the end of 2003, savings deposits in state banking institutions of Beijing rose by 15.9% to RMB 1,832.19 billion (USD 221 billion). The year-end value of loans rose by 23.6% to RMB 1,134.33 billion (USD 137 billion). This growth rate is much faster than the country's average. Meanwhile, personal consumption loans totaled RMB 164.63 billion (USD 19.9 billion), an increase of 12.3%.

In recent years, the financial sector in Beijing has started introducing and improving on a variety of services to cater to the ordinary residents of the city. RMB 50 billion (about USD 6 billion) in bank loans were spent in financing construction of housing projects. By 2003, the outstanding volume of housing loans for individuals topped RMB 80 billion (about USD 9.64 billion), greatly fostering the development of real estate in Beijing.

The loan structure of the city's financial system also improved immensely with loans to high-technology sectors reaching RMB 34.5 billion (USD 4.17 billion), up 64.1% from 2000.

Since 1997, the financial sector had written off more than RMB 10 billion (USD 1.2 billion) of loans owed by 3,853 bankrupted or merged enterprises and had helped 33 enterprises carry out debt-for-equity swaps, which alleviated the burden on state-owned enterprises and ensured Beijing is on-course in reforming state-owned enterprises.

Cash-in value of financial institutions in Beijing totaled RMB 3,132 billion (USD 378.7 billion) in

2002, and cash-out, RMB 1,742 billion (USD 210 billion), with the amount of currency withdrawn from circulation standing at RMB 11.82 billion (USD 1.43 billion).

Beijing Banking Service Annual Statement 2003 (USD Billion)

Item	Deposit / Loan Services	% Change
Total Cash Inflow	138.8	-
Total Cash Outflow	174	-
Total RMB Deposits	221.5	+19.9
Total Corporate Deposits	120.7	-23.4
Total Resident Deposits	31.36	+5.9
Total Corporate Loans	137	+23.6
Total Consumer Loans	19.9	+12.3

Source: Beijing Statistics Bureau

Insurance

Insurance premiums increased in 2003. At the end of the year, insurance premiums totaled RMB 28.25 billion (USD 3.41 billion), up by 22.5% over the previous year. Of this total, property insurance premiums were RMB 4.8 billion (USD 0.58 billion), up by 13.3%; and life insurance premiums, RMB 23 billion (USD2.78 billion), up by 22.5%.

Currently, some 51.1% of Beijing families have insured themselves against various personal risks, of which personal insurance accounts for 69.6%; endowment insurance, 53.4%; life insurance, 47.4%; insurance against major diseases and accidents, 38.3% and 29.3% respectively.

China's Insurance Market 2003

Total Premium	USD 409.68 billion
1 Property Insurance	USD 10.51 billion
2 Personal Insurance	USD 36.41 billion
1) Personal Accidence Insurance	USD 12.04 billion
2) Health Insurance	USD 2.83 billion
3) Life Insurance	USD 3.23 billion
Compensation payment	USD 10.17 billion
1) Property Insurance	USD 57.6 million
2) Personal Insurance	USD 4.41 billion
Personal Accidence Insurance	USD 44.1 million
Health Insurance	USD 84.52 million
Life Insurance	USD 31.92 million
Operating Cost	USD 43.67 million
Bank Deposits	USD 5.5 billion
Investment	USD 46.30 billion
Total Assets	USD 110.31 billion

Source: Beijing Statistics Bureau

Beijing Insurance Company Premium/Compensation 2003

Item	Value	% Change
Total Premiums	USD 3.41 billion	+20.7
– Property Insurance	USD 62.8 million	+13.3
– Life Insurance	USD 2.78 billion	+22.5
Total Compensation	USD 58.1 million	+2.3

Source: Beijing Statistics Bureau

Growth in Insurance Premiums in China (USD billion)

Source: CIRC, XLWI

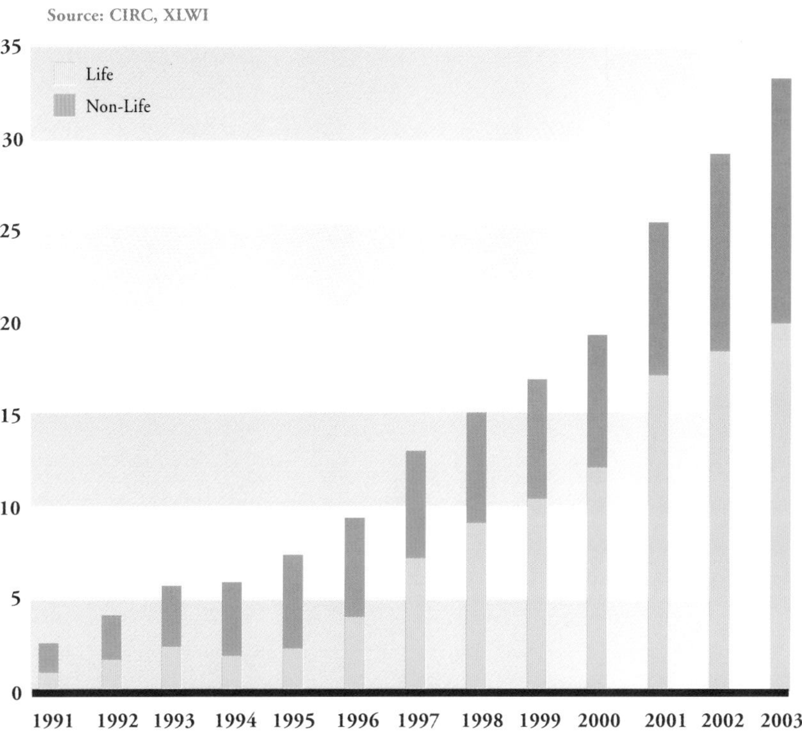

Beijing Insurance Market Share 2003

Source: CIRC. XLWI

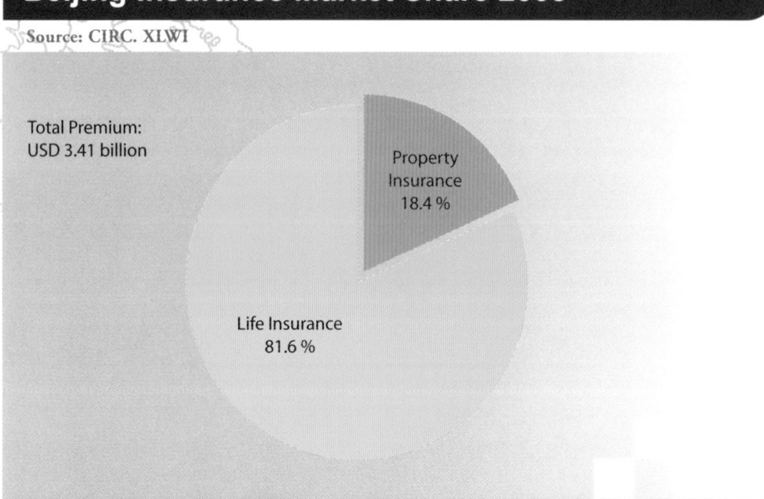

China's Top Insurers, 2002

Company	Base of Operations	Type of Insurance	Geographic Scope
China Life Insurance	Beijing	Life	National
China Property Insurance	Beijing	Property	National
China Reinsurance	Beijing	Reinsurance	National
China Pacific Insurance Co.	Shanghai	Comprehensive	National
Ping An Insurance Co.	Shenzhen	Comprehensive	National
Tian An Insurance Co.	Shanghai	Property	Shanghai
Dazhong Insurance Co.	Shanghai	Property	Shanghai
Hua An Insurance Co.	Shenzhen	Property	Shenzhen
Xin Hua Life Insurance Co.	Beijing	Life	National
Taikang Life Insurance Co.	Beijing	Life	Beijing, Guangzhou, Wuhan
Huatai Life Insurance Co.	Beijing	Property	Beijing, Nanjing, Shanghai
Yong An Property Insurance	Xi'an	Property	Xi'an

Source: China Insurance Regulatory Commission (CIRC)

Foreign Insurance Companies in China, 2002

Company	Country	Type of Insurance	Geographic Scope
Min An Insurance Co.	Hong Kong	Property	Shenzhen, Hainan
AIG	US	Life & Property	Shanghai, Guangzhou
Tokio Marine & Fire Insurance Co.	Japan	Property	Shanghai
Manulife Financial	Canada	Life	Shanghai
Winterthur Schweizerische	Switzerland	Property	Shanghai
Allianz AG	Germany	Life	Shanghai
Aetna Inc.	US	Life	Shanghai
Royal & Sun Alliance	UK	Property	Shanghai
Colonial Mutual Life Insurance	Australia	Life	Shanghai
AXA-UAP & Mining Corp.	France	Life	Shanghai

Source: CIRC

Stock market

The stock market also saw prosperous development in 2003. The transaction value of various securities on the stock market totaled RMB 2,336.98 billion (USD 282.9 billion), rising a sharp 86% over the previous year.

Of this total, transaction value of stocks was RMB 504.14 billion (USD 60.96 billion), up by 33.1% over the previous year. By the end of 2003, the number of listed enterprises in Beijing amounted to 64 (6 newly listed enterprises), compared to 11 in 1997. Capital raised from the domestic stock market totaled RMB 61.5 billion (USD 7.44 billion), almost three times that of 1997.

Beijing Financial Street

The biggest beneficiary of the influx of foreign business in Beijing is the Financial Street, Beijing's business hub, also known as China's Wall Street. Located in the western part of Beijing, the Financial Street has long been a decision-making center for the country's monetary policies. After nine years of construction, Beijing Financial Street has is today a rising financial center and hotspot for developing China's banking and financial services.

Within the circumference of 1 km^2, the Street is now home to the headquarters of over 300 state-owned banks, economic regulatory bodies and famous industrial firms.

They include the three major financial regulatory bodies of China, the People's Bank of China, China Securities Regulatory Commission and China Insurance Regulatory Commission; the three major commercial banks, the Industrial and Commercial Bank of China, Bank of China and China Construction Bank; the largest insurance company in China, the People's Insurance Securities Co.; important financial service institutions such as the national clearance center and reputable industrial companies such as China Telecom, China Mobile, and China Netcom.

In the coming four years, the Beijing government will continue to extend the Street to accommodate more financial institutions. An estimated 1,000 financial companies are expected to rent offices in the financial hub.

The Financial Street consists of seven districts, ranging from A to G, with B and F as its central districts. Investment for the central part of he Financial Street is expected to reach between RMB 12 and 15 trillion. Construction is expected for completion by the end of 2005.

WTO commitments in the banking and finance industry

Since formally becoming a WTO member in December 2001, China has issued a number of new regulations and detailed measures, translating its WTO commitments into specific rules governing foreign participation in its financial market. For foreign financial services companies eager to gain access to the China market, it is crucial to understand these regulatory changes.

Banking

Currently, the major business of foreign banks remains in foreign currency business dealings with foreign-funded enterprises and a limited number of Chinese enterprises. According to the WTO agreements, China will gradually, region by region, lift restrictions imposed on foreign banks in handling RMB business:

- Kunming, Beijing, and Xiamen by 11 December 2004;
- Shantou, Ningbo, Shenyang and Xi'an by 11 December 2005;
- All geographic restrictions will be removed by 11 December 2006.

In addition, China will also gradually abolish client restrictions on foreign banks in RMB business.

- In December 2003, China begun allowing foreign banks to handle RMB business for Chinese enterprises.
- By 11 December 2006, China will permit foreign banks to provide services for all Chinese clients. It will also allow them to set up business outlets in the same region. The requirements of examination and approval are the same with domestic banks.
- By December 11 2006, China will abolish all existing restrictions imposed on foreign banks in their ownership, forms of operation and establishment, including their branches, representative offices and the issuance of licenses.

Insurance

The main commitments of the Chinese government in opening up the insurance business are as follows.

In terms of business form:

- Immediately upon China's entry to the WTO, foreign non-life insurance companies are allowed to set up branches or joint ventures in China. These firms will be allowed to hold as much as 51% of the stake in the joint ventures.
- Foreign life insurance companies are allowed to set up joint ventures in China, and hold no more than 50% stake in the joint

ventures. They will also be allowed to choose their partners independently.

- Immediately upon China's WTO accession, the foreign stake in Sino-foreign joint venture insurance brokerage companies may reach 50%; the proportion may not exceed 51% within three years of the accession.
- Two years after joining the WTO, foreign non-life insurance firms will be allowed to set up wholly owned sub-firms in China, i.e. there will be no restriction regarding the form of enterprise establishment.
- Five years after WTO entry, foreign insurance brokerage companies will be permitted to set up wholly owned subsidiary firms. With gradual cancellation of geographical limitations, foreign insurance companies will, after approval, be permitted to set up branches. The qualification conditions for initial establishment do not apply to the establishment of internal branches.

In terms of geographical restrictions:

- Immediately upon WTO entry, foreign life and non-life insurance firms are allowed to offer services in Shanghai, Guangzhou, Dalian, Shenzhen and Foshan.
- Two years after entry, foreign insurance companies' business can be extended to Beijing, Chengdu, Chongqing, Fuzhou, Suzhou, Xiamen, Ningbo, Shenyang, Wuhan and Tianjin.
- All geographical restrictions will be lifted three years after entry.

In terms of business scope:

- Immediately upon WTO entry, foreign non-life insurance companies from abroad are permitted to engage in general insurance and large-scale commercial insurance without any geographical limitation.

  They may also offer non-life services to overseas enterprises, property insurance to foreign-funded enterprises in China, and related liability insurance and credit insurance services.

- Immediately upon entry, foreign life insurance companies are permitted to provide individual (non-group) life insurance services to foreign citizens and Chinese citizens.
- Immediately upon WTO entry, foreign reinsurance companies are permitted to provide life and non-life reinsurance services in the form of branch company, joint-venture company or wholly owned subsidiary firm. There are no geographical restrictions or quantity limits in license granting.
- Two years after WTO entry, non-life insurance companies from abroad will be able to offer all kinds of non-life insurance services to Chinese and foreign customers.
- They will also be permitted to provide health insurance, group insurance, pension insurance and annual pay insurance services to Chinese and foreign citizens.

In terms of business license issuance:

- Immediately upon WTO entry, China is committed to abolishing restrictions on the number of licenses issued to foreign insurance companies.

  Foreign insurance companies must satisfy the following conditions before applying for licenses in China: a business history of more than 30 years in a WTO member, operating a representative office in China for two consecutive years, and holding no less than USD 5 billion in total assets by the end of the year prior to the application.
- In terms of legal insurance scope, China is committed to leaving unchanged the regulation of 20% proportion provided by Sino-foreign direct insurance companies to Chinese reinsurance companies immediately upon WTO entry. This will be lowered to 15% one year after WTO entry, 10% two years after, 5% three years after, and cancelled four years after the entry.

  However, foreign capital insurance companies will not be permitted to engage in third party liability insurance of motor vehicles, liability insurance for public transport vehicles, commercial vehicle drivers and carriers, and other legal insurance services.
- In terms of general insurance policy, national treatment will be

granted. However, the geographical scope for opening to foreign capital insurance brokerage companies will follow that of foreign insurance companies.

This means they will be allowed to do business in Shanghai, Guangzhou, Dalian, Shenzhen and Foshan immediately upon WTO entry, in 10 more cities two years later, and in all cities three years after WTO entry.

- In terms of insurance brokerage qualification, aside from the conditions of a 30-year operating history and having run a representative office in China for two consecutive years, there are also conditions in the aspect of asset scale, that is, in excess of USD 500 million at the time of entry, in excess of USD 400 million one year after entry, in excess of RMB 300 million two years after entry, and in excess of RMB 200 million four years after entry.

Besides, the Chinese government has, in accordance with the General Agreement on Service Trade, made commitments with regard to trans-territory delivery, for example, in international marine shipping, aviation and freight transport insurance and reinsurance, and large-scale commercial insurance and reinsurance brokerage services.

Securities

At the end of 2001, the China Securities Regulatory Commission (CSRC) announced specific contents of the policy to open up the securities market after China's WTO entry:

- Within three years after accession, foreign securities institutions will be permitted to establish joint ventures, with foreign minority ownership not less than 25% but not exceeding 33%.
- Securities JVs may engage in underwriting A shares; underwriting and trading of B and H shares; and underwriting and trading of government and corporate debts.
- More competent domestic enterprises are encouraged to list overseas. While still encouraging them to list in the Hong Kong market, global securities markets are to be tapped in other

overseas markets such as New York, London, Tokyo, Singapore and Australia.

- Qualified foreign-funded enterprises are to be gradually permitted to issue stocks and get listed in China when conditions are mature.

Fund management

Upon accession to WTO, foreign investors are allowed to either invest in an existing fund management company or jointly establish a new enterprise. Initially, their investment ratio can be more than 25% while less than 33%; in three years that percentage of ownership may grow to 49%.

Other financial services

Upon WTO entry, foreign non-bank financial institutions are allowed to set up wholly foreign-owned or joint venture automobile financing service companies. Within five years of WTO entry, China foreign-funded banks can provide automobile credit services to individual Chinese residents. Foreign-funded financial leasing companies, like Chinese firms, are allowed to provide financial leasing services.

Entry requirements for financial services providers

Foreign financial institutions should meet asset and experience requirements before applying for establishing wholly owned foreign enterprises or joint ventures. They also have to meet minimum registered capitalization and define their business scope before starting their operations.

Banking services

The State Council approved the Regulations of the People's Republic of China on Administration of Foreign-Invested Financial Institutions on 12 December 2001. They were promulgated on 20 December 2001 and came into effect on 1 February 2002.

The Regulations cover wholly owned foreign banks, branches of foreign banks, JV banks, wholly owned foreign financial companies and JV financial companies in China.

The minimum registered capital (in a freely convertible currency) for wholly owned foreign banks and JV banks is equivalent to RMB 300 million (USD 36.23 million). For wholly owned foreign financial companies and JV financial companies (in a freely convertible currency), it is equivalent to RMB 200 million (USD 24.15 million).

In both cases, the actual paid-up capital shall be 50% of the minimum registered capital. In addition, parent companies should allocate at least (in freely convertible currency) the equivalent of RMB 100 million (USD 12.07 million) to their branches in China as operating funds.

The total assets of a party applying to establish a wholly owned foreign bank or wholly-owned foreign finance company must not be less than USD 10 billion at the end of the year preceding the application.

The total assets of a party that applies to establish a foreign bank branch must be at least USD 20 billion at the end of the year preceding the application.

The total assets of a foreign joint venture partner applying to establish a joint venture bank or joint venture finance company must be USD 10 billion at the end of the year preceding the application.

The Regulations provide that a foreign-invested financial institution must meet the following requirements in order to carry out Chinese currency business:

- It must have conducted business in China for at least three years before the application.
- It must have made a profit in the two successive years preceding the application.

- It must meet other prudent requirements stipulated by the People's Bank of China.

Wholly foreign-owned banks, branches of foreign banks and JV banks may:

- Issue short-term, medium-term and long-term loans;
- Bill acceptance and discount;
- Purchase and sell government and financial bonds and securities in foreign currency other than shares;
- Engage in credit and guarantee services;
- Handle domestic and foreign account settlements;
- Purchase and sell foreign exchange;
- Engage in foreign currency conversion;
- Execute inter-bank call loans;
- Engage in bankcard services;
- Handle safe keeping services;
- Offer credit investigation and consulting services; or
- Other operations approved by People's Bank of China (PBC).

Insurance services

The conditions for establishing a foreign funded insurance company in China are as follows:

- A track record of operating insurance business for more than 30 years;
- A representative office in China for more than two years; and,
- Total assets of no less than USD 5 billion in the year immediately prior to the submission of the application.

For insurance brokers, the asset requirement is USD 500 million. Within two years of China's accession to the WTO, it will be reduced to USD 300 million, and further reduced to USD 200 million three years later.

The minimum registered capital for a joint venture insurance company or a wholly owned insurance company should not be less than RMB 200 million or equivalent in foreign exchange. The registered capital should be paid up.

A branch is not deemed as a separate legal entity in China. Therefore, the concept of limited liability does not apply. The parent company is required to allocate a minimum of RMB 200 million or equivalent in foreign exchange as the branch's operating capital.

A foreign-funded insurance company, in accordance with its business scope verified by China Insurance Regulatory Commission (CIRC), is permitted to carry out either of the following categories of business, but not both.

- Property insurance, including property loss insurance, liability insurance, credit insurance and other insurance; and,
- Personal insurance including life insurance, health insurance, accident insurance and so on.

Securities

According to legislation on Sino-Foreign joint venture securities companies ("Securities JV Rule"), the conditions on a securities JV are as follows:

- It must have registered capital of not less than RMB 500 million;
- The Chinese and foreign parties as well as the proportion and methods of their capital contributions must comply with the provisions of the "Securities JV Rule";
- It must have no less than 50 practitioners with professional qualifications for securities business, as well as the necessary accounting, legal and IT professionals;
- It must have a sound international management and risk control system and a standardized system for the separate management of personnel, finance and information for underwriting, brokerage and proprietary trading businesses, and have an appropriate technical system for internal control;
- It must have the required business premises and proper trading facilities; and,

- Other conditions specified by China Securities Regulatory Commission (CSRC).

Conditions to be satisfied by a foreign party before setting up a Securities JV:

- It must be located in a country with sound securities laws and regulatory systems, and the relevant securities regulatory authority must have concluded a memorandum of understanding on securities regulatory cooperation with the CSRC;
- It must possess the legal qualification to conduct securities business in its home country, operated financial business for more than 10 years, and received no material punishment from the securities regulatory authority or judicial bodies in the last three years;
- Every risk monitoring ration in the past three years must be in compliance with the provisions of laws and the requirements of the securities regulatory authority of its home country;
- It must have a sound internal control system; and,
- It must have a satisfactory reputation and performance in the international securities market.

CONSTRUCTION

In the past decade, Beijing has seen continuous changes in its urban landscape. Infrastructure construction has been one important engine for Beijing's economic development. In the ninth 5-Year Plan period (1996-2000), investment in the city's infrastructure development amounted to USD 16.7 billion. It is expected to grow to USD 21.5 billion in the 10th 5-Year period (2001-2005).

In 2003, the GDP of the construction sector reached RMB 130.67 billion (USD 15.8 billion), accounting for 7.8% of the city's GDP. Meanwhile, the total value-added of the sector amounted to RMB 28.12 billion (USD 3.4 billion), an impressive increase of 11.6% over 2002. Labor productivity was USD 16,200 per capita, up 14.5%, while profits of the industry as a whole was RMB 3.06 billion (USD 0.37 billion), an increase of 23.9%.

Total investment in fixed assets reached RMB 215.71 billion (USD 26 billion), increasing 18.9% over 2002. RMB 41.78 billion (USD 5.05 billion) of this amount was invested in urban infrastructure development, an increase of 1.4%. Investments in the real estate sector amounted to RMB 69.24 billion (USD 8.37 billion), a moderate rise of 9.1% over 2002. This was due to a slowdown in residential housing development, which constituted 32.1% of total real estate investment, a drop of 2.9% over 2002.

The total construction area of commercial property in 2003 was 90.70 million m^2, increasing 20.8% over 2002. Construction on 25.9 million m^2 has been completed, increasing completed land area by 8.8%. Today, commercial property development remains a hotspot in Beijing, making up 52.6% of total real estate investment, an increase in investment of 7.9%.

Opportunities & challenges

Beijing has taken steps to further open its construction sector. From year 2000, contractors for all large-scale construction projects in the municipality will be selected through international tendering. The areas covered include surveying, planning, design, work inspection, and purchase of key materials and equipment.

From 2002, foreign and domestic construction firms had been receiving equal treatment towards bidding for large construction projects. The move towards liberalization is set to attract more foreign investment to Beijing's construction sector. A host of opportunities is in store for foreign businesses to invest in the planning, design and work inspection of construction projects as well as real estate development in Beijing.

Beijing 2008 Olympics

Having won the bid to host the 2008 Summer Olympic Games, Beijing has launched various massive programs for construction and investment in preparation for the Games. A huge project, this is one of the most ambitious and impressive infrastructure undertakings Beijing has committed itself to. It involves the extensive construction, refurbishment and maintenance of Olympic-related sports venues and facilities, major enhancements to transportation and telecommunications networks, and installation of environmental protection systems. Around 75% of the factories, large-scale agricultural commodity and trade markets, house decoration and commodity wholesale markets will be moved out of Beijing and reconstructed.

According to the budget plan, USD 2.06 billion will be invested for the construction of the Olympic village, stadia and venues; USD 3.6 billion for urban infrastructure; and USD 8.6 billion for improving the environment. This presents tremendous opportunities for international construction firms. Construction and renovation of all new Olympic venues will be open for international bidding, including designing, construction, and operation and management of sports venues and surrounding facilities.

Numerous construction projects have been planned. These include a total of 37 stadia and venues to stage the Olympic events. Of these, 10 are existing venues requiring few modifications and five require some renovation. The remaining 22 will be newly-built facilities.

In addition, Beijing also plans to develop the city's transport, education and utilities infrastructure. These projects include construction of over 100 km of new rail lines, construction or renovation of over 900 km of roads, building a second natural gas pipeline from Shaanxi to Beijing, excellent information systems, improving water quality and increasing electricity supply.

Existing Facilities Requiring No Construction Work

Venue	Owner/ Manager
Urban Highway Circuit	Beijing Municipal Government
Beijing Shooting Range	State Administration for Sports
Shenyang Wulihe Stadium (Liaoning)	Shenyang Municipal Government
Olympic Sports Center Gym	State Administration for Sports
Beihang Gymnasium	Beijing University of Aeronautics and Astronautics
Workers' Stadium	Beijing Municipal Federation of Trade Unions
Workers' Indoor Arena	Beijing Municipal Federation of Trade Unions
Shanghai Stadium (Shanghai)	Shanghai Municipal Government
Forbidden City Triathlon Circuits	Beijing Municipal Government
Capital Indoor Stadium	State Administration for Sports

Source: www.bda.gov.cn

Existing Venues Requiring Modification, Construction, Renovation

Venue	Owner/ Manager	Total Estimated Cost (USD million)
Olympic Sports Center Stadium	State Administration for Sports	28.57
Olympic Sports Center Softball Field	State Administration for Sports	36.32
Ying Tung Natatorium	State Administration for Sports	28.41
Laoshan Mountain Circuits	State Administration for Sports	7.49
Beijing Country Equestrian Park	Shunyi County Government	150.74

Source: www.bda.gov.cn

New Venues to be Built

Venue	Owner/ Manager	Total Estimated Cost (USD million)
New China International Exhibition Center, Hall A*	Beijing Municipal Government	13.24
New China International Exhibition Center, Hall B*	Beijing Municipal Government	10.61
New China International Exhibition Center, Hall C*	Beijing Municipal Government	12.25
New China International Exhibition Center, Hall D*	Beijing Municipal Government	13.52
National Stadium	Beijing Municipal Government	247.51
National Swimming Center	Beijing Municipal Government	46.21
Olympic Green Archery Field	Beijing Municipal Government	108.76
National Tennis Center	State Administration for Sports	45.71
National Hockey Stadium	State Administration for Sports	70.17
Beijing Shooting Range	State Administration for Sports	37.91
Aoshan Velodrome	State Administration for Sports	43.13
Wukesong Indoor Stadium	Haidian District Government	283.05
Wukesong Baseball Field	Haidian District Government	36.24
Fengtai Baseball Field	Fengtai District Government	28.88
Shunyi Olympic Aquatic Park	Shunyi District Government	79.50

Shoutiyuan Indoor Stadium	Beijing Municipal Education Committee	34.72
Beitidao International Marina	State Administration for Sports	14.66
Tian'anmen Beach Volleyball Pits	Beijing Municipal Government	10.14
Qingdao International Marina (Shandong)	Qingdao City Government	89.09
Tianjin Stadium (Tianjin)	Tianjin Municipal Government	83.61
Qinhuangdao Stadium (Hebei)	Qinhuangdao City Government	36.54

Source: www.bda.gov.cn *renovation and modifications

WTO agreements on construction

Contract construction

According to the WTO agreements, within three years of WTO accession, wholly owned foreign enterprises are allowed in China, but they are restricted to the following projects:

- Projects solely funded by foreign investment or foreign donation;
- Projects financed by international financial institutions' loan through international tendering;
- Projects jointly undertaken by Chinese and foreign enterprises with foreign investment over 50%; or,
- Joint venture projects or special domestic projects that are technically difficult for a domestic enterprise to undertake by itself, and are approved by the relevant government bodies as joint venture projects between domestic and foreign contractors.

At present, a joint venture contractor, which has the status of a Chinese legal person, is theoretically capable of undertaking all construction projects in China.

Within three years of WTO accession, Sino-foreign joint ventures can enjoy national treatment; and within five years of WTO accession, wholly owned foreign enterprises are allowed without project restrictions.

Survey and consulting

- Equity joint ventures or cooperative joint ventures are allowed to operate in China.
- Architects, engineers or enterprises who wish to undertake survey or consulting businesses in China are required to have received the requisite licenses in their home country to operate as such.
- Within five years of WTO accession, wholly owned foreign enterprises will be allowed to operate in China.

Real estate

- Wholly owned foreign enterprises are allowed to undertake real estate development but are disallowed from participation in high-grade projects (high-grade hotels, condominiums, golf courses etc.)
- Sino-foreign joint ventures are allowed in real estate agency services (real estate valuation, management etc.)
- Within five years of WTO accession, wholly owned foreign enterprises will be allowed.

City planning

- Sino-foreign joint ventures are allowed in area planning, but disallowed from overall city planning.
- Foreign individuals or enterprises who undertake businesses in this area must be planners or enterprises who have received the requisite licenses in their home country.

Entry requirements for foreign construction companies

Foreign-invested construction enterprises will be established according to the *Law on Sino-foreign Equity Joint Ventures of PRC*, the *Law on Sino-Foreign Cooperative Enterprises of PRC*, the *Regulation on the Control of the Qualifications of Construction Enterprises* and other related laws, decrees and regulations.

Apart from meeting the above legal requirements, the establishment of a foreign-funded construction enterprise must meet the following conditions:

- The Chinese partner to a foreign-funded construction enterprise shall be a construction enterprise with at least the second-grade qualification certificate; the foreign partner shall be a construction enterprise with the status of a legal person that has a high level of technology and management and a good reputation;
- The applicant foreign-funded construction enterprise can import or adopt advanced international technology and equipment for construction, as well as train Chinese personnel in engineering and management.
- The registered capital must meet the following requirements:

(1) The registered capital must not be less than USD 10 million for first-grade construction engineering enterprises; USD 5 million for second-grade construction engineering enterprises and USD 1.6 million for third-grade construction engineering enterprises.

(2) The registered capital shall not be less than USD 2 million for first-grade construction, decoration and fitting enterprises; USD 1.5 million for second-grade decoration and fitting enterprises, and USD 600,000 for third-grade decoration and fittings enterprises.

Relevant rules & regulations

According to the *Regulations of Beijing Municipality on the Administration of Construction Market*, the Beijing Municipal Construction Commission (BMCC) is the general administrative authority responsible for the municipality's construction market. The district/county construction administrative departments are responsible for the administration of the construction market in the area under their jurisdiction.

Individuals or organizations have to register at the Industrial and Commercial Administrative Department and obtain certificates of professional qualifications issued by the relevant ministry or the BMCC before they undertake the following work:

- To undertake survey, design and construction for building projects;
- To undertake sub-contracting, supervision and cost consultation for construction projects.

Individuals or organizations from Hong Kong and Macau Special Administrative Regions, Taiwan and others, who wish to engage in construction activities, are required to, upon approval by both the Beijing Foreign Economic Relations and Trade Commission and the BMCC, obtain the business contracting permit, and register at the Industry and Commerce Administration, before they are allowed to engage in construction activities in Beijing.

Project proposals and feasibility studies for establishing foreign-funded construction enterprises will be examined and approved by the relevant administrative departments in charge of construction.

Examination and approval are carried out at different levels. Applications for establishing first-grade foreign-funded construction enterprises will be examined and determined by the Ministry of Construction and approved by the Ministry of Foreign Trade and Economic Cooperation (MOFTEC); applications for establishing foreign-funded construction enterprises of second-grade and lower will be examined and determined by the provincial administrative department in charge and approved by the provincial foreign trade and economic cooperation departments.

If the Chinese partners are enterprises directly affiliated to State Council departments, the applications are examined by the Ministry of Construction and approved by the Ministry of Foreign Trade and Economic Cooperation.

A foreign-funded enterprise is to be established according to the following procedures:

(1) The Chinese partner shall submit to the relevant administrative department the project proposal, feasibility study report and related documents of the proposed foreign-funded construction enterprises for examination. If all requirements are met, a 'Recommendation for the Examination of Foreign-Funded Construction Enterprises' will be issued.

(2) The Chinese partner shall, on the strength of the 'Recommendation for the Examination of Foreign-Funded Construction Enterprises', submit the contract, articles of association and related documents for establishing foreign-funded construction enterprise for examination and approval by the department in charge under the Ministry of Foreign Trade and Economic Cooperation. If all the requirements are met, a 'Certificate of Approval for the Establishment of Foreign-Founded Enterprises' will be issued.

(3) The Chinese partner shall go through the legal person registration procedures with the administrative department for industry and commerce upon the strength of the "Recommendation for the Examination of Foreign-Funded Construction Enterprises", the "Certificate of Approval for the Establishment of Foreign-Funded Enterprises" and other related documents.

(4) After obtaining the license of a corporate person, the foreign-funded construction enterprise will go through the qualification examination and approval procedures with the administrative department in charge of construction.

In applying to establish as a foreign-funded construction enterprise, the Chinese partner is required to submit the following documents to the administrative department in charge of construction:

(1) Report of application for the establishment of foreign-funded construction enterprises;

(2) Qualification certificates of the Chinese partner;

(3) Documents of examination by relevant departments;

(4) Project proposals for establishing foreign-funded construction enterprises;

(5) Feasibility study reports jointly compiled by all partners to a joint venture;

(6) Certificates of all partners for registration with administrations for industry and commerce;

(7) Credit rating certificates of all partners; and,

(8) Other documents.

In applying for the establishment of foreign-funded construction enterprises, the following documents are to be submitted to the department in charge under the Ministry of Foreign Trade and Economic Cooperation according to the procedures prescribed in Article 5 of these Provisions:

(1) The Recommendation for the Examination of Foreign-Funded Construction Enterprises;

(2) Contracts and articles of association of the foreign-funded construction enterprises to be established;

(3) Project proposals and feasibility study reports;

(4) Registration certificates of all partners issued by administrations for industry and commerce;

(5) Credit rating certificates of all partners;

(6) Certificates for the approval of names issued by administrations for industry and commerce; and,

(7) The list of the board of directors and the appointments of directors of all parties involved in the joint venture.

EDUCATION

Overview

China's education system consists of four components: basic school education, vocational education, general higher education and adult education. Types of schools in China include preschool, primary school, secondary general school, secondary vocational school, university and college, as well as graduate school education.

Children above three years old enter kindergarten for a term of three years. China's law stipulates that education at primary and junior secondary stages is compulsory – the so called "nine-year compulsory basic education". In most areas of China, children at the ages of six or seven attend primary schools for a term of six years. Following this, they enter secondary general school, where they attend a term of three years at junior secondary schools and another term of three years at senior secondary schools.

Secondary vocational schools are divided into two types. The first type accepts junior secondary school graduates, usually for a three-year

schooling term. The second type recruits senior secondary school graduates, normally with a two-year schooling term.

The schooling term of full-time university undergraduates is four or five academic years (seven or eight years at some medical universities). The schooling term for polytechnic students is two or three years.

Graduate education is divided into the Masters and PhD programs, each with a term of two or three academic years.

Statistics on Beijing's Education, 2003

Item	2003 Unit	2002 Unit	% change
Number of schools			
Postgraduate Schools	164	170	-3.5
General Higher Schools	73	62	+17.7
General Secondary Schools	977	998	-2.1
Primary Schools	1,652	1,824	-10.4
Special Education Schools	25	23	+8.7
Kindergartens	1,430	1,540	-7.0
Teachers			
General Higher Schools	38,296	34,783	+11
General Secondary Schools	64,648	66,059	-2.0
Primary Schools	49,843	52,840	-5.7
Special Education Schools	667	681	-2.1
Kindergartens	13,056	12,127	+7.7
Student population			
Postgraduate Schools	120,386	97,734	+23.2
General Higher Schools	457,353	390,995	+17.0
General Secondary Schools	968,255	984,117	-1.6
Primary Schools	546,530	594,241	-8.0
Special Education Schools	6,177	5,405	+11.43
Kindergartens	199,390	213,794	-6.7
Student enrolment			
Postgraduate Schools	47,580	38,904	+22.3
General Higher Schools	142,391	124,642	+14.2
Number of graduates			
Postgraduate Schools	22,496	17,303	+30
General Higher Schools	83,551	65,937	+26.7

Source: Beijing Statistics Bureau

Opening up of education sector

As all schools were supported by the government or state-owned enterprises, education was not formerly an industry in China. However, public schools are far from sufficient in meeting the demands for education at different levels and for different types of education.

With a population of 1.3 billion, the country has just about 1,000 public universities. As a result, only 6% of its youths are admitted to universities. In addition, there is increasing demand from enterprises and government bodies for staff education and training services.

The private education sector began to emerge after China launched its reforms in 1978, and this sector has experienced a rapid expansion in recent years. Statistics indicate that by 2002, 45,000 private schools had been approved by Chinese education authorities, ranging from kindergartens to non-degree-awarding higher education institutions. There are currently more private non-degree-awarding higher education institutions than ever before – 1,300 institutions with 1.5 million registered students, or about 40% of total college and university students nationwide.

At present, private higher education institutions and senior high schools are relatively concentrated in economically developed areas, including Beijing, Shanghai, Guangdong and Zhejiang.

Foreign investment in the education market

Restricted by China's foreign education policy, China's education market did not open to foreign capital until very recently as a result of the country's membership to WTO. For foreign education institutions and investors, cooperating with Chinese partners is an effective way to break into the market.

In accordance with the "Industry Catalogue of Directing Foreign Investment" released in April 2002, the higher education sector falls into the "encouraged" category for foreign investment, although it was restricted only to joint ventures. The secondary education sector was another "restricted" area, permitting foreign investment only in joint ventures. The primary education sector was altogether prohibited from foreign investment.

It was reported that, within three to five years after its WTO entry, China will try to promote the development of education by issuing government bonds and asking for loans from international financial organizations, foreign governments and individual investors.

Business opportunities

China's private education market is one of the fastest growing markets in the world. Beijing, as the country's culture and education center, has seen a rapid expansion of its education sector.

According to statistics, Beijing's per capita expenditure on education reached RMB 1,803 in 2003, much higher than the country's average. A research report indicated that Beijing residents spend some RMB 2 billion (USD 241 million) every year on improving their English.

Major Players in Private Education Sector

Beijing New Oriental School

Based in Beijing and formerly established as a test-oriented English training center, New Oriental School is China's largest private English education institution. With 200,000 students enrolled every year in its programs in Beijing, Shanghai and Guangzhou, New Oriental constitutes 80% of the English training market in Beijing and 50% of the country's total.

Informatics Group

Informatics set up its first school in Shanghai in 1993. Currently, it has a network of 25 schools throughout the country, including Beijing, Wuhan, Chongqing, Chengdu, Xi'an, Xiamen, Guangzhou, Tianjin, Nanjing, Suzhou, Kunming, Shenzhen, Ningbo, Hangzhou and Changzhou. They offer both IT and business education programs.

Education expenditure was ranked second only to food in the consumption list.

Statistics from the Beijing Statistics Bureau also show that Beijing residents spent an average 16.8% of their household savings on their children's education. Schools jointly run by Chinese and international education organizations have been growing at an unprecedented rate.

The increasing demand for private education was spurred, on the one hand, by increasing household incomes of the Beijing people, and on the other hand, by the continuously growing fees of public education institutes.

In addition, with China's entry into the WTO, the Chinese government and enterprises face an urgent need for highly skilled professionals and talented personnel in many fields, resulting in a huge demand for an updated educational system and the introduction of advanced training methods.

Beijing residents spend some RMB 2 billion (USD 241 million) every year on improving their English. Education expenditure was ranked second only to food in the consumption list.

Education and training plan for civil servants

The following are outlined in Beijing's education and training plan for civil servants:

- Each civil servant should have at least 56 training hours every year;
- ***Orientation Training*** From 2001 onwards, 98% of newly recruited civil servants are required to go through orientation training with a term of no less than 80 training hours;
- ***Training before promotion*** Comprises at least 240 training hours; and 95% of civil servants should be receiving such training before promotion by 2005;

- ***Knowledge Updates Training*** This involves encouraging civil servants to read higher academic degrees, e.g. MBA. It also promotes e-government expertise. Specialized knowledge training for all civil servants under the age of 50 will also be conducted;
- ***English training for Olympics 2008*** All civil servants should be able to communicate in English by 2004; and 1,000 civil servants will be selected to participate in at least three months' extensive training program for international exchange;
- 400 civil servants will go abroad for international exchange programs every year; and international experts will be invited to conduct training programs for civil servants.

Training education market

Training expenses spent by Chinese enterprises exceeded RMB 40 billion (USD 4.84 billion) in 2003. Some experts estimate that the training expenses of Chinese enterprises will exceed USD 5 billion in 2005. The training market in China is huge and has unlimited prospects.

In view of the training content and customer demand, China's training market could be divided into foreign language training, exam training, IT training, HR training, soft skills training, senior management training and EMBA education.

Average per capita expenditure of Beijing residents on education, 2003

Type	2003	2002	% Increase
General education	RMB 971	RMB 870	10.3
Adult education	RMB 114.4	RMB 90.8	20.6

Source: Beijing Statistics Bureau

REAL ESTATE

Market overview

The real estate market generally maintained a steady growth trend. In the whole of 2003, the value-added of the industry reached RMB 18.59 billion (USD 2.25 billion), a hefty increase of 86% over the previous year, constituting 8.4% of total value-added of the third industry, and contributing 5.1% to the city's overall GDP.

Total investment in real estate development for the year reached RMB 12.03 billion (USD 1.45 billion), an expansion of 21.5% over 2002. Total value of investment in real estate made up 55.7% of the city's total investment in 2003, an increase of 1.2% over the previous year.

As for commercial property, total construction area was 90.7 million m^2, with 25.9 million m^2 completed, and total sales of real estate reaching 18.95 million m^2, an increase of 20.8%, 8.8% and 11% respectively. The sales value of commercial property hit RMB 89.8 billion (USD 10.9 billion), up 10.4%.

Residential property remained a hotspot in the real estate market. Total value of investment committed was RMB 63.3 billion (USD 7.65 billion), an increase of 7.9%, constituting 52.6% of total investment in the property market. The total area of construction for residential property was 63.5 million m^2, up 17.7%, and completed area was 20.8 million m^2 in total, up 8%.

Beijing's districts and counties

Located in northeast China 180 km from the ocean, Beijing is the second largest city and the capital of the People's Republic of China. Beijing municipality's total area is 16,808 km^2 and includes 18 districts and counties.

Beijing Municipality's Districts and Counties

City Proper:
Dongcheng District, Xicheng District, Chongwen District, Xuanwu District
City Area:
Chaoyang District, Fengtai District, Shijingshan District, Haidian District
Inner Suburbs:
Mentougou District, Fangshan District, Tongzhou District, Shunyi District, Changping District, Daxing District, Pinggu District, Huairou District
Outer Suburbs:
Miyun County, Yanqing County

Source: Beijing Statistics Bureau

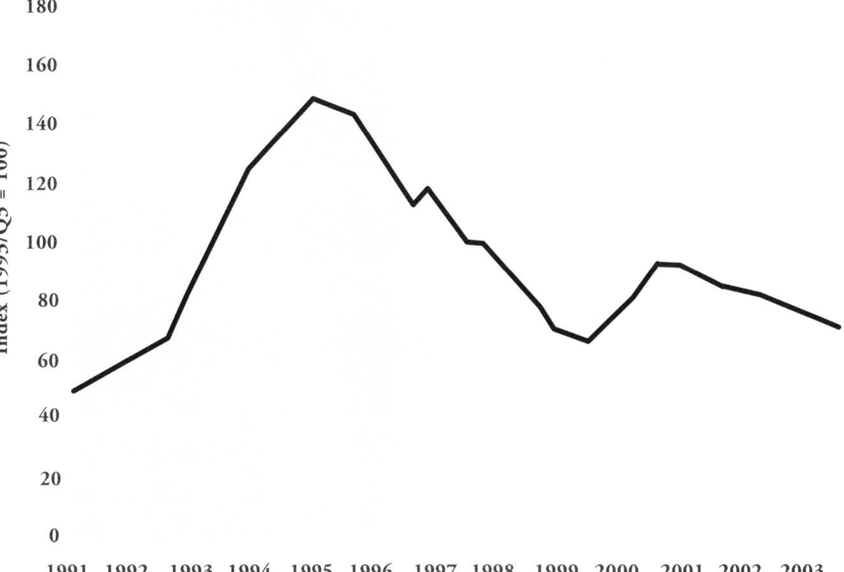

Average Housing Prices by District

	Total Stock (sqm)	Vacancy (%)	Base Rent (USD/sqm/mo)	Occupancy Cost (USD/sqft/yr)	%change (from Jan 03)	6 month Forecast
Chaoyang	1,180,640	13.5	25.40	34.50	- 8.3	▼
Dongcheng	378,350	19.4	28.40	37.90	- 6.2	▼
Xicheng	321,020	10.9	26.50	35.80	-12.9	▼
Haidian	277,700	18.2	21.60	30.30	-13.8	▼
Chongwen	42,000	10.0	17.60	25.90	N/A	▼
Overall	2,199,710	14.8	25.35	34.50	-8.0	▼

Source: DTZ Research

Note: Total stock and vacancy statistics reflect the overall Grade A office market. Rent exclusive of management fees and other outgoings. Occupancy cost is rent plus all outgoing. All units are based on net floor area.

Beijing Area & Population

Municipal Area Features	City Proper	City Area	Inner Suburbs	Outer Suburbs
Permanent Population (10,000 people)	237.6	439.2	309.5	134.5
Area (km^2)	87.1	1,282.8	7,490	7,947.9
Population Density	27,279	3,423	413	169

Source: Beijing Statistics Bureau

Major planned and zoned areas

Government departments at the central, city, and district levels are responsible for zoning regulations. On the national level, it is the National Land and Building Administration. This bureau sets national regulations on city planning issues.

As Beijing is the capital, the central government's role in zoning is greater than in other cities. A major zoning initiative undertaken in recent years was the development of special zones. This was a cooperative effort of the city planning authorities of the municipal, district and central governments.

Central Business District

Located in Chaoyang District, the new CBD covers 3.9 km^2. At the time of its establishment in 1999, more than 60% of the land area was occupied by factories and warehouses. Government policy required all factories inside the 4th Ring Road to relocate by 2012. Future development potential was the key criteria in demarcating the boundaries of the new CBD.

The new CBD is zoned for office, residential, retail, and hotel space. Developers planning large-scale projects get preferential treatment for purchase and transfer. The majority of projects are multi-use integrated projects with a combination of property types. Many of these planned projects have significant construction areas – 300,000 to 1 million m^2. Most projects, with an expanded area of 5 million m^2 of office and residential space, are scheduled for completion in phases, by 2007.

Central Industrial District

Approved by the State Council in May 1988, the municipal government had designated the 100-km^2 Zhongguancun as a high-tech research and development area. The west zone covers 51.44 ha, of which 1 million m^2 is slated for office buildings and will be completed by 2012.

Central Finance District

The new Central Finance District covers 3 ha with proposed construction of 2 million m^2. The "Financial Street" has the headquarters of four of China's largest state-owned banks, two largest insurance companies, and major securities and state-owned companies.

Olympics Village Area

A 1,215-ha Olympic Green has been zoned for the 2008 Olympic Games. In addition to sports facilities, an Olympic Village consisting of hotel, residential, retail and office zones was also approved. Directly north of the Olympic Village, a 760-ha Olympic Park and surrounding green belts have been planned.

Planned Residential Communities

In order to alleviate urban housing pressures, the Comprehensive City Plan in 1992 delineated 10 communities between the city proper and the counties. These 10 communities are separated from the city by a green belt currently under construction. In addition, 14 satellite towns are planned in the outer suburbs.

Planned Satellite Towns

Name	Current Population (10,000 persons)	Planned Population (10,000 persons)	Zoning Features
Tongzhou	15.5	30.8	-
Shunyi	8.8	22.5	Tourism
Miyun	6.5	19	-
Pinggu	3.6	10	Tourism
Huairou	7	17	Tourism
Yanqing	4.6	10.5	Tourism
Changping	11.4	21.6	Higher Education
Shahe	2.2	7.5	Higher Education
Mencheng	14	18.8	Tourism
Liangxiang	12.5	19.6	Higher Education
Changxindian	11.6	23.1	-
Huangcun	13.3	27	-
Fengshan	16	18	-
Yizhuang	3	15	High-tech manufacturing area

Source: Beijing City Planning Bureau

Planned Residential Communities

Name	Current Population (10,000 persons)	Planned Population (10,000 persons)
Qinghe	8.96	40
Beiyuan	6	28
Wangjing	16.75	39
Dongba	1.78	22
Dingfuzhuang	10.93	30
Fatou	5.57	18
Nanyuan	4.4	22.8
Fengtai	12.35	40
Shijingshan	30.68	33
Nanyuan	6.9	10

Source: Beijing City Planning Bureau

Demand and supply

In year 2000, total area of new housing completed in Beijing was 184.5 million m², including 30 million m² in the city, 119.8 million m² in the inner suburbs, and 34.4 million m² in the outer suburbs. In 2001 alone, 17.074 million m² was completed. A total of 11.275 million m² of commercial property was sold for RMB 53.17 billion (USD 6.43 billion). This yields an average sales price of RMB 4,716 (USD 570.25) per m².

However, the market had experienced a slowdown since 2002. Demand only began to pick up in the first quarter of 2004. The commencement of Olympics-related works has been a push factor as potential buyers expect demand to become stronger in the coming years.

In view of uneven market supply in different parts of the city, prices for areas with shortage of supply are expected to increase at a faster rate, while in areas within and around the CBD, increases are likely to be marginal. Prices in these areas had experienced a downward trend in the past few quarters.

Market outlook

First-time buyers making their purchases are likely to be major drivers of growth. The majority of these are educated individuals with stable income. Urban resettlement should also contribute to further market growth in 2004 and beyond.

Strong demand is foreseen for local housing along with increased requirements for high quality and high value segments. A secondary housing market is expected to emerge after housing prices drop to levels below the prices of first-time purchases. Additional changes in legal and property ownership regulations are expected in the near future. These changes will boost the secondary market.

Construction of new residential units will continue in Beijing in the next few years as part of overall urban resettlement plans and various projects will be accelerated in preparation for the 2008 Olympics.

All in, Beijing will continue to experience a surge in demand, particularly in the Zhongguancun and Financial Street regions. Suburbanization will become a major trend in Beijing as development will be largely focused on the Beijing government's planned communities.

Land area completed and sold

Source: Beijing City Planning Bureau

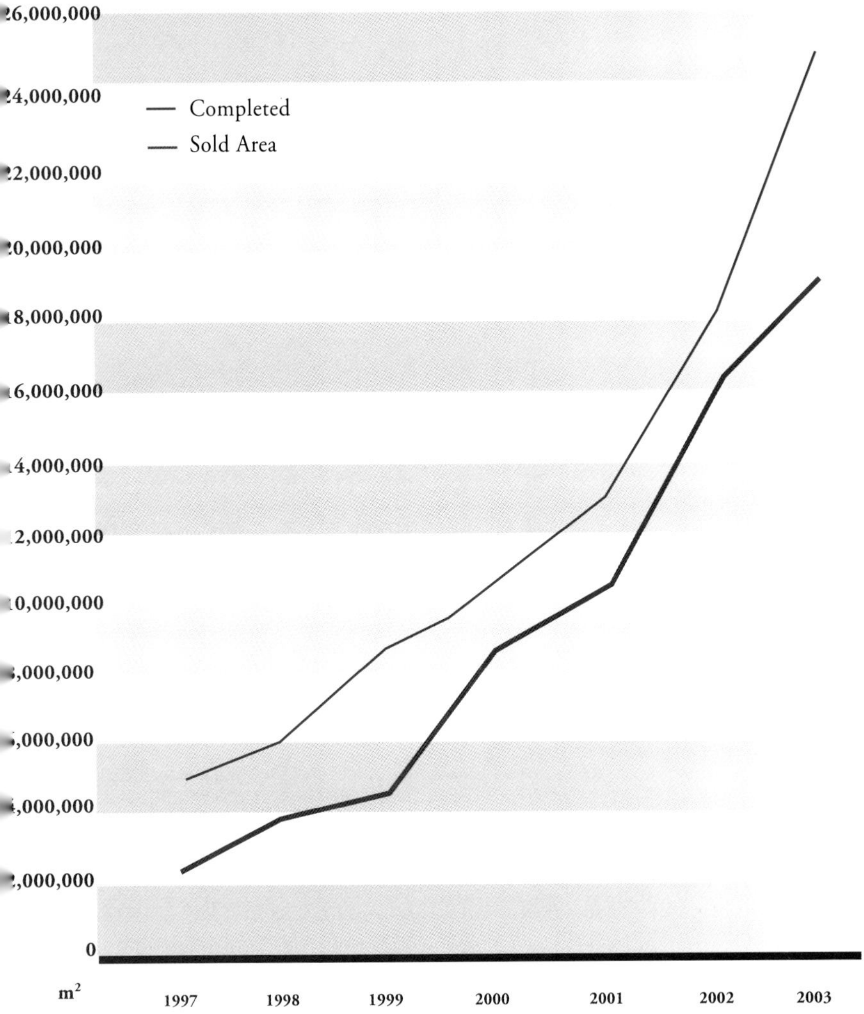

TOURISM

Beijing is a top tourist city in China in terms of tourism resources and tourist facilities. As an ancient capital and the nation's political and cultural center, Beijing has innumerable cultural relics and tourist attractions.

The most popular historical scenic spots include the Forbidden City – one of the most marvelous ancient architectural sites in the world; the Great Wall – a symbol of China and one of the Eight Wonders in the world; the Ming Tombs – the densest royal tombs; the Summer Palace – the old royal gardens; and the Temple of Heaven - the place to worship and pray for bountiful harvests in the olden days.

The Great Wall, the relics of Zhoukoudian, the Forbidden City, the Temple of Heaven and the Summer Palace have been listed by the United Nations Education, Science and Culture Organization (UNESCO) as World Cultural Heritages. The grand Tian'anmen Square, the gorgeous royal gardens, the solemn temples and luxurious princes' residences bespeak the magnificence of oriental civilization.

Beijing also boasts rich reserves of beautiful natural landscape. It owns a national scenic spot, two national natural protective areas, three national forest parks and a number of newly developed scenic spots. Apart from that, Beijing's events calendar also features various cultural events such as Beijing Opera, Hutong tours and local folk customs.

Beijing enjoys the most developed tourist service system in China. Star-level hotels are all around the city. Tourist service standards are improving and tourist reception capacity has been expanding. Facilities are being enhanced with transport and communication lines linking up all parts of the city, bringing great convenience to domestic and international tourists.

The Beijing Capital International Airport, with 69 international air routes opened, is connected to 56 large cities of 36 countries and regions. It is the largest international airport in the country. It has two runways, two airport bays, and handles up to 35 million passengers each year.

Beijing Tourism 2003

In 2003, Beijing's tourism market was severely affected by the outbreak of the Severe Acute Respiratory Syndrome (Sars), especially in the first half of the year. In spite of speedy recovery in the second half of the year, the industry's performance had declined substantially when compared to previous years.

The number of foreign tourists dropped to 1.85 million, down 40.4%; and foreign exchange earnings from tourism was USD 1.9 billion, a sharp decline of 38.9% from 2002. As for domestic tourists, the number was 87.37 million, down 24%. Income from domestic tourism was RMB 70.6 billion (USD 8.54 billion), 23.9% lower than the year before.

At the end of the year, the total number of hotels was 659, of which 614 are star-level hotels. The total number of rooms reached 10,900 units, an increase of 6,000 units. The occupancy rate, however, was 51.7%, down 10.3% from end of 2002.

Prior to Sars, the tourism industry had also been affected by the 9/11 terrorist attacks in the US. The growth rate of tourist volume from main source countries had dropped considerably. As a result, tourism in 2002 had also suffered a severe setback.

According to China National Tourism Administration, there are 490 tourism agencies in Beijing at present. These include some of the largest ones in China, such as China Travel Service (CTS), China International Travel Service (CITS), China Youth Travel Service (CYTS), Beijing Capital Travel Co. Ltd (BCT), China Comfort Travel Service, China Xinhua Travel Service, CITIC Travel Service, COSCO Travel Service and others.

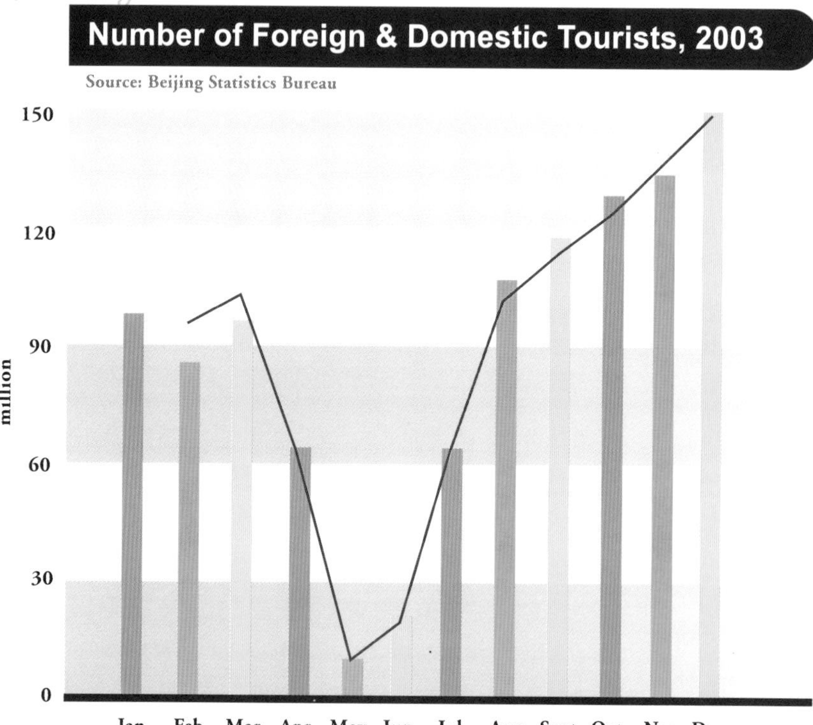

Established in 1949, CTS is the first travel agency since the establishment of P. R. China. It now has over 200 branches across China and 14 overseas branches. Presently, it is a formal member of many international tourism organizations such as PATA, USTOA, IATA, ASTA and the Travel Service Association of China. Languages used by tour guides cover Chinese,

English, Japanese, German, French, Thai, Malay, Italian, Spanish, Korean, Spanish and Russian etc.

The CITS Group was established in 1989 with 160-plus members. The CYTS Alliance was established in April 2002, with CYTS Holdings as the core member. Beijing Capital Travel Co. Ltd was established in February 1999 and was listed on the Shanghai Stock Exchange in 2000.

Development of Beijing's tourism industry

With rich tourism resources and facilities, Beijing has remained the leading tourist city in China. Foreign exchange reaped by the city made up one-fifth of the country's total. The contribution of the tourism sector to the city's GDP was over 19% in 2003, the highest among the cities in China.

Foreign investment

Tourism has been one of the fastest growing sectors in China. Beijing's tourism industry enjoys unique advantages in the aspects of resources, infrastructure, human resources and information. With an improved investment environment, favorable investment policies and numerous tourism development programs, Beijing exerts a strong appeal on investors from home and abroad.

There are many opportunities for foreign travel service operators, especially in the process of Beijing's preparations for the 2008 Olympics. Foreign companies have been invited to assist with tourism resources planning and management, marketing, hotel management and renovation, and the training of senior managers. They may also participate in financing and jointly-operating related projects and be involved in market information and agency services.

Overseas Tourists and Tourism Revenue in Beijing, 1992-2003

Source: Beijing Statistics Bureau

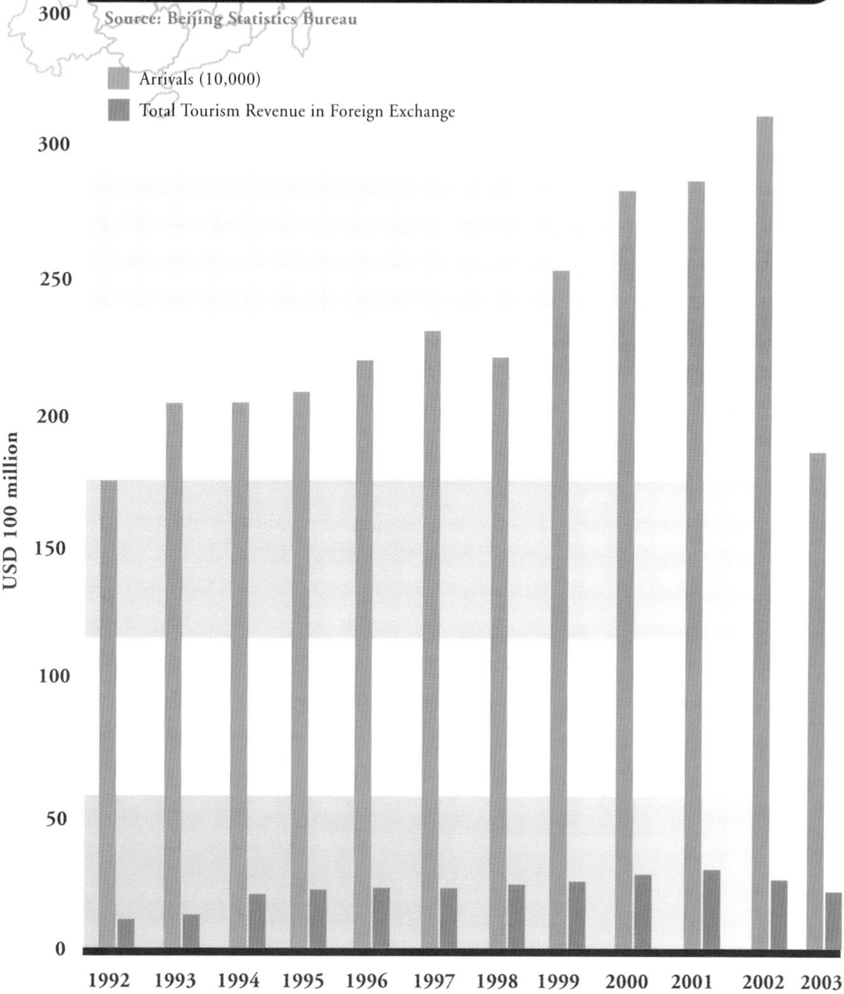

300

Arrivals (10,000)

Total Tourism Revenue in Foreign Exchange

300

250

200

USD 100 million

150

100

50

0

1992 1993 1994 1995 1996 1997 1998 1999 2000 2001 2002 2003

Main Overseas Tourists to Beijing, 2003 (1,000)

Country/Region	No. Of Tourists
Taiwan	97.5
Hong Kong	21.7
Japan	29.2
Korea	24.5
United States	19.4
United Kingdom	8.1
Germany	6.3
France	5.5
Russia	5.15
Malaysia	4.4
Singapore	4.3
Canada	3.78
Australia	3.45
Mongolia	2.57
Thailand	2.3
Sweden	2.26
Switzerland	1.95
Italy	1.9
Netherlands	1.57
Indonesia	1.55
Spain	1.11
India	1.06
Macau	1.0
Philippines	0.55
New Zealand	0.46

Source: Beijing Statistics Bureau

WTO agreements related to tourism industry

China joined the World Trade Organization (WTO) on 11 December 2001. China's commitments pertaining to the tourism industry focused on two categories – hotel (including serviced apartment) and restaurant sectors; and travel agencies. There were no commitments pertaining to tourist guides and other services.

Hotels/Restaurants

Market Access

- Foreign investors are permitted to establish, refurbish and operate hotels and restaurants in the form of joint ventures. Currently, only majority ownership is allowed. Within four years of WTO accession, there will be no restriction on the ownership proportion. Wholly owned foreign enterprises will be allowed.
- Foreign parties are permitted to hold the majority of shares.
- Limitations on the form of company and share ratio were lifted on 31 December 2003.

Restrictions on Human Resources

- Managers, professionals, and senior management of the foreign party can only begin services after signing a contract with the joint-venture hotel or restaurant.

Travel Agencies

Market Access

- Foreign travel agencies with business revenue of more than USD 50 million are permitted to set up joint travel agencies at national scenic resorts approved by the State Council and in four cities, namely, Beijing, Shanghai, Guangzhou and Xi' an.
- The foreign party is allowed to form joint ventures from 1 January, 2003.
- Wholly foreign-owned travel agencies will be allowed to set up by 31 December, 2005.
- For investors from the USA, the registered capital of joint travel agencies should be no less than RMB 5 million (USD 604,000);
- For investors from the European Union, the registered capital of joint travel agencies should be no less than RMB 4 million (USD 483,000) when China joins the WTO, and will be lowered to RMB 2.5 million (USD 302,000) three years after China's WTO accession. They can enjoy national treatment with regards to the registered capital six years after.

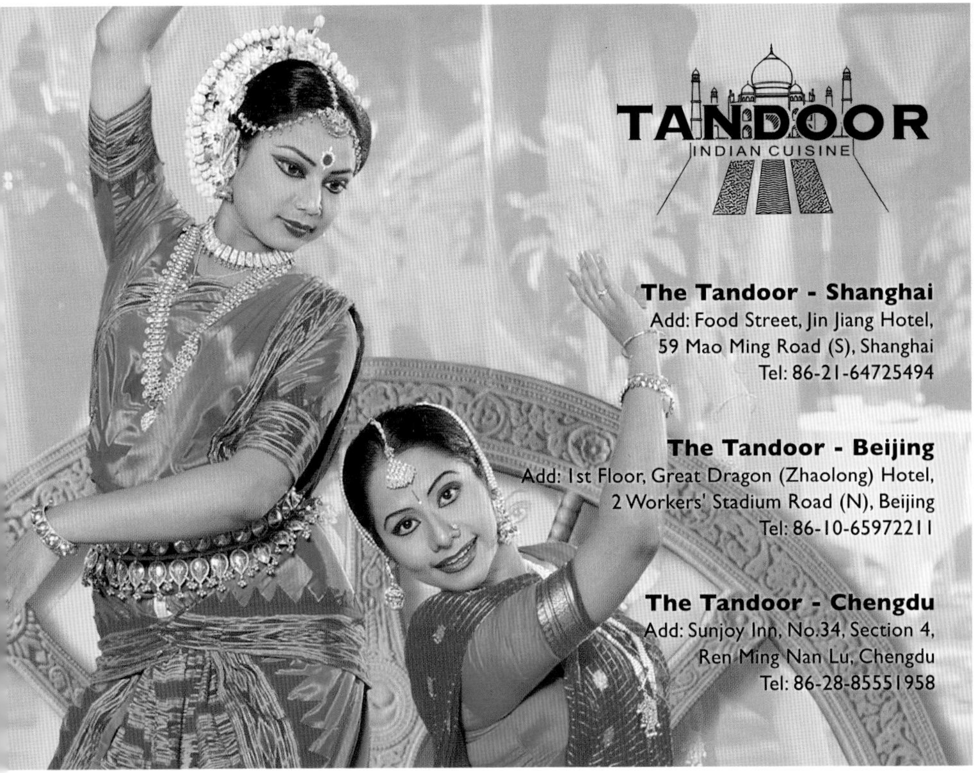

TANDOOR
INDIAN CUISINE
The Tandoor - Shanghai
Add: Food Street, Jin Jiang Hotel,
59 Mao Ming Road (S), Shanghai
Tel: 86-21-64725494
The Tandoor - Beijing
Add: 1st Floor, Great Dragon (Zhaolong) Hotel,
2 Workers' Stadium Road (N), Beijing
Tel: 86-10-65972211
The Tandoor - Chengdu
Add: Sunjoy Inn, No.34, Section 4,
Ren Ming Nan Lu, Chengdu
Tel: 86-28-85551958

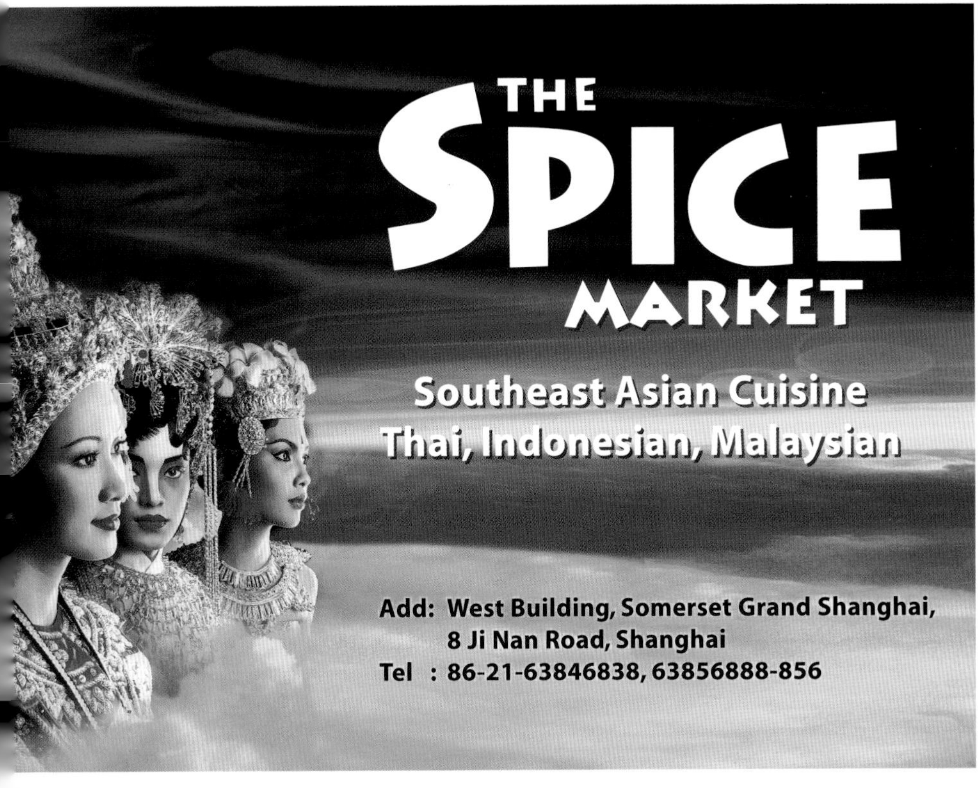

THE SPICE MARKET
Southeast Asian Cuisine
Thai, Indonesian, Malaysian
Add: West Building, Somerset Grand Shanghai,
8 Ji Nan Road, Shanghai
Tel : 86-21-63846838, 63856888-856

No. of star-level hotel guest rooms in Beijing, 1992-2003

Source: Beijing Statistics Bureau

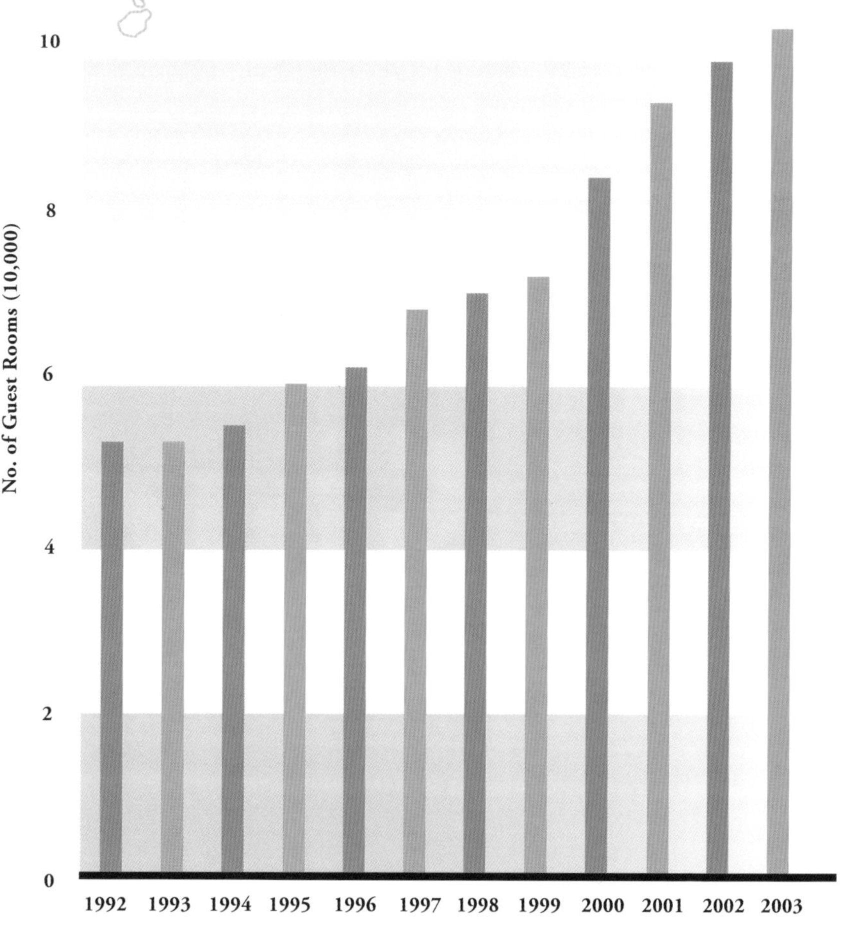

Business Scope

- Foreign-invested travel agencies are permitted to directly engage transportation and hotel operators in China to provide travel and hotel accommodation services to foreign travelers as well as Chinese domestic travelers.
- They are also permitted to conduct tours for both foreign and domestic travelers and provide traveler's check-cashing services within China.
- Restrictions for foreign-invested travel agencies to set up branches and outlets within China will be lifted no later than 31 December 2005.

Limitations on Joint and Wholly Foreign-owned Travel Agencies

Joint and wholly foreign-owned travel agencies are not permitted to engage in outbound travels by Chinese citizens, including travels to HK, Macau and Taiwan.

Tourist Info Centers

Place	Address	Tel.	Email
Haidian District	South lobby, Modern Plaza, 40 Zhongguancun Dajie	8262 2895 6257 6688 ext 6127/ 6118	haidian@bjta.gov.cn
Dongcheng District	10 Dengshikou Xijie	6512 3043	dongcheng@bjta.gov.cn
Xicheng District	1/f, Xidan Science and Technology Plaza, 131 Xidanbei Dajie	6616 0108 6612 0110	xicheng@bjta.gov.cn
Xuanwu District	3 Hufang Lu	6351 0018	xuanwu@bjta.gov.cn
Shijingshan District	22 Shijingshan Lu	6868 6201 6868 6202	shijingshan@bjta.gov.cn
Fangshan District	Haotian Holiday Hotel, 1 Gongchenbei Dajie, Liangxiang	8936 0123	fangshan@bjta.gov.cn
Mentougou District	35 Xinqiao Dajie	6985 3974 6983 6677	mentougou@bjta.gov.cn
Changping District	Activity Center for Retired Workers, Changping	8974 0051 8974 0061	changping@bjta.gov.cn
Chaoyang District	27 Gongtibei Lu	6417 6627 6417 6656	chaoyang@bjta.gov.cn
Yanqing County	2A Weihe Nanlu, Yanqing	8119 1011 8119 7633	yanqing@bjta.gov.cn

INFORMATION TECHNOLOGY & COMMUNICATIONS

Overview

In the past decade, China's total telecommunications turnover had increased by 35 times. To date, the fixed and mobile communication networks of China are the largest in the world. After China's entry into the WTO, Beijing, as well as other cities, have opened up their telecommunications market, encouraging competition and developing more efficient telecommunications networks.

In terms of network infrastructure, by the end of 2003, total local exchange capacity in Beijing had amounted to 8.34 million lines, an increase of 3.8%. The number of fixed-line telephone subscribers had reached 6.8 million, up 16.2% over the previous year. This means that ownership of phone lines by Beijing residents had reached 47.3 per 100 residents.

The city has established IP phone networks to offer domestic and international IP phone services, with 7.53 billion minutes of usage recorded in 2003, up 150%.

The mobile phone network is growing fast too. Mobile phone subscribers in Beijing have increased to 10.96 million in 2003, an increase of 19.2% over 2002. GSM 900, GSM 1800 and CDMA are now adopted in Beijing. The use of new technologies such as multimedia, Internet, SMS and digital communications has spread rapidly.

In terms of data network, China also saw great growth. China is able to provide various data transmission services such as DDN, Frame Relay, X.25, VSAT and other advanced systems. These services do not merely cover China, but extend internationally as well. China can also provide VPN service based on Frame Relay, ATM and IP. As for IP services, by the end of August 2002, there were 43.3 million Internet users in China. The total number of domain names registered with ". cn" is now more than 100,000.

The information technology and communications industry is a pillar industry in Beijing. The development and industrialization of advanced technologies such as microelectronics, computers, communications, bio-pharmaceuticals, new materials and laser technology have been actively promoted, among which, communications, IT and modern biomedical science have had some initial results.

In 2003, the total value-added of Beijing's IT and communications industry was RMB 17.48 billion (USD 2.1 billion), an increase of 12.4% over 2002. The manufacturing industry of communications equipment focuses on developing large broadband communications equipment, multimedia and other types of communication devices.

New targets and investments

The wave of "information superhighway" that had swept across the world in 1997 had stimulated Beijing to build an "information harbor" with several fundamental projects outlined. Beijing is determined to keep abreast with Hong Kong and Singapore in terms of information technology status. It is turning into one of the most important communication hubs in the Asia Pacific region. The government encourages cooperation and alliance among enterprises, universities and research institutes.

High-tech communications

Beijing has established five major high-tech communications networks over the past five years. These include a foreign trade data network, a social security network and a community service network. The municipality had also set up a series of key information systems with a focus on urban planning, finance, employment and industrial & commercial administration.

Beijing has stressed many times that the high-tech communications sector was one of the key growth areas of its economy. Over the past few years, this sector has manufactured top-quality integrated circuits, computers, mobile telecommunications facilities and a series of other profitable high-tech communication products.

The new digital communications and multimedia market have enjoyed fast-track advancement. The ISDN network and ATM technology facilitate high speed and obstruction-free data exchange. Customers are now provided with a new variety of advanced products and services.

Software sector

Beijing has declared various favorable policies to promote its software and integrated circuit (IC) sector. The information office together with other related departments of the Beijing Municipal Government had offered a series of favorable conditions to attract foreign investments in the development of software and IC industries, following the central government's announcement of new policies.

According to the Beijing Statistics Bureau, the export value of the city's software sector in 2003 was USD 138 million, an increase of 48.2% over the previous year. The number of new software enterprises was 514, with 1,213 newly registered products. The total number of software enterprises was thus 1,749, with an accumulated 4,820 software products.

High technology sectors

Focusing on modern telecommunications, modern biology, pharmaceuticals, and new materials, Beijing's high-tech sectors have achieved sound progress. In 2003, the expenditure of the high technology sector totaled RMB 45.75 billion (USD 5.53 billion), an increase of 11.3% over 2002.

Total expenditure on R&D reached RMB 25.28 billion (USD 3 billion), which constituted 7% of the city's GDP. In 2003, the value-added of the information technology industry was RMB 16.13 billion (USD 1.95 billion), increasing 13% over the previous year. The telecommunications sector achieved a total production value of RMB 28.2 billion (USD 3.4 billion), up by 18.9%.

Information highway

Information highways give access to services and contents, and allow circulation and processing of information. They have considerable economic and cultural implications, creating new forms of exchange and networking. UNESCO promotes three areas of action to encourage the development of electronic networks.

The first is to prepare and implement development policies, including the social and cultural aspects. The second is to support the development of information sources and services. Finally, it is to train professionals for the design, implementation, operation and utilization of information and communication technologies. In this context, UNESCO supports the development of regional networks.

Beijing leads many cities in Information Technology

Beijing Economic Information Center has reported that Beijing led all other Chinese cities in terms of the level of development of the IT industry.

According to the analysis compiled into a Blue Paper on Beijing's development and published by the Social Sciences Documentation Publishing House, Beijing's index of information in 1998 was 89.87%, 18% higher than Shanghai, which was ranked 2nd in the field. In fact, the average index nationwide was only 25.89%. As for information levels, Beijing has surpassed some developed countries, according to the analysis.

Many Beijing-based companies are among the top 100 Chinese electronics enterprises. These include Putian Information Industry, Lenovo Group, Founder Group, Tongfang Group, Datang Telecom, Panasonic Color Tube, Oriental Electronics, LG Shuguang and Tsinghua Unisplendour etc. Meanwhile, more than one-third of Internet Service Providers and Internet Content Providers in China run their businesses in Beijing.

In addition, one-third of the nation's computer software engineers, as well as half of the professionals specialized in systematic integration and semi-conductors work in Beijing.

Changes in the IT & Communications sector in Beijing

The IT and communications sector has witnessed many changes in Beijing in recent years. The practical application of information resources is greatly promoted in Beijing.

At the same time, considerable technological advancement and achievements in IT and communications have expanded information resources. Due to the dramatic increase in the number of MNCs having established their offices and agencies in Beijing, as much as 23.6% of China's on-line databases are concentrated in Beijing, as reflected in statistics from the China Internet Information Center.

The Internet in Beijing has contributed immensely to the rapid development of the city. The city WB Internet is generally functional in all areas of the city, and the information infrastructure, namely the Capital Public Information Platform, has already taken shape. In fact, a series of information application systems such as e-business, e-office, social security, information community and so on are all supported by the project. Various business networks have been set up, providing an assortment of services.

The SDH Network of Beijing Telecommunications is to-date the largest SDH transforming network in the world. Beijing also boasts three sets of Pacific Ocean Satellite systems and three sets of Indian Ocean Satellite systems. In addition, 10 international telecommunication optical cables have been set up, allowing international communications with over 200 countries and regions worldwide.

Beijing has seen an extensive application of information technology. The main sponsors of international Internet transferring system with WB823M include China Telecom, China Netcom (CNC) and Jitong China Golden Bridge Network.

The rapid growth of the information industry has boosted economic development in Beijing. The third industry, especially, offers substantial opportunities for foreign participation. In 2003, investment by foreign enterprises in the computer and information service industries grew by 42.3% and 38.1% respectively. There were altogether 32,173 technological development contracts signed in the year, with total contract value reaching RMB 26.54 billion (USD 3.2 billion).

Of the total computer software products exported by China, 70% was developed in Beijing. Take Zhongguancun as an example, it was responsible for two-thirds of the total export of Beijing's software industry.

Greater attention has been paid to the training of IT professionals. At the end of 2003, Beijing had 274,000 professionals working in the IT sector, representing 5.4% of the population of employees. As many as 59 universities and colleges offer IT-related majors, providing around 36,000 graduates annually. Rich supply of human resources is helpful in promoting the IT industry. Meanwhile, the development environment for IT industries has also been further improved.

The IT industry in Beijing and other developed countries

Differences might be found between Beijing's IT industry and that of developed countries. In the late 1990s, international economic growth rate hovered around 3%, while the growth rate of IT-related industries was two to three times that figure.

In Beijing, the IT industry is rather young. Despite the fact that 25.1% of the GDP increase was contributed by IT-related industries, the development of these industries is still far from maturity. In fact, the government has been actively promoting the healthy development of IT-related industries.

The R&D of certain key technologies was not developing fast enough compared to international standards. Manufacturing technologies had been focused on medium and low-class products. As a result, hardware and software enterprises are lacking core technologies.

The Indian software industry is a leading power in terms of IT development. It is responsible for as much as 20% of the international market. In 2000, the output of Indian software reached USD 6.2 billion, while for China, as a whole, the figure was USD 1 billion. Still, Beijing, as the technological center of China, is trying to improve the investment environment as well as certain technologies so that its IT related industries can develop more healthily.

IT industry in Beijing and Shanghai

In terms of the IT industry, Shanghai has a larger scale of capital commitment than Beijing. In 2003, the total added value of the IT industry in Shanghai reached RMB 35 billion (USD 4.24 billion), while that of Beijing was RMB 16.13 billion (USD 1.95 billion). In terms of growth rate, Beijing enjoyed a faster speed than Shanghai. For expenditure on R&D, for example, Beijing's total investment jumped by 15.2%, constituting 7% of the city's GDP; while Shanghai's total expenditure made up only 2.06% of the municipality's GDP.

On the other hand, in terms of service income, business profit, total capital and number of professionals, the IT industry of Beijing saw a more exciting picture than that of Shanghai in 2003. To be specific, the service income of the IT industry of Beijing was twice that of Shanghai's; the business profit of Beijing was almost three times that of Shanghai's; the total capital of Beijing was 2.2 times that of Shanghai's; and the number of professionals in Beijing was 2.7 times that of Shanghai's.

ENVIRONMENTAL PROTECTION

Overview

Beijing has a vast array of textile mills, iron and steel works, chemical plants and factories manufacturing heavy machinery, electronic equipment, locomotives, plastics, synthetic fibers, and rolling stock.

In recent years, especially after its successful bid for host nation of the 2008 Olympics, Beijing has been attaching greater importance to the city's environmental protection. Reducing industrial pollution is a key focus of this effort.

About 200 industrial enterprises in the downtown area are shifting production or moving out so as to reduce the amount of pollution in the urban areas. The Capital Iron & Steel Group, for example, invested RMB 320 million (USD 38 million) in its environmental programs in 2001 alone. The company has successfully cut its output of iron and steel and shifted its business focus to high-tech products and real estate development. The company has also taken various measures to help improve the environment in the city.

The Beijing Municipal Government has identified air quality as a major health and environmental issue. In 1999, Beijing introduced tougher vehicle emission standards that require an 80% reduction in emissions by 2005. From 2004 to 2007, Beijing will adopt more rigorous standards to further reduce emissions by 60%.

Coal will be banned except for use in designated large power plant boilers. It is being replaced with cleaner fuels, such as natural gas, electricity, LPG and coal gas. A natural gas pipeline from Shaanxi province to Beijing is to be completed by 2008. When completed, it will supply five billion cubic meters of natural gas to the capital so that 80% of all fuel used will be clean.

Beijing has committed to investing RMB 147.8 billion (USD 17.9 billion) to improve its infrastructure and environmental quality, with USD 6.6 billion to be spent on energy and environmental projects between 2003 and 2007.

Many of the activities simply represent an acceleration of existing environmental goals. For instance, Beijing's 10th Five-Year Plan (2001-2005) for environmental protection had already called for the relocation of 100 factories, including the relocation of 20 heavy polluters to sites outside of Beijing's 4th Ring Road.

The development of the city's environmental protection industry will not only raise the overall level of Chinese enterprises in this field, but also provide a huge market and many opportunities for foreign companies. It can be expected that, with the implementation of the environmental plan and the preparation for the 2008 Olympics, Beijing will have a rapidly expanding environmental protection market.

Business opportunities and challenges

Environmental protection is a young but fast-growing industry in China. In the past 10 years, the number of enterprises engaging in environmental protection had increased by four folds and the number of employees grew by six folds. In the same period, the output value of China's environmental protection industry also rose 25 folds with a yearly output hitting RMB 10 billion, making the industry a new focus point in China's economic growth.

It is estimated that China needs to invest RMB 50.4 billion (USD 6.09 billion) to construct 443 urban sewage treatment and refuse disposal plants in the period 2001-2005. The government alone cannot meet such great demand for financial resources. Various possible means such as BOT and stock system are likely to be introduced to attract capital and promote market-oriented operation.

The State Environmental Protection Administration is to open the market to domestic and foreign investors for the construction and operation of urban sewage treatment and refuse disposal plants.

Estimates place urban wastewater discharged in China annually at 32,800 million cubic meters, while the treatment rate is lower than 37%. The collected and transported urban domestic refuse amounts to 140 million tons, half of which is not properly disposed but piled up at open areas. This not only takes up a large area of land, but causes pollution to water, soil and air.

China's revenue from environmental protection was estimated to be RMB 169 billion (about USD 20.4 billion), including profits of RMB 16.7 billion (about USD 2.0 billion).

Currently, development of the environmental protection business is restricted by the lack of finance, technology, advanced management expertise, inadequate policies and a disorganized market. But there are positive factors in the environmental protection industry that investors can look forward to. Major development, and hence profits, can be expected.

The coming years will see China pump more investment into the environmental protection industry in a bid to promote its growth. In the meantime, the state will also work out favorable policies for the extension of subsidies and discount loans to major enterprises carrying out environmental protection and other related projects.

The central government has outlined the goal for ecological construction and environmental protection in the 10th Five-year Plan (2001-2005) for national economic development. The goal is to stop further ecological deterioration in China in five years, to improve the environmental quality in cities, reduce the emission of pollutants by 10% from 2000 onwards, and make progress in conserving and protecting natural resources.

According to the Plan, the focus of the environmental protection industry will be the development of advanced technologies, equipment and materials for environmental protection, e.g. for desulphurization and exhaust treatment. It will also give priority to the comprehensive utilization of resources and to the development of information, consulting and technology services.

To reach that goal, China will go all out to develop the environmental protection industry. It is estimated that about RMB 700 billion (USD 84.8 billion), or 1.3% of the GDP, will be put into the environment sector in the period 2001-2005, of which RMB 550 billion (USD 66.6 billion) will be used for air and water pollution prevention and treatment.

However, as the industry is still in its infancy in China, it has so far attracted limited capital investment and technology. China is now seeking diversified investments, putting in place financing mechanisms and opening its market to foreign technology and equipment.

Air quality

Beijing hopes to raise its air quality to national and WHO standards by 2008. In order to achieve this target, Beijing has already introduced strict exhaust gas emission standards for motor vehicles. Stricter standards will be enforced in 2007 to reduce exhaust gas emission by 60%.

At present, gas fuel is used by 60% of public buses and 40% of taxis in the Chinese capital. These ratios will be raised to 90% and 70% respectively by 2008.

Garbage treatment

By 2008, all garbage in Beijing will be treated, with 30% of which re-cycled and 50% sorted and disposed. All garbage generated at Olympic venues will be sorted and centrally treated with a recycling rate of 50%. Regenerated materials will be used as building materials and the making of temporary furniture and billboards for the Games.

Sewage treatment

By 2008, Beijing will be able to treat 2.8 million tons of sewage daily (the daily treatment capacity was 1.08 million tons in 1999). Over 90% of urban sewage will be treated and 50% will be recycled.

The quality of drinking water will be improved to WHO standards. Water-saving equipment will be used in the Olympic Village and all competition venues; rain water collection and recycling facilities will be built; and eco-toilets that require no water for flushing will be used.

Energy

The use of natural gas will be increased by five times by 2007 and clean energy will be used in all urban households. Wind-generated energy will be used as much as possible in the Olympic Village and all competition venues; geothermal and solar energy will be used in the supply of hot water; and natural light will be utilized to the fullest extent to reduce energy consumption.

Satellites to monitor the environment

The central government plans to launch three satellites in 2006 to monitor the environment and predict natural disasters.

China has so far established more than 2,200 monitoring stations nationwide, which provide about 30 million items of data every year on the atmosphere, water and ecological environment.

However, the current monitoring means do not fully meet the needs of environmental protection yet. The satellites will greatly improve the standard of environmental monitoring and disaster prediction.

Market Segments of Environmental Industries in China

Source: National Environmental Protection Administration

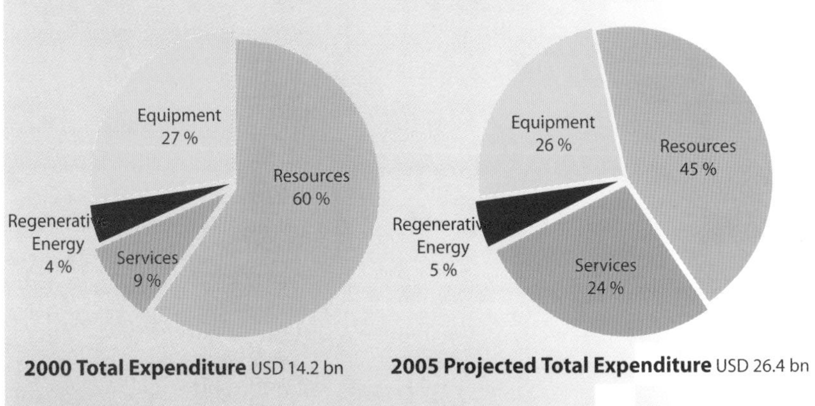

Beijing curbs environmentally unfriendly automobiles

Beijing has introduced measures to limit the movement, within the second-ring urban area, of automobiles with 19 seats that have not achieved the mark of environmental friendliness. Only those automobiles with 19 seats or over that are environmentally friendly, namely up to the Euro I standard, may enter downtown Beijing.

The Beijing Environmental Protection Administration and the Bureau of Traffic Control are taking joint action to reduce air pollution caused by heavy vehicles. The pollutants discharged from the vehicles cannot be dispersed in the downtown area as there are many high-rise buildings.

The area under control is being gradually expanded in stages after 1 November 2003 in view of the heavy air pollution. It will expand to within downtown Beijing's third ring by end-2004.

This move will affect 300,000 heavy vehicles, of which 130,000 of them are stationed in downtown Beijing.

Source: www.xinhuanet.cn

Future outlook

Beijing will invest a total of USD 12.2 billion to protect the ecological environment in the period 1998 – 2007. Since 1998, Beijing has invested a total of USD 3.63 billion in encouraging the use of clean fuels, controlling gas pollutant emission, treating wastewater, advising safe disposal of solid waste and protecting wild life species.

Since 1999, Beijing has also adopted strict emission standards. During the period 2004 – 2007, Beijing will adopt even stricter standards so as to further reduce emission by 60%.

By 2007, 90% of the buses and 70% of the taxis will use clean natural gas. By the same year, Beijing will consume five times as much natural gas as in 2000. No fuel coal will be used except in a few large boilers in power plants.

By 2007, 14 more wastewater treatment plants will be built to increase the treating capacity to 90% of the total that the city produces. 50% of the treated wastewater will be reused. In addition, Beijing will maintain the balance between demand and supply of water by expanding water sources and encouraging water-saving.

Beijing already has 80% of urban garbage safely disposed, at present. By 2007, the amount will increase to 100%. At the same time, 50% of all domestic waste will be sorted before being collected and 30% will be recycled.

By 2007, trees will cover 70% of Beijing's mountainous areas. The capital city will also develop more than 23,000 ha of green belt along major rivers and roads, and 12,000 ha of forest strips to separate the city from the surrounding countryside.

WHOLESALE AND RETAIL

Market overview

Despite the short-term negative economic effects of Severe Acute Respiratory Syndrome (Sars), Beijing's wholesale and retail sales of consumer products in 2003 achieved impressive results.

Continued upsurge of per capita income of urban residents in the city was the most significant contributory factor. In 2003, the per capita disposable income of urban residents was RMB 13,882 (USD 1,679), up 11.4% over 2002. Increases in household consumption fueled the development of the retail sector.

The multi-faceted development of the economy contributed directly to commercial prosperity. For the year as a whole, the wholesale and retail business, together with the booming food and beverage industry attained an added value of RMB 27.13 billion (USD 3.28 billion), an increase of 7.8%. Total sales of consumer goods hit RMB 458.7 billion (USD 55.5

billion), a hefty increase of 31.6%; and total purchases reached RMB 434.49 billion (USD 52.5 billion), a 31.6% leap from 2002.

Currently, Beijing has a total of 230,000 retail stores. These stores are expanding from downtown areas to suburban areas and neighboring areas, and hire over 1.2 million employees throughout the area.

Economic indicators that reflect business profitability and solvency are encouraging. For example, the level of gross profit for large and medium-sized commercial enterprises increased from 8.39% in 2002 to 24.4% in 2003, achieving total profits of USD 95 million; product sales increased from 1.4% in 2002 to 31.6% in 2003, with sales value rising to USD 55.5 billion; and total purchase value reaching USD 52.5 billion, an increase of 35.8%.

Restrictions on retail sector to be lifted

The Ministry of Commerce reiterated recently the further liberalization of China's retail sector in view of its WTO agreements. Coming into 2004, foreign ownership has been permitted in the retail sector, with no geographic or quantitative restrictions.

Since 1992, the retail sector has utilized USD 3 billion of foreign investment. As at September 2003, 264 foreign-funded retailers and 2,200 chain stores have been approved. Most of these retailers are involved in new retail businesses.

Foreign retailers have played an important role in accelerating the modernization of China's retail sector. In the meantime, domestic retailers have learned valuable lessons in management and marketing skills from their foreign counterparts.

Famous shopping centers in Beijing include Lufthansa Center, Shuang'an Plaza, Shidu Department Store, Dong'an Market, Ganjiakou Department Store, New Oriental Plaza, Wangfujing Department Store and Xi'dan Plaza etc.

Major foreign retail groups are Carrefour, Sogo, Er Chok Lotus, OBI, B & Q, Letto, WalMetro, Lawson, 7-Eleven and Auchan. Total retail sales of foreign-invested commercial enterprises in Beijing was estimated to be over RMB 10 billion (USD 1.2 billion) in 2003, an increase of 13.2% over 2002.

The retail market of automobiles also had a remarkable showing in 2003. In the year, over 408,000 cars of various kinds were sold, with a total value of USD 3.7 billion, representing increases of 56.6% and 51.2% respectively over the previous year.

The annual expenditure on transportation by urban residents reached USD 204 per capita, up 32.8%; while rural household annual expenditure increased 10.5% to USD 563 per capita. The bulk of consumer expenditure was on transport and communication, housing, education and entertainment, which together constituted 45.3% of consumer expenditure on goods and services.

China's service trade tops the developing world

Trade-related services are growing rapidly in China, particularly in major cities such as Beijing, Shanghai and Guangzhou. According to annual statistics provided by the World Trade Organization for 2003, China's service traders have contributed significantly to the export value internationally.

Meanwhile, the import value created by service traders worldwide reached USD 1.734 trillion, of which USD 53.8 billion or 3.1% was created by China, making it the 8th largest service importer in the world.

Chain stores in Beijing

Chain stores in Beijing appeared in the early 1990s and have been developing well in the past decade. In 2003, the retail sales of chain stores in Beijing reached RMB 46.3 billion (USD 5.59 billion), up 23.7% over

2002. This is 24.2% of total retail sales in Beijing. Based on figures from the China Chain Store Association, there were more than 20 chain store groups in Beijing in 2003. They include the following, which are ranked among the top 100 in China: Beijing Hualian Supermarket, Beijing Guomei Electronics, Wangfujing Department Store, Supermarket Tiankelong, Wumei Commercial Group, Legend Co. Ltd. and Jingkelong Center.

Share of World Service Trade Export

Country	Total Export Value	% of World Service Trade
United States	USD 282 billion	16%
UK	USD 129.5 billion	7.3%
Germany	USD 111.7 billion	6.3%
France	USD 98 billion	5.6%
Spain	USD 76.4 billion	4.3%
Japan	USD 70.2 billion	4.0%
Chinese mainland	USD 44.5 billion	2.5%
Chinese Hong Kong	USD 4.32 billion	2.5%

Source: WTO

The rapid emergence and outstanding performance of chain stores herald the modernization of the retail business in Beijing. The more than 300 convenience stores all across the city also play an important role. Their total sales value reached USD 1.51 billion, a more than one-fold increase over the previous year.

According to the China Chain Store Association, the total sales of the top 100 chain store groups in 2002 reached RMB 162 billion (USD 19.59 billion), an increase of 48% over 2001. Among them, the sales of the top 10 accounted for RMB 71.8 billion (USD 8.67 billion) or 44% of the total.

WTO agreements on distribution, wholesale and retail

Before China's accession to the WTO, foreign companies were prohibited from distributing imported products or providing repair and maintenance services. China is now liberalizing its distribution system to delegate full distribution rights to foreign firms, with a comprehensive set of commitments covering commissioned agent services, wholesaling, retailing, franchising, sales away from a fixed location, and related services such as inventory management or repair and maintenance.

China has also agreed to open up rental and leasing services, air courier services, freight forwarding and packing services. Current restrictions for most distribution-related services will be phased-out within three years of the date of WTO accession, although the schedule of commitments varies according to the services involved.

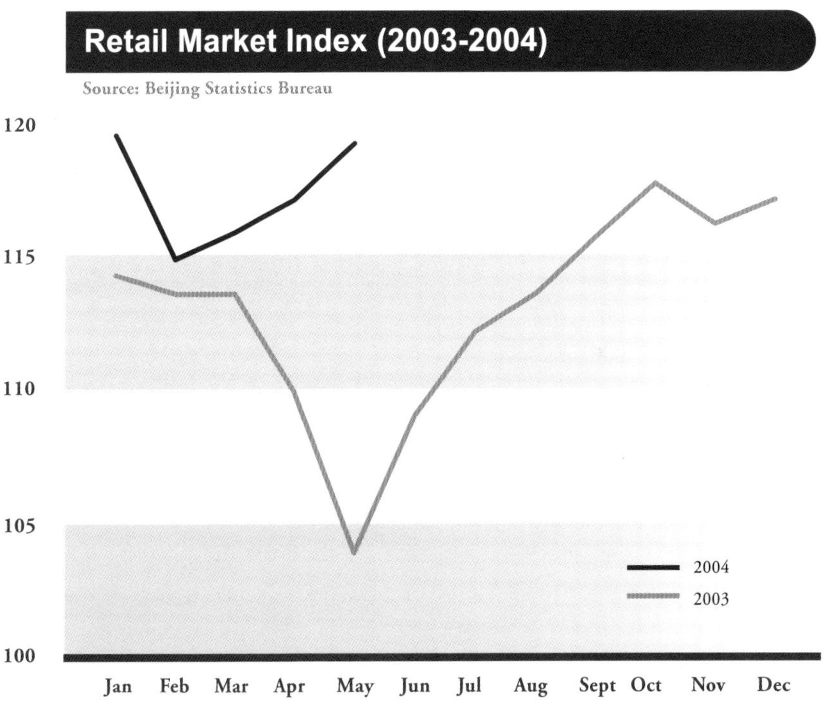

Enterprise Business Performance Index (2003-2004)

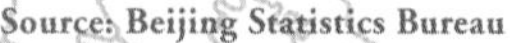

Source: Beijing Statistics Bureau

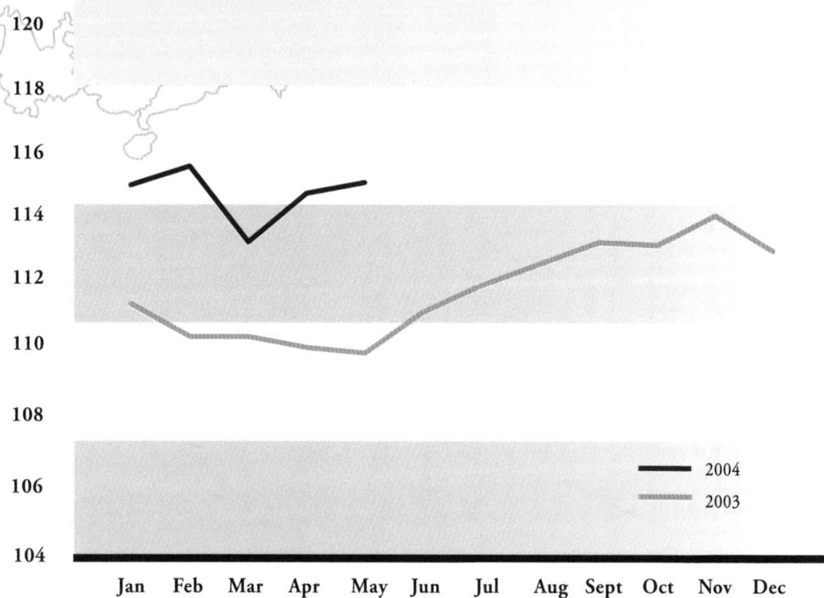

Beijing Consumption Expenditure Breakdown, 2003

	2003 (USD billion)	Increase over 2002
Consumption Expenditure	23.18	14.05%
Food	6.02	6.7%
Clothes	25.5	1.8%
Family appliances	13.7	18.9%
Housing	9.54	10.1%
Vehicles	3.69	51.2%
Others	1.93	25.14%

Source: Beijing Statistics Bureau

Wangfujing/ Beijing Overall Business Index (2003-2004)

Source: Department of Commerce, Beijing

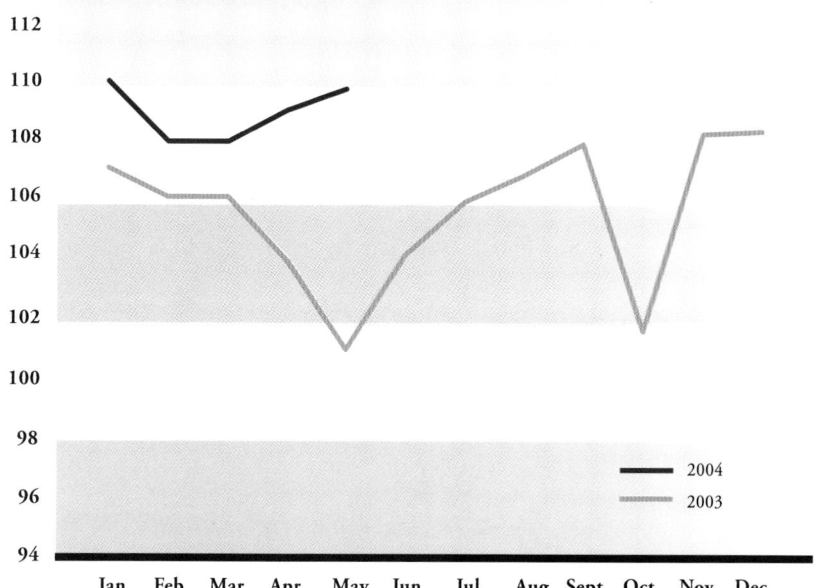

Consumer durables owned by Beijing residents (per 100 households)

Item	Unit	Year 2003	% change
Air-conditioner	Sets	119.3	+12.0
Shower heater	Sets	85.4	+2.3
Color TV	Sets	147.0	- 0.9
Refrigerator	Sets	100.4	-1.2
Washing machine	Sets	99.3	+0.7
Personal computer	Sets	68.3	+23.1
Microwave oven	Sets	79.2	+8.3
Kitchen ventilator	Sets	81.3	+3.6
Cooking appliance	Sets	107.8	+9.9

Source: Beijing Statistics Bureau

Retail business

Foreign ownership restrictions

- Within one year after WTO accession, foreign investment of up to 50% is allowed;
- Within two years after accession, foreign investors may have controlling shareholdings;
- Within three years after accession, wholly owned foreign investments will be allowed;
- Foreign investors are not allowed to be controlling shareholders in the operation of any business on cars (restrictions will be removed no later than 11 December 2006), books, newspapers, magazines, pharmaceuticals, pesticides, mulching film, chemical fertilizers, processed petroleum products, rice, vegetable oil, sugar, tobacco and cotton.

Product restrictions

- Within one year after WTO accession, foreign investment is allowed in business activities involving books, newspapers, magazines and publications;
- Within three years after accession, foreign investment is allowed in business activities involving pharmaceuticals, pesticide, mulching film and processed petroleum products;
- Within five years after accession, foreign investment is allowed in the chemical fertilizer business;
- Within three years after accession, foreign investment is allowed in franchising and wholesale and retail at unfixed points of sale.

Geographical and Quantitative Restrictions

- Upon WTO accession, foreign service suppliers will be permitted to establish joint ventures in Zhengzhou and Wuhan;
- Two years after accession, foreign majority equity share was allowed in joint ventures, and geographic restrictions had been further lifted to include all provincial capitals, Chongqing and Ningbo.

- Within three years after accession, there will be no restrictions on equity, geographic areas, or the number of service suppliers.

Exceptions for Distribution, Retailing and Wholesaling

- China's WTO commitments do not include wholesaling for salt, and wholesaling and retailing for tobacco.
- For joint venture retail department stores and chain stores, only minority equity participation is allowed.
- There are different schedules for commission-based distribution and wholesale services relating to the following product categories: chemical fertilizers, books, magazines, newspapers, pharmaceuticals, pesticides, mulching film, crude oil and processed petroleum products.

For pharmaceutical products, pesticides and mulching films, foreign investment will be allowed within three years of China's WTO accession; for chemical fertilizers, processed oil and crude oil products, foreign investment will be allowed within five years of China's accession.

Other distribution, wholesaling, retailing related services

Courier Services

Courier services refer to all services related to international shipment being handled by an express carrier, except for those currently specifically reserved to China Post Administration by law.

- Upon China's accession, foreign investment in courier services will be allowed in the form of joint ventures;
- Within one year after accession, foreign majority ownership is allowed;
- Within four years after accession, there will be no restrictions on foreign investment in courier services, and foreign suppliers of courier services will be allowed to establish wholly owned subsidiaries.

Freight Transportation

Road Freight Transportation

- Upon China's accession, foreign investments in road freight transportation are allowed in the form of joint ventures, with foreign ownership not exceeding 49%;
- Within one year after accession, foreign majority ownership is allowed;
- Within three years after accession, there will be no restriction on foreign investment in road freight transport services, and foreign firms will be allowed to establish wholly owned subsidiaries.

Rail Freight Transportation

- Within four years after accession, foreign majority ownership will be allowed in rail transport services;
- Within six years after accession, there will be no restriction on foreign investment in rail transport services, and foreign firms will be allowed to establish wholly owned subsidiaries.

Packaging, Storage and Warehousing Services

- Upon China's accession, foreign investments in storage and warehousing services are allowed in the form of joint ventures, with foreign investment not exceeding 49%;
- Within one year after accession, foreign majority ownership will be allowed;
- Within three years after accession, there will be no restriction on foreign investment in storage and warehousing services, and foreign firms will be allowed to establish wholly owned subsidiaries.

Freight Forwarding Agency Services

- Upon China's accession, freight forwarding agencies which have at least three consecutive years of experience and registered capital of no less than USD 1 million, are allowed to set up freight forward agency joint ventures in China, with foreign investment not exceeding 50%;

- Within a year after accession, foreign majority ownership is allowed. After having operated in China for one year, joint ventures engaged in freight forwarding agency services may set up branches when registered capital of both sides has been provided. Another RMB 1 million shall be added to the original registration capital of the joint venture for the set-up of each branch. A freight forwarding agency may set up a second joint venture after its first joint venture has been in operation for five years;
- Within four years after accession, there will be no restriction on foreign investment in freight forwarding agency services, and foreign firms will be allowed to establish wholly owned subsidiaries, provided that the minimum registered capital of such joint ventures is no less than USD 1 million and the operation term of such joint ventures shall not exceed 20 years.

Corporate Goods Price Indices (CGPI)
previous corresponding period = 100

	Overall Index	Agricultural Product	Mining Product	Coal,Oil & Electricity	Processed Product
2003.01	100.59	99.29	102.08	113.65	99.48
2003.02	101.01	97.72	102.55	115.78	100.39
2003.03	101.74	99.93	103.20	115.31	100.72
2003.04	101.59	100.33	103.09	113.02	100.63
2003.05	100.97	99.42	103.48	108.14	100.58
2003.06	100.83	99.39	103.88	106.55	100.54
2003.07	101.49	101.12	103.81	106.70	100.91
2003.08	101.91	102.38	103.43	106.38	101.17
2003.09	102.17	103.52	104.21	106.22	101.14
2003.10	103.67	106.88	105.65	104.17	102.46
2003.11	105.47	109.88	108.51	104.42	104.03
2003.12	106.31	110.54	109.33	106.67	104.73

Source: Department of Commerce, Beijing

Maintenance and Repair Services

- Upon WTO membership, foreign investment in maintenance and repair services must be in the form of joint ventures.
- Starting no later than a year after WTO entry, foreign majority ownership will be permitted.
- Starting no later than three years after WTO entry, foreign suppliers of maintenance and repair services will be permitted to establish wholly owned subsidiaries.

Set-up requirements

To establish a domestic commerce joint venture, the foreign party has to meet the following requirements:

- Possess strong financial ability, advanced commercial management experiences, extensive sales networks, good reputation and healthy track record;
- Capable of helping the export of Chinese products via the proposed joint venture;
- For foreign investors who wish to set up a retail joint venture, its assets in the year immediately prior to the application year should be more than USD 200 million and its average annual sales for three years prior to the application should be more than USD 2 billion;
- For foreign investors who wish to set up a wholesale joint venture, its assets in the year immediately prior to making the application must be more than USD 300 million and its average annual sales for three years prior to the application should be more than USD 2.5 billion.

The Chinese party must meet the following requirements:

- Possess strong financial and operational ability;
- Its assets in the year immediately prior to making the application are more than RMB 50 million (RMB 30 million for applicants in central and western regions);

- If the Chinese party is a commercial enterprise, its average annual sales for three years prior to the application shall be more than RMB 300 million (RMB 200 million for applicants in central and western regions);
- If the Chinese party is a foreign trade company, its average annual import & export trade volume (not including those conducted on behalf of others on an agency basis) for three years prior to the application shall be more than USD 50 million, with export volume of not less than USD 30 million.

From the prescribed qualifications and regulations, it is apparent that for foreign retailers to operate in China, they must cooperate with a local partner. The size of their investment, store location and even a decision to withdraw from the market require government approval. It is not easy for small companies to qualify, given these requirements. Even if the foreign investor does qualify, they may also find difficulties in locating the qualified Chinese party to set up a joint venture with.

EXHIBITIONS AND TRADE EVENTS

Overview

As the nation's capital and a major international metropolis, Beijing has unique advantages for the development of its exhibition industry. Robust economic development, international reputation, geographical location and large numbers of professionals are key factors boosting its conference and exhibition industry.

Nevertheless, due to the outbreak of Sars in early 2003, the total number of international conventions and exhibitions fell slightly by 7.7% to 3,160. Of the total number, 51.5% were trade and technical exhibitions, while 26% were cultural and educational in nature. The activities generated a total revenue of USD 19.9 million for the hotel industry. For the city itself, the events contributed USD 3.42 billion in revenue, or 2% of overall GDP.

In the same year, there were 1,063 international conventions held, of which 48.3% were trade and technical in nature.

In 2003, there were 1,700 Beijing-based companies providing various kinds of exhibition services to local and foreign exhibitors. Most large-scale events were held at the city's 13 major exhibition centers, which together had total exhibition and convention areas of 240,000 m^2 and 160,000 m^2 respectively.

Within the next five to eight years, Beijing is expected to become a hub for international exhibitions while also attracting tourists who will visit the city for the 2008 Olympic Games. Before the opening of the exciting event, Beijing will build a larger group of exhibition facilities, expanding its total exhibition area to 400,000 m^2.

The China International Exhibition Center will be rebuilt at another location to make it the largest in Asia, covering an exhibition area of 200,000 m^2. The rebuilt exhibition hall is expected to be operational in 2006.

Apart from that, a group of exhibition centers in downtown Beijing are on the way to completion, each with around 10,000 m^2 of floor space and will be suitable for small and medium-sized exhibitions. Several other centers of between 30,000 to 50,000 m^2 will also be built around the city.

Meanwhile, in the suburban region of Beijing, some large and modern exposition centers exceeding 200,000 m^2 will be built to cater to business functions and entertainment. The total area set aside for the construction of these exhibition centers is estimated to be between 500,000 to 800,000 m^2.

Major exhibition events

China International Machine Tool Exhibition (CMIT)

China Machine Tool & Tool Builders' Association (CMTBA) is the largest and best-known international machine tool exhibition in China. To date, Beijing has successfully hosted seven sessions of the China International Machine Tool Show (CIMT). Domestic and overseas machine tool manufacturers consider CIMT an important event at which to demonstrate their new products, conduct technological exchanges, promote trade and seek cooperative partners.

CIMT 2001 saw a total of 1,078 exhibitors from 25 countries and regions in the world participate in the exhibition which took up 15 exhibition halls. Nine countries were represented by their delegations: Germany, Spain, South Korea, Switzerland, Great Britain, Italy, Japan, the Republic of Czech and the United States. More than 130,000 visitors, mostly professionals and businessmen, toured the exhibition.

CIMT 2001 Visitor Profile

Source: Ministry of Commerce

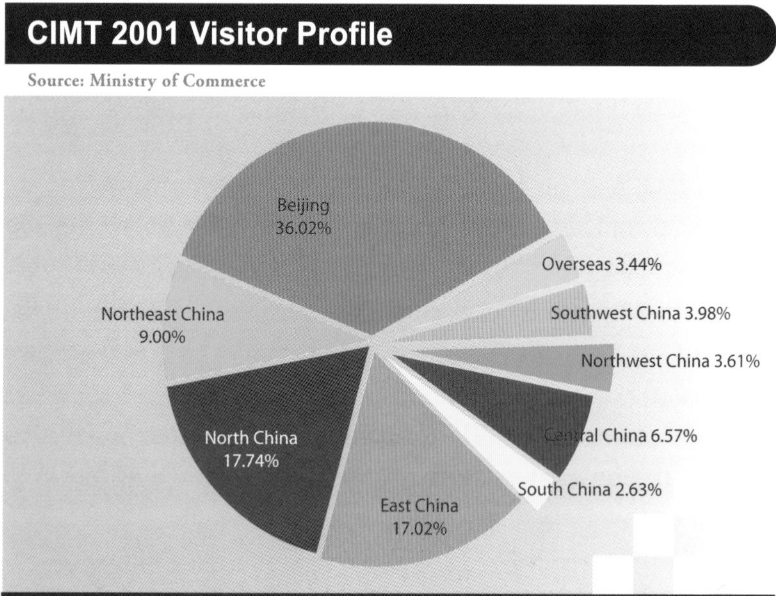

In 2003, the 8th China International Machine Tool Show, also known as CIMT 2003, was held at the China International Exhibition Center in Beijing, 16-25 April 2003. The 7-day exhibition was badly affected by the sudden outbreak of Sars and additional last-minute arrangements were made to ensure the safety of all exhibitors as well as visitors. While the final three days saw a sharp drop in visitors, the show went better than expected.

1,200 exhibitors from 27 countries and regions had participated in the event. Total exhibition area was 72,000 m². The number of visitors was estimated to be 104,000 and the quality of the exhibits was considered high. Most of the exhibits were new machines and tools, and many were sold. Sales by local exhibitors was estimated at RMB 8.35 million (USD 1.09 million), while the sales performance of foreign participants was estimated to have exceeded that in the last CIMT show in 2001.

Other important events

Other important exhibition events held in Beijing were the China International Clothing & Accessories Fair, China Building 2002, Hardware China 2002, International Medical Instruments & Equipment Exhibition, Environment & Health Industries Exhibition, COMDEX China 2002,

China International Wide Exposition, International Exhibition for Agriculture, Animal Breeding and Food Processing Techniques, China Beijing International High-tech Industries Week, Beijing International Automotive Industry Exhibition, Beijing International City Landscaping Expo, Pharmatec China 2002, International Advertising Show, International Chemical Industry Fair and China International Franchise Exhibition etc.

Major exhibition venues

China International Exhibition Center

China International Exhibition Center, a subsidiary of China International Exhibition Corporation (CIEC) under the China Council for the Promotion of International Trade (CCPIT) and China Chamber of International Commerce (CCIC), organizes and hosts international fairs, trade shows and foreign exhibitions in China. It aims at strengthening economic and technological exchanges and cooperation, as well as, promoting economic development and prosperity between China and other countries.

Being a member of Union des Foires Internationals (UFI) and International Association for Exposition Management (IAEM), China International Exhibition Center actively takes part in events held among the international exhibition circles and strives to make the Chinese exhibition industry meet international standards.

Since its establishment in 1985, China International Exhibition Center has hosted and organized around 350 international exhibitions, many of which are well-known in the world. These include China International Machine Tool Exhibition (CIMT), China International Textile Machinery Exhibition (CITME), and Metal & Metallurgy China, which are ranked among the four most important shows of their kind in the world.

China Print, CIMT and Metal & Metallurgy China are approved by UFI as its member events. In addition, Auto China, China International Chemical Industry Fair (ICIF), PT Expo Comm China, China Computer World, China Foodtech and Aviation China are influential trade shows, known around the world. Beijing International Fair and Asia Pacific International Trade Fair are also famous as the general fairs held at CIEC. At present, 50 exhibitions are listed on CIEC's schedule as regular events. Most of these are held once every one or two years.

China International Exhibition Center owns a total indoor exhibition space of 60,000 m^2, an outdoor space of 7,000 m^2, car parking facilities of 10,000 m^2, a container-ground of 10,000 m^2 and a Customs-bonded warehousing space of 3,000 m^2. All the exhibition halls have ready access to electricity and power, water supply and drainage, telecommunications, as well as, heating and air-conditioning systems, fully meeting the requirements of international exhibitions.

A general service building offers Chinese and Western restaurants, seminar and meeting rooms and lecture halls. Exhibitors can easily obtain the services they need in this exhibition complex, such as Customs, transportation, booth set-up, business tour, hotel accommodation and article renting.

Located at the north-east corner of urban Beijing, China International Exhibition Center is only 8 km away from downtown Beijing, 5 km from the diplomatic area and 20 km from the airport, with highways leading in all directions and more than 20 hotels in the surrounding areas. Exhibitors will find CIEC pleasant and convenient.

Beijing International Convention Center

The Beijing International Convention Center, a key member of the Beijing North Star Industrial Group, specializes in staging national and international conferences, exhibitions and other large events, and also leases office space. It is generally used by the Beijing Municipal Tourism Administration to host events by international clientele.

The BICC, with a floor area of 77,000 m^2, consists of the Conference Building, the Chenxin House, the Chenyun House and the East Annex to the Conference Building.

Located within the magnificent Asian Games Village, the BICC lies in close proximity to Beijing's major sports facilities and scenic spots. The National Olympic Sports Center is just across the street. The BICC is 9 km from Tian'anmen Square and 8 km from the Beijing Railway Station.

The Capital International Airport is 20 km to the east, while the Summer Palace is 12 km to the west. To its north are two world-famous attractions, namely, the Great Wall and the Ming Tombs.

China Hall of Science & Technology

China Hall of Science & Technology (CHST) is a multi-functional and comprehensive building for scientific and technological activities. CHST hosts domestic and international academic exchanges of science and technology as well as large and medium-sized meetings. It covers 61,000 m^2 and has all the necessary fittings.

The convention center of CHST comprises a 600-seat conference hall with facilities for simultaneous interpretation in multinational languages and modern acoustic equipment; a 300-seat performance hall with advanced facilities for audio-visual, video, broadcast and screening; and 20 meeting rooms for holding meetings, media liaison, academic lectures, business negotiations, performances and film screening. The 1,000-m^2 multi-function hall is an ideal place for scientific and technological exhibitions, product launches and public gatherings.

National Agricultural Exhibition Center

China National Agricultural Exhibition Center (CNAEC) was built in 1959 and is well-known as one of the 10 famous architectural sites in Beijing built in the early years of the founding of the new republic.

Located in Chaoyang District in northeast Beijing, CNAEC enjoys the advantage of being near Capital International Airport. Facing the foreign diplomatic area in the west, this exhibition center is surrounded by magnificent office buildings, shopping centers, night clubs and star hotels such as the Great Wall Sheraton Hotel and Kunlun Hotel.

Occupying an area of 52 ha, the CNAEC consists of 10 exhibition halls built in Chinese traditional architectural style and seven light-duty showrooms with a total floor area of 30,000 m^2.

With 18,000 m^2 indoor exhibition area, 40,000 m^2 outdoor exhibition area and 4,000 m^2 warehousing area, the CNAEC is able to satisfy different needs from international and domestic clients.

Since its establishment, with the strong support of the Agriculture Ministry, the Ministry of Science & Technology, the Foreign Trade & Economic Cooperation Commission as well as other important government departments, the CNAEC has hosted more than 300 national and international exhibitions.

MAJOR HOTLINE NUMBERS

SPECIAL SERVICES

Police	110
Telephone Repair	112
Telephone Number Inquiry	114
Time Inquiry	117
Fire	119
Ambulance	120
Weather Report	121
Traffic Police	122

GOVERNMENT

Beijing Municipal Government	12345
Beijing Municipal Industrial & Commercial Administration	12315
Beijing Municipal Quality & Technology Supervision Administration	12365
Beijing Municipal Consumer Association	62241234
Beijing Municipal Environment Administration	68413817
Legal Service Hotline	1600148
Taxi Complaint	68351150

TELECOM & POST SERVICES

Beijing Telecom Customer Service	189
Ministry of Information Industry Feedback Center	96123
Beijing Mobile Customer Service	1860
Beijing Unicom Service Hotline	1252
Beijing Post Service Hotline	185

TICKETING SERVICES

Airplane Information Inquiry	2580
Air Ticket Booking Hotline	2581
Beijing Railway Station Inquiry Hotline	65634432
Beijing West Railway Station Inquiry Hotline	63216253
Beijing South Railway Station Inquiry Hotline	63030031
Beijing North Railway Station Inquiry Hotline	65636223
Train Tickets Booking Hotline	63217188

OTHER SERVICES

Tap Water Maintenance	66189955

Electricity Maintenance	63129999
Gas Maintenance	96777
Public Bus	96166
Automobile Help Service	8008100198
Exit & Entry Administration Information	26611266

MINISTRIES AND STATE ADMINISTRATIONS

Ministry of Foreign Affairs 2 Chaoyangmen South Avenue	(8610) 6596 1114
State Development and Planning Commission 38 Yuetan South Street	(8610) 6850 1240
State Economic and Trade Commission 26 Xuanwumen West Avenue	(8610) 6319 2299
Ministry of Education 37 Damuchang Hutong	(8610) 6609 6114
Ministry of Science and Technology 15 Fuxing Road	(8610) 6851 5544
Ministry of Public Safety 14 East Chang'an Boulevard	(8610) 6520 2114
Ministry of State Security 14 East Chang'an Boulevard	(8610) 6524 4072
Ministry of Supervision 4 Zhaojun Temple	(8610) 6212 4129
Ministry of Civil Affairs 147 North Heyan Avenue	(8610) 6513 5333
Ministry of Justice 10 Chaoyangmen South Avenue	(8610) 6520 5114
Ministry of Finance 3 Sanlihe South No. 3 Street	(8610) 68551624
Ministry of Personnel 7 Hepingli Middle Street	(8610) 6492 1155

Ministry of Labor and Social Insurance 12 Hepingli Middle Street	(8610) 8420 1114
Ministry of State Land Resources 37 Guanying Garden West Zone	(8610) 6612 7114
Ministry of Construction 9 Sanlihe Road	(8610) 6839 4114
Ministry of Railway 10 Fuxing Road	(8610) 6324 0114
Ministry of Transportation 11 Jiannei Avenue	(8610) 6529 2114
Ministry of Information Industry 13 West Chang'an Boulevard	(8610) 6602 1290
Ministry of Water Resources 2 Baiguang Road No. 2 Zone	(8610) 6320 2114
Ministry of Agriculture 11 Agriculture Exhibition Center South Street	(8610) 6419 3366
Ministry of Foreign Trade and Economic Cooperation 2 East Chang'an Boulevard	(8610)6519 8114
Ministry of Culture 10 North Chaoyangmen Avenue	(8610) 6555 1114
Ministry of Health 1 Xizhimenwai South Road	(8610) 6879 2114
State Population Planning Commission 14 Zhicun Road	(8610) 6204 6622
People's Bank of China 32 Chengfang Street	(8610) 6619 4114
The General Auditing Office 1 Beilu Garden Exhibition Road	(8610) 6830 1114
The General State Customs 6 Jianguomennei Avenue	(8610) 6519 4114

The General State Taxation Administration 5 Yangfangdian West Road	(8610) 6341 7114
The General State Environmental Protection Administration 115 Xizhimennei South Street	(8610) 6615 3366
The Civil Aviation Administration of China 155 Dongshi West Boulevard	(8610) 6409 1114
The State Broadcasting, Film and Television Administration 2 Fuxinmenwai Boulevard	(8610) 6609 3114
The State Sports Administration 9 Stadium Road	(8610) 6711 2233
The State Statistics Bureau 75 Yuetan South Street	(8610) 6857 3311
The State Industrial & Commercial Administration 8 Sanlihe East Road	(8610) 6803 2233
The State News Publishing Administration 85 Dongsi South Boulevard	(8610) 6512 2800
The State Forestry Administration 18 Hepingli East Road	(8610) 8423 8800
The State Quality and Technology Supervision Administration 4 Zicun Road	(8610) 6202 2288
The State Drug Administration 38 North Lishi Road	(8610) 6831 3344
The State Intellectual Property Administration 6 West Tucheng Road	(8610) 6209 3114
The State Tourism Administration 9 Jiannei Avenue	(8610) 6520 1114
The State Religion Affairs Administration 22 Xi'anmen Avenue	(8610) 6402 3355

The State Council Consultancy Office 11 Qianmen East Avenue	(8610) 6513 0941
The State Council Taiwan Affairs Office 35 Fuwai Avenue	(8610) 6832 8320
The State Council News Office 225 Chaonei Avenue	(8610) 8652 1199
The State Archives Administration 21 Fengsheng Hutong	(8610) 6617 6354
Xinhua News Agency 57 Xuanwumen West Avenue	(8610) 6307 1114
Chinese Academy of Sciences 52 Sanlihe Road	(8610) 6859 7114
Chinese Academy of Social Sciences 5 Jianguomennei Avenue	(8610) 6513 7744
Chinese Academy of Engineering 3 Fuxin Road	(8610) 6851 8822
State Development Research Center 225 Chaoyangmennei Avenue	(8610) 6513 5566
State Public Administration Institute 6 Changchunqiao	(8610) 6842 7894
China Earthquake Administration 63 Fuxin Road	(8610) 6821 5522
China Meteorology Administration 46 Zhongguancun South Avenue	(8610) 6840 6114
China Securities Regulatory Commission 16 Jinrong Avenue	(8610) 8806 1000
State Safety Supervision Administration 21 Hepingli North Street	(8610) 6421 7766
State Mechanical Industry Administration 46 Sanlihe Road	(8610) 6859 4114

State Light Industry Administration 22 Fuchengmenwai Avenue	(8610) 6839 6114
State Textile Industry Administration 12 East Chang'an Boulevard	(8610) 6308 1114
State Construction Materials Industry Administration 11 Sanlihe Road	(8610) 6831 1144
State Foreign Experts Administration 1 Zhongguancun South Avenue	(8610) 6849 8888
State Tobacco Administration 26 Xuanwumen West Avenue	(8610) 6360 5678
State Ocean Administration 1 Fuxinmenwai Avenue	(8610) 6804 7634
State Cultural Treasury Administration 10 North Chaoyangmen Avenue	(8610) 6555 1572
State Chinese Medicines Administration 13 Baijiazhuang East Street	(8610) 6506 3322
State Foreign Exchange Administration 18 Fucheng Avenue	(8610) 6840 1188
State Quality Supervision, Inspection and Quarantine Administration 10 Chaoyangmenwai Avenue	(8610) 6599 4600

BEIJING MUNICIPAL GOVERNMENT AGENCIES

CPC Beijing Committee 3 Taijichang Avenue	(8610) 6512 1118
Beijing Municipal Government 2 Zhengyi Road	(8610) 6519 2233

Beijing Municipal Development and Planning Commission 2 Fuxinmen South Avenue	(8610) 6641 5588
Beijing Municipal Economic Commission 2 Zhengyi Road	(8610) 6519 3323
Beijing Municipal Construction Commission 3 Taijichang Avenue	(8610) 6308 8159
Beijing Municipal Commerce Commission 190 Chaonei Avenue	(8610) 6523 6688
Beijing Municipal Education Commission 109 Qianmen West Avenue	(8610) 6607 4354
Beijing Municipal Science & Technology Commission 16 Xizhimen South Avenue	(8610) 6615 3395
Beijing Municipal Personnel Administration 3 Taijichang	(8610) 6524 9721
Beijing Municipal Broadcasting and Television Administration 14 Jianwai Avenue	(8610) 65150033
Beijing Municipal Chinese Medicines Administration 5 Xiaoqudeng Hutong	(8610) 8403 6773
Beijing Municipal Industrial & Commercial Administration 9 Daozuomiao	(8610) 8269 0900
Beijing Municipal Health Administration 2 Huaibaishu Street	(8610) 6301 1386
Beijing Municipal Town & Village Enterprises Administration 6 Huixing East Street	(8610) 6496 8314
Beijing Municipal Land Resources & Housing Administration 1 Nanwanzhi Hutong, Nanheyan Avenue	(8610) 6512 4104

Beijing Municipal Culture Administration 7 West Chang'an Boulevard	(8610) 6602 2588
Beijing Municipal Public Safety Administration 9 Qianmen East Avenue	(8610) 8522 5050
Beijing Municipal Agriculture Administration 6 Yuming Middle Road	(8610) 6201 5149
Beijing Municipal Labor and Social Insurance Administration 2 Huaibaishu Street	(8610) 8801 1135
Beijing Municipal Quality and Technology Supervision Administration 3 Yuhui South Road	(8610) 6495 1177
Beijing Municipal Finance Administration 15 Fucheng Road	(8610) 6842 3355
Beijing Municipal Auditing Administration 73 Nancaiyuan Street	(8610) 63546664
Beijing Municipal Forestry Administration 8 Yuming Middle Road	(8610) 6205 2244
Beijing Municipal Price Administration 7 Binhe East Road	(8610) 6204 6644
Beijing Municipal Intellectual Property Administration 3 South Lishi Road	(8610) 6803 7177
Beijing Municipal Urban Planning Commission 60 South Lishi Road	(8610) 6801 1122
Beijing Municipal State Tax Administration 10 Chegongzhuang Avenue	(8610) 8837 2266
Beijing Municipal Customs House 6 Jianguomennei Avenue	(8610) 6519 4114
Beijing Municipal Statistics Administration 2 Huaibaishu Street	(8610) 6301 1066

Beijing Municipal Tourism Administration 28 Jianwai Avenue	(8610) 6515 8844
Beijing Municipal Local Tax Administration 8 Chegongzhuang Avenue	(8610) 8837 1766
Beijing Municipal Environmental Protection Administration 14 Chegongzhuang West Road	(8610) 6841 3817
Beijing Municipal Drug Administration 7 Xiaoyunli	(8610) 8455 1498
Beijing Municipal News Publishing Administration 24 Heping Street 11th Zone	(8610) 84251187
Bejing Municipal Government Foreign Affairs Office 2 Zhengyi Road	(8610) 6519 2708
Beijing Municipal Transportation Administration 2 Huaibaishu Street	(8610) 6302 1418

DISTRICT GOVERNMENT AGENCIES

Dongcheng District

District Government	(8610) 6403 4477
Development and Planning Committee	(8610) 6407 9927
Foreign Trade and Economic Trade Committee	(8610) 6405 8830
Foreign Affairs Office	(8610) 6403 4477

XICHENG DISTRICT

District Government	(8610) 8806 4477
Development and Planning Committee	(8610) 6603 2719
Foreign Trade and Economic Trade Committee	(8610) 6803 3197
Foreign Affairs Office	(8610) 6605 1208

CHONGWEN DISTRICT

District Government	(8610) 6711 0088
Development and Planning Committee	(8610) 6711 0311
Foreign Trade and Economic Trade Committee	(8610) 6711 0088
Foreign Affairs Office	(8610) 6711 0088

XUANWU DISTRICT

District Government	(8610) 6353 3366
Development and Planning Committee	(8610) 6353 1285
Foreign Trade and Economic Trade Committee	(8610) 6354 3202
Foreign Affairs Office	(8610) 6353 3366

CHAOYANG DISTRICT

District Government	(8610) 6509 4114
Development and Planning Committee	(8610) 6501 2644
Foreign Trade and Economic Trade Committee	(8610) 6509 4524
Foreign Affairs Office	(8610) 6509 4323

HAIDIAN DISTRICT

District Government	(8610) 6841 3388
Development and Planning Committee	(8610) 6255 3519
Foreign Trade and Economic Trade Committee	(8610) 8845 4762
Foreign Affairs Office	(8610) 6841 3388

FENGTAI DISTRICT

District Government	(8610) 6381 2244
Development and Planning Committee	(8610) 6381 5308
Foreign Trade and Economic Trade Committee	(8610) 6381 7907
Foreign Affairs Office	(8610) 6381 2244

SHIJINSHAN DISTRICT

District Government	(8610) 6887 3631
Development and Planning Committee	(8610) 6882 4023
Foreign Trade and Economic Trade Committee	(8610) 6886 3681
Foreign Affairs Office	(8610) 6886 0089

MENTOUGOU DISTRICT

District Government	(8610) 6984 3375
Development and Planning Committee	(8610) 6984 2187
Foreign Trade and Economic Trade Committee	(8610) 6984 4038
Foreign Affairs Office	(8610) 6984 3657

FANGSHAN DISTRICT

District Government	(8610) 8935 0012
Development and Planning Committee	(8610) 6937 9331
Foreign Trade and Economic Trade Committee	(8610) 8935 0395

Foreign Affairs Office	(8610) 8935 0488

TONGZHOU DISTRICT

District Government	(8610) 6955 2434
Development and Planning Committee	(8610) 6954 6553
Foreign Trade and Economic Trade Committee	(8610) 6954 3319
Foreign Affairs Office	(8610) 6954 3233

SHUNYI DISTRICT

District Government	(8610) 6944 3788
Development and Planning Committee	(8610) 6944 1363
Foreign Trade and Economic Trade Committee	(8610) 6944 3513
Foreign Affairs Office	(8610) 6944 3788

CHANGPING DISTRICT

District Government	(8610) 8974 1523
Development and Planning Committee	(8610) 6974 2252
Foreign Trade and Economic Trade Committee	(8610) 6974 1224
Foreign Affairs Office	(8610) 6974 3764

DAXING DISTRICT

District Government	(8610) 6924 3711
Development and Planning Committee	(8610) 6924 4968
Foreign Trade and Economic Trade Committee	(8610) 6924 3711
Foreign Affairs Office	(8610) 6924 3711

PINGGU DISTRICT

District Government	(8610) 6996 2218
Development and Planning Committee	(8610) 6996 1357
Foreign Trade and Economic Trade Committee	(8610) 6996 2876
Foreign Affairs Office	(8610) 6997 2744

HUAIROU DISTRICT

District Government	(8610) 6964 4113
Development and Planning Committee	(8610) 6964 1622
Foreign Trade and Economic Trade Committee	(8610) 6964 6342
Foreign Affairs Office	(8610) 6964 4545

MIYUN COUNTY

County Government	(8610) 6904 1684

Development and Planning Committee	(8610) 6904 2988
Foreign Trade and Economic Trade Committee	(8610) 6904 3521
Foreign Affairs Office	(8610) 6904 1869

YANQING COUNTY

County Government	(8610) 6911 2345
Development and Planning Committee	(8610) 6910 1063
Foreign Trade and Economic Trade Committee	(8610) 6914 4034
Foreign Affairs Office	(8610) 6916 6222

AIRLINE OFFICES

Aeroflot Russian International	(8610) 6500 2412
Air China	(8610) 6601 7755
Air Canada	(8610) 6468 2001
Air France	(8610) 6588 1388
Air Koryo	(8610) 6501 1557
Air Macau	(8610) 6515 8988
All Nippon Airways	(8610) 6590 9191
Asiana Airlines	(8610) 6468 4000
Austrian Airlines	(8610) 6462 2161
British Airways	(8610) 6512 3637
China United Airlines	(8610) 6340 2590
China Southern Airlines	(8610) 6567 2203
China Southwest Airlines	(8610) 6601 7579
China Eastern Airlines	(8610) 6468 1166
China Northern Airlines	(8610) 6601 7755
Ethiopian Airlines	(8610) 6459 1156
Finnair	(8610) 6512 7180
Hainan Airlines	(8610) 6603 9548
Hungarian Airlines	(8610) 6526 3091
Italian Airlines	(8610) 6505 6657
Iran Airlines	(8610) 6512 4940
Japan Airlines	(8610) 6513 0888
Korean Air	(8610) 8453 8888
KLM Royal Dutch Airlines	(8610) 6505 3505
Lufthansa German Airlines	(8610) 6465 4488
Malaysia Airlines	(8610) 6505 5640
Mongolian Airlines	(8610) 6507 9297
Northwest Airlines	(8610) 6505 3505
Pakistan International Airlines	(8610) 6505 1681

Romanian Airlines	(8610) 6500 2233
Royal Brunei Airlines	(8610) 6505 1681
SAS Scandinavian Airlines	(8610) 8527 6800
Sichuan Airlines	(8610) 6603 9529
Singapore Airlines	(8610) 6505 2233
Shandong Airlines	(8610) 6608 8777
Shanghai Airlines	(8610) 6456 4016
Shenzhen Airlines	(8610) 6605 0726
Thai Airways International	(8610) 6460 8899
United Airlines	(8610) 6463 8551
Wuhan Airlines	(8610) 6605 0727
Xiamen Airlines	(8610) 6601 7755
Xinhua Airlines	(8610) 6674 0118
Xinjiang Airlines	(8610) 6602 4084
Yugoslavia Airlines	(8610) 6590 3166
Yunnan Airlines	(8610) 8401 7871

FOREIGN CHAMBERS

AMERICAN CHAMBER OF COMMERCE

19-03 China Resources Tower, Dongcheng District
Tel: (8610) 8519 1920 Fax: (8610) 8519 1910

AUSTRALIAN CHAMBER OF COMMERCE

#03-18 Great Wall Sheraton Hotel, Chaoyang District
Tel: (8610) 6590 5566 Fax: (8610) 6590 5281

BRITISH CHAMBER OF COMMERCE

Room 1001, China Life Tower, 16 Chaoyangmenwai Avenue, Beijing
Tel: (8610) 8525 1111 Fax: (8610) 8525 1100

CANADA-CHINA BUSINESS COUNCIL

#18-22 CITIC Building, 19 Jianguomenwai Avenue
Tel: (8610) 6512 6120 Fax: (8610) 6512 1125

CHINA INTERNATIONAL CHAMBER OF COMMERCE

1 Fuxinmenwai Avenue
Tel: (8610) 6801 3344 Fax: (8610) 6803 0747

ECONOMIST CORPORATE NETWORK

Tel: (8610) 65102152

EUROPEAN UNION OF COMMERCE

Tel: (8610) 6462 2065

FRENCH CHAMBER OF COMMERCE

S123 Lufthansa Center Apartments, Chaoyang District
Tel: (8610) 8451 2071

GERMAN CHAMBER OF COMMERCE

#08-11 Landmark Tower Two, Chaoyang District
Tel: (8610) 6590 0926 Fax: (8610) 6590 6313

HONG KONG CHAMBER OF COMMERCE

7 Jiannei Avenue, Dongcheng District
Tel: (8610) 6510 1583 Fax: (8610) 6510 1584

JAPAN CHAMBER OF COMMERCE

Changfugong Center Office Building, Chaoyang District
Tel: (8610) 6513 0829 Fax: (8610) 6513 9859

ITALY CHAMBER OF COMMERCE

#36-05 Jingguang Tower, Chaoyang District
Tel: (8610) 6597 3078 Fax: (8610) 6597 3066

KOREAN CHAMBER OF COMMERCE

32 Landmark Bridge Road, Chaoyang District
Tel: (8610) 6464 3621 Fax: (8610) 6464 3620

SWEDISH CHAMBER OF COMMERCE

#03-13 Radisson Hotel
6A North 3rd Ring East Road, Chaoyang District
Tel: (8610) 6466 3388 Fax: (8610) 6468 4190

US-CHINA BUSINESS COUNCIL

Tel: (8610) 6592 0721

EMBASSIES

AFGHANISTAN, EMBASSY OF ISLAMIC STATE OF

8 Dongzhimenwai Avenue Beijing 100600
Tel: (8610) 6532 1582 Fax: (8610) 0 6532 2269

ALBANIA, EMBASSY OF REPUBLIC OF

28 Guanghua Road, Jianguomenwai Beijing 100600
Tel: (8610) 6532 1120 Fax: (8610) 6535 451

ALGERIA, EMBASSY OF DEMOCRATIC PEOPLE'S REPUBLIC OF

7 Sanlitun Road, Sanlitun Beijing 100600
Tel: (8610) 6532 1231 Fax: (8610) 6532 1648

ANGOLA, EMBASSY OF REPUBLIC OF

1-8-1 Taiyuan Diplomatic Office Building Beijing 100600
Tel: (8610) 6532 6968 Fax: (8610) 6532 6992

ARGENTINA

11 East No. 5 Road, Sanlitun Beijing 100600
Tel: (8610) 6532 2090 Fax: (8610) 6532 2319

ARMENIA

9-2-62 Tayuan Diplomatic Apartments Beijing 100600
Tel: (86) (10) 6532 5677 Fax: (86) (10) 6532 5654

AUSTRALIA

15 Dongzhimenwai Avenue, Dongcheng District Beijing 100600
Tel: (8610) 6532 2331 Fax: (8610) 6532 4606

AUSTRIA

5 Xiushui South Street, Chaoyang District Beijing 100600
Tel: (8610) 6532 2061 Fax: (8610) 6532 1505

AZERBAIJIAN

3-2-32 Sanlitun Diplomatic Apartments Beijing 100600
Tel: (8610) 6532 4614 Fax: (8610) 6532 4615

BANGLADESH

42 Guanghua Road Beijing 100600
Tel: (8610) 6532 2521 Fax: (8610) 0 6532 4346

BELARUS

1 Ritan East No. 1 Street Beijing 100600
Tel: (8610) 6532 6749 Fax: (8610) 6532 6417

BELGIUM

6 Sanlitun Road Beijing 100600
Tel: (8610) 6532 1736 Fax: (8610) 6532 5097

BENIN

38 Guanghua Road Beijing 100600
Tel: (8610) 6532 2741 Fax: (8610) 6532 5103

BOLIVIA

2-3-2 Tayuan Diplomatic Apartments Beijing 100600
Tel: (8610) 6532 3074

BOSNIA AND HERZEGOVINA

1-5-1 Tayuan Diplomatic Office Building Beijing 100600
Tel: (8610) 6532 6587 Fax: (8610) 6532 6418

BOTSWANA

IBM Tower Pacific Century Place
2A Gongti North Road Beijing 100027
Tel: (86) (10) 6539 1616

BRAZIL

27 Guanghua Road Beiing 100600
Tel: (86) (10) 6532 2881 Fax: (86) (10) 6532 2751

BRUNEI DARUSSALAM

Villa 3, Qijiayuan Diplomatic Apartments Beijing 100600
Tel: (86) (10) 6532 4094 Fax: (86) (10) 6532 4095

BULGARIA

4 Xiushui North Street Beijing 100600
Tel: (8610) 6532 1946 Fax: (8610) 6532 4502

BURUNDI

25 Guanghua Road Beijing 102600
Tel: (8610) 0 6532 2328

CAMBODIA

9 Dongzhimenwai Avenue Beijing 100600
Tel: (8610) 6532 1889 Fax: (8610) 6532 3207

CAMERON

7 Sanlitun East No. 5 Street Beijing 100600
Tel: (8610) 6532 1818 Fax: (8610) 6532 1761

CANADA

19 Dongzhimenwai Chaoyang District Beijing 100600
Tel: (8610) 6532 3031 Fax: (8610) 6532 4311

CHILE

1 Sanlitun East No. 4 Street Beijing 100600
Tel: (8610) 6532 1591 Fax: (8610) 6532 3170

COLUMBIA

34 Guanghua Road Beijing 100600
Tel: (8610) 6532 3377 Fax: (8610) 6532 1969

CONGO

7 Sanlitun East No. 4 Street Beijing 100600
Tel: (8610) 6532 1658

COTED IVOIRE

9 North Little Street, Sanlitun Beijing 100600
Tel: (8610) 6532 1482 Fax: (8610) 6532 2407

CROATIA

2-7-2 Sanlitun Diplomatic Apartments Beijing 100600
Tel: (8610) 6532 6241 Fax: (8610) 6532 6257

CUBA

1 Xiushui South Street Beijing 100600
Tel: (8610) 6532 6568 Fax: (8610) 6532 2017

CYPRUS

2-13-2 Tayuan Diplomatic Office Building Beijing 100600
Tel: (8610) 6532 5057 Fax: (8610) 6532 4244

CZECH REPUBLIC

Ritan Road, Jianguomenwai Beijing 100600
Tel: (8610) 6532 6902 Fax: (8610) 6532 5653

DENMARK

1 Sanlitun East No. 5 Street Beijing 100600
Tel: (8610) 6532 2431 Fax: (8610) 6532 2439

KOREA, EMBASSY OF THE DEMOCRATIC PEOPLE'S REPUBLIC OF

11 Ritan North Road, Chaoyang District Beijing 100600
Tel: (8610) 6532 1186 Fax: (8610) 6532 4862

ECUADOR

2-62 Sanlitun Diplomatic Office Building Beijing 100600
Tel: (8610) 6532 3849 Fax: (8610) 6532 4371

EGYPT

2 Ritan East Road Beijing 100600
Tel: (8610) 6532 1825 Fax: (8610) 6532 5365

EQUATORIAL GUINEA

2 Sanlitun East No. 4 Street Beijing 100600
Tel: (8610) 6532 3679 Fax: (8610) 6532 3805

ERITREA

2-10-1 Tayuan Diplomatic Apartments Beijing 100600
Tel: (8610) 6532 6534 Fax: (8610) 6532 6532

ESTONIA

C-617 Kampinski Hotel Beijing 100016
Tel: (86) (10) 6463 7913

ETHIOPIA

3 Xiushui South Street Beijing 100600
Tel: (8610) 6532 5258

FINLAND

26F Kerry Center South Tower, 1 Guanghua Road, Chaoyang District Beijing 100020
Tel: (8610) 8529 8541 Fax: (8610) 8529 8544

FRANCE

3 Sanlitun East No. 3 Street Beijing 100600
Tel: (8610) 6532 1331 Fax: (8610) 6532 4841

GABON

30 Guanghua Road Beijing 100600
Tel: (8610) 6532 2810 Fax: (8610) 6532 2621

GERMANY

17 Dongzhimenwai Avenue Beijing 100600
Tel: (8610) 6532 2161 Fax: (8610) 6532 5335

GHANA

8 Sanlitun Road Beijing 100600
Tel: (86) (10) 6532 1319
Fax: (86) (10) 6532 3602

GREECE

19 Guanghua Road Beijing 100600
Tel: (8610) 6532 1317 Fax: (8610) 6532 1277

GUINEA

2 Sanlitun West No. 6 Street Beijing 100600
Tel: (8610) 6532 3649 Fax: (8610) 6532 4957

GUYANA

1 Xiushui East Street Beijing 100600
Tel: (8610) 6532 1337 Fax: (8610) 6532 5741

HUNGARY

10 Dongzhimenwai Avenue Beijing 100600
Tel: (8610) 6532 1431 Fax: (8610) 6532 5053

ICELAND

802 Landmark Tower
8 East 3rd Ring North Road Beijing 100004
Tel: (8610) 6590 7795 Fax: (8610) 6590 7801

INDIA

1 Ritan East Road Beijing 100600
Tel: (8610) 6532 1856 Fax: (8610) 6532 4684

INDONESIA

Sanlitun Diplomatic Apartments Tower B Beijing 100600
Tel: (8610) 6532 5488 Fax: (8610) 6532 5368

IRAN

13 Sanlitun East No. 6 Street Beijing 100600
Tel: (8610) 6532 2040

IRAQ

25 Xiushui North Street Beijing 100600
Tel: (8610) 6532 3385 Fax: (8610) 6532 1596

IRELAND

3 Ritan East Road Beijing 100600
Tel: (8610) 6532 2691 Fax: (8610) 6532 6857

ISRAEL

No. 17 Tianze Road, Chaoyang District Beijing 100600
Tel: (8610) 6532 7788 Fax: (8610) 6505 0328

ITALY

2 Sanlitun East No. 2 Street Beijing 100600
Tel: (8610) 6532 2131 Fax: (8610) 6532 4676

JAPAN

7 Ritan Road Beijing 100600
Tel: (8610) 6532 2361 Fax: (8610) 6532 4625

JORDAN

5 Sanlitun East No. 6 Street Beijing 100600
Tel: (8610) 6532 1558 Fax: (8610) 6532 4305

KAZAKHSTAN

9 Sanlitun East No. 6 Street Beijing 100600
Tel: (8610) 6532 6182 Fax: (8610) 6532 6183

KENYA

4 Sanlitun West No. 6 Street Beijing 100600
Tel: (8610) 6532 3381 Fax: (8610) 6532 1770

LAOS

11 Sanlitun East No. 4 Street Beijing 100600
Tel: (8610) 6532 1224 Fax: (8610) 6532 6748

LEBANON

10 Sanlitun East No. 6 Street Beijing 100600
Tel: (8610) 6532 2197 Fax: (8610) 6532 2770

LESOTHO

302 Dongwai Diplomatic Office Building Beijing 100600
Tel: (8610) 6532 6842 Fax: (8610) 6532 6845

LIBYA

3 Sanlitun East No. 6 Street Beijing 100600
Tel: (8610) 6532 3666 Fax: (8610) 6532 3391

LITHUANIA

18 Xiaoyun Road, Chaoyang District Beijing 100600
Tel: (8610) 6468 1152 Fax: (8610) 6468 1150

LUXEMBURG

21 Neiwubu Street Beijing 100600
Tel: (8610) 6513 5937 Fax: (8610) 6513 7268

KUWAIT

21 Guanghua Road Beijing 100600
Tel: (8610) 6532 2216 Fax: (8610) 6532 1607

MADAGASCAR

3 Sanlitun East No. 3 Street Beijing 100600
Tel: (8610) 6532 1353 Fax: (8610) 6532 2102

MALAYSIA

13 Dongzhimen Avenue Beijing 100600
Tel: (8610) 6532 2531 Fax: (8610) 6532 5032

MALI

8 Sanlitun West No. 4 Street Beijing 100600
Tel: (8610) 6532 1704 Fax: (8610) 6532 1618

MALTA

1-5-2 Sanlitun Diplomatic Apartments Beijing 100600
Tel: (8610) 6532 3114 Fax: (8610) 6532 6125

MAURITANIA

9 Sanlitun East No. 3 Street Beijing 100600
Tel: (8610) 6532 1346 Fax: (8610) 6532 1685

MAURITIUS

23 Dongzhimenwai Avenue Beijing 100600
Tel: (86) (10) 6532 5695 Fax: (8610) 6532 5706

MEXICO

5 Sanlitun East No. 5 Street Beijing 100600
Tel: (8610) 6532 2574 Fax: (8610) 6532 3744

MOLDOVA

2-4-2 Tayuan Diplomatic Office Building Beijing 100600
Tel: (8610) 6532 5494 Fax: (8610) 6532 5379

MONGOLIA

2 Xinshui North Street Beijing 100600
Tel: (8610) 6532 1203 Fax: (8610) 6532 5045

MOROCCO

16 Sanlitun Road Beijing 100600
Tel: (8610) 65321796 Fax: (8610) 65321453

MOZAMBIQUE

1-7-2 Tayuan Diplomatic Office Building Beijing 100600
Tel: (8610) 6532 3664 Fax: (8610) 6532 5189

MYANMAR

6 Dongzhimenwai Avenue Beijing 100600
Tel: (8610) 6532 1425 Fax: (8610) 6532 1344

NAMIBIA

2-9-2 Tayuan Diplomatic Office Building Beijing 100600
Tel: (8610) 6532 4810 Fax: (8610) 6532 4549

NEPAL

1 Sanlitun West No. 6 Street Beijing 100600
Tel: (8610) 6532 1795 Fax: (8610) 6532 3251

NETHERLANDS

4 Liangmahe South Road Beijing 100600
Tel: (8610) 6532 1131 Fax: (8610) 6532 4689

NEW ZEALAND

No. 1 Ritan Road East Chaoyang District Street Beijing 100600
Tel: (8610) 6532 2731 Fax: (8610) 6532 4317

NIGERIA

2 Sanlitun West No. 5 Street Beijing 100600
Tel: (8610) 6532 3631 Fax: (8610) 6532 1650

NORWAY

1 Sanlitun East Beijing 100600
Tel: (8610) 6532 2261 Fax: (8610) 6532 2392

OMAN

6 Liangmahe South Road Beijing 100600
Tel: (8610) 6532 3692 Fax: (8610) 6532 7185

PAKISTAN

1 Dongzhimenwai Avenue Beijing 100600
Tel: (8610) 6532 6600 Fax: (8610) 6532 2715

PALESTINE

2 Sanlitun East No. 2 Street Beijing 100600
Tel: (8610) 6532 1361 Fax: (8610) 6532 3241

PAPUA NEW GUINEA

2-11-2 Tayuan Diplomatic Apartments Beijing 100600
Tel: (8610) 6532 4312 Fax: (8610) 6532 4689

PERU

2-9 Sanlitun Foreign Diplomatic Office Building Beijing 100600
Tel: (8610) 6532 3719 Fax: (8610) 6532 2178

PHILIPPINES

23 Xiushui North Street Beijing 100600
Tel: (8610) 6532 2451 Fax: (8610) 6532 3761

POLAND

1 Ritan Road Beijing 100600
Tel: (8610) 6532 1235 Fax: (8610) 6532 1745

PORTUGAL

8 Sanlitun East, Chaoyang District Beijing 100600
Tel: (8610) 6532 3497 Fax: (8610) 6532 4796

REPUBLIC OF KOREA

2 Sanlitun West No. 6 Street Beijing 100600
Tel: (8610) 6532 6774 Fax: (8610) 6532 6778

ROMANIA

Ritan Road East No. 2 Street Beijing 100600
Tel: (8610) 6532 3442 Fax: (8610) 6532 5728

RUSSIAN FEDERATION

4 Dongzhimennei Middle Street Beijing 100600
Tel: (8610) 6532 2051 Fax: (8610) 6532 4851

RWANDA

30 Xiushui North Street Beijing 100600
Tel: (8610) 6532 2193 Fax: (8610) 6532 2006

SAUDI ARABIA

1 Sanlitun North Little Street Beijing 100600
Tel: (8610) 6532 4825 Fax: (86) (10) 6532 5324

SIERRA LEONE

7 Dongzhimenwai Avenue Beijing 100600
Tel: (8610) 6532 1222 Fax: (8610) 6532 3752

SINGAPORE

1 Xiushui North Road, Chaoyang District Beijing 100600
Tel: (8610) 8529 6256 Fax: (8610) 8529 6244

QATAR

Xijiao Garden Apartments Beijing 100600
Tel: (8610) 6532 2231 Fax: (8610) 6532 5274

SLOVENIA

Yaqu Garden of King's Garden Villa Beijing 100016
Tel: (8610) 6468 1030 Fax: (8610) 6468 1040

SLOVAK

Ritan Road, Chaoyang District Beijing 100600
Tel: (8610) 6532 1531 Fax: (8610) 6532 4814

SOUTH AFRICA

5 Dongzhimenwai Avenue, Dongcheng District Beijing 100600
Tel: (8610) 6532 0172 Fax: (8610) 6532 0177

SPAIN

9 Sanlitun Road, Chaoyang District, Beijing 100600
Tel: (8610) 65321986 Fax: (8610) 65323401

SRI LANKA

3 Jianhua Road, Jianguomenwai Beijing 100600
Tel: (8610) 6532 1861 Fax: (8610) 6532 5426

SUDAN

1 Sanlitun East No.2 Street Beijing 100600
Tel: (8610) 6532 3516 Fax: (8610) 6532 1207

YUGOSLAVIA

1 Sanlitun East No. 6 Street Beijing 100600
Tel: (8610) 6532 3516 Fax: (8610) 6532 1207

SWEDEN

3 Dongzhimenwai Avenue Beijing 100600
Tel: (8610) 6532 3331 Fax: (8610) 6532 5008

SWITZERLAND

3 Sanlitun East No. 5 Street Beijing 100600
Tel: (8610) 6532 2736 Fax: (8610) 6532 4353

SYRIA

6 Sanlitun East No. 4 Street Beijing 100600
Tel: (8610) 6532 1372

TAJIKISTAN

9-1-101 Tayuan Diplomatic Apartments Beijing 100600
Tel: (8610) 6532 2598 Fax: (8610) 6532 3039

THAILAND

40 Guanghua Road Beijing 100600
Tel: (8610) 6532 1903

TOGO

11 Dongzhimenwai Avenue Beijing 100600
Tel: (8610) 6532 2202 Fax: (8610) 6532 5884

SOMALIA

2 Sanlitun Road Beijing 100600
Tel: (8610) 6532 1752

SURINAME

1-3-32 Jianwai Diplomatic Apartments Beijing 100600
Tel: (8610) 6532 2939 Fax: (8610) 6532 2941

TANZANIA

8 Liangmahe South Road Beijing 100600
Tel: (8610) 6532 1491 Fax: (8610) 6532 4351

TUNISIA

1 Sanlitun East Road Beijing 100600
Tel: (8610) 6532 2435 Fax: (8610) 6532 5818

TURKEY

9 Sanlitun East No. 5 Street Beijing 100600
Tel: (8610) 65321715

UGANDA

5 Sanlitun East Street Beijing 100600
Tel: (8610) 6532 1708

UNITED STATES

3 Xiushui North Street Beijing 100600
Tel: (8610) 6532 3831

UKRAINE

11 Sanlitun East No. 6 Street Beijing 100600
Tel: (8610) 6532 6359 Fax: (8610) 6532 6765

UNITED KINGDOM

11 Guanghua Road Beijing 100600
Tel: (8610) 6532 1961 Fax: (8610) 6532 1937

URUGUAY

2-7-2 Tayuan Office Building Beijing 100600
Tel: (8610) 6532 4445 Fax: (8610) 6532 4357

UZBEKISTAN

11 Sanlitun North Street Beijing 100600
Tel: (8610) 6532 6305 Fax: (8610) 6532 3621

VENEZUELA

14 Sanlitun Road Beijing 100600
Tel: (8610) 6532 1295

YEMEN

5 Sanlitun East No. 3 Street Beijing 100600
Tel: (8610) 6532 1558 Fax: (8610) 6532 4305

ZIMBABWE

7 Sanlitun East No. 3 Street Beijing 100600
Tel: (8610) 6532 3795 Fax: (8610) 6532 5383

LOCAL BANKS

Industrial & Commercial Bank of China Beijing	(8610) 6641 0055
• Dongcheng	(8610) 8403 7286
• Wangfujing	(8610) 6525 1290
• Xicheng	(8610) 6605 6108
• Chongwen	(8610) 6727 1188
• Xuanwu	(8610) 6348 0658
• Haidian	(8610) 6255 1286
• Chaoyang	(8610) 6599 1155
• Fengtai	(8610) 6381 5968
• Shijingshan	(8610) 6887 4128
• Daxing	(8610) 6924 3119
• Changping	(8610) 6974 6269
• Mentougou	(8610) 6984 4598
• Tongzhou	(8610) 6954 6362
• Fangshan	(8610) 6913 4765
• Miyun	(8610) 6904 2424
• Huairou	(8610) 6964 2388
• Pinggu	(8610) 6996 1425
• Shunyi	(8610) 6944 3932
• Yanqing	(8610) 6914 3392
China Construction Bank Beijing	(8610) 95533
Agricultural Bank of China Beijing	(8610) 6835 3756
• Dongcheng	(8610) 6559 4210
• Xicheng	(8610) 6804 3405
• Chongwen	(8610) 6760 3862
• Xuanwu	(8610) 6360 2266
• Haidian	(8610) 6253 3660
• Chaoyang	(8610) 6552 2914
• Fengtai	(8610) 6381 2148
• Shijingshan	(8610) 6883 6236

• Daxing	(8610) 6924 3488
• Changping	(8610) 6974 2829
• Fangshan	(8610) 6931 3609
• Miyun	(8610) 6904 1923
• Huairou	(8610) 6964 4982
• Pinggu	(8610) 6996 1393
• Shunyi	(8610) 6944 4435
• Yanqing	(8610) 6914 4474
Bank of China Beijing	(8610) 6519 9114
• Dongcheng	(8610) 6406 3180
• Wangfujing	(8610) 8518 1155
• Xicheng	(8610) 6800 1383
• Chongwen	(8610) 6702 6696
• Xuanwu	(8610) 6304 4230
• Haidian	(8610) 6261 3913
• Chaoyang	(8610) 6410 8145
• Fengtai	(8610) 6385 8131
• Shijingshan	(8610) 6886 4968
• Changping	(8610) 6970 4842
• Tongzhou	(8610) 6955 8124
• Fangshan	(8610) 8935 6533
• Miyun	(8610) 6904 3884
• Huairou	(8610) 6964 4815
• Pinggu	(8610) 6996 2353
• Shunyi	(8610) 6944 5330
• Yanqing	(8610) 6914 1843
Beijing City Commercial Bank	(8610) 8422 7800
• Wangfujing	(8610) 6522 0955
• Xicheng	(8610) 8808 7435
• Chongwen	(8610) 6701 0568
• Xuanwu	(8610) 6326 4141
• Haidian	(8610) 6257 2919
• Chaoyang	(8610) 6436 2269
• Shijingshan	(8610) 6887 8220
Huaxia Bank Beijing	(8610) 6318 8214
• Xidan	(8610) 6615 0176
• Fuxinmen	(8610) 6608 2003
• Zhongguancun	(8610) 6261 7603
• Jianguomen	(8610) 6522 5305
• Jingguang Center	(8610) 6597 2812
• Shijingshan	(8610) 6829 4148

• Asian Villages	(8610) 6492 6417
CITIC Industrial Bank Beijing	(8610) 6621 9988
• International Plaza	(8610) 6512 5578
• Capital Tower	(8610) 6466 0187
• Chaoyang	(8610) 6538 9582
• Haidian	(8610) 6261 3873
• Chongwen	(8610) 6715 1791
• Wangfujing	(8610) 6526 8282
China Everbright Bank Beijing	(8610) 6856 5577
• Wangfujing	(8610) 6527 9070
• Jianguomen	(8610) 6592 6247
• Xuanwu	(8610) 6326 3651
• Haidian	(8610) 6251 0230
• Chaoyang	(8610) 6552 0322
• Zhongguancun	(8610) 6262 7243
• Xicheng	(8610) 6800 2203
China Minsheng Banking Corporation Beijing	(8610) 6857 9321
• Fuchengmen	(8610) 6858 8449
• Jianguomen	(8610) 6532 5937
• Zhongguancun	(8610) 6262 9093
• Chaoyang	(8610) 6588 4529
China Merchants Bank Beijing	(8610) 6642 6969
• Chang'an Boulevard	(8610) 6529 2004
• Zhongguancun	(8610) 6254 4826
• Wangfujing	(8610) 6527 2079
• Chaoyang	(8610) 8528 2371
• Chongwen	(8610) 6708 9485
Shanghai Pudong Development Bank Beijing	(8610) 6834 7529
• Financial Street	(8610) 68091855
• Xuanwu	(8610) 6351 5446
• Zhongguancun	(8610) 6255 0716
• Chaoyang	(8610) 6599 2606
• Jianguo Road	(8610) 6581 2275
• Haidian	(8610) 8266 4290
• Yabao Road	(8610) 8519 2332
• Capital Stadium	(8610) 8802 6239
• East 3rd Ring	(8610) 8458 4706
Guangdong Development Bank Beijing	(8610) 6526 9966
• Xinjiekou	(8610) 6204 8191

- Hangtianqiao (8610) 8841 5104
- Asian Games Village (8610) 6491 0397
- Zhongguancun (8610) 6251 0781
- Yuetan (8610) 6808 3560
- Jianguo Road (8610) 6566 6953
- International Exhibition Center (8610) 84603165
- West Railway Station (8610) 6395 6520
- Dongcheng (8610) 6418 2990

China Bank of Communications Beijing (8610) 6610 1190

- Dongdan (8610) 6513 6078
- Wangfujing (8610) 6528 9470
- Asian Games Village (8610) 6491 2517
- Huixing East Street (8610) 6498 0665
- Hepingli (8610) 6423 4670
- Fuwai Avenue (8610) 6809 5539
- Haidian (8610) 6262 4766
- Xizhimen (8610) 6225 0032
- Xidan (8610) 6607 8436

Shenzhen Development Bank Beijing (8610) 6642 1728

- Anhua (8610) 6442 2721
- West 3rd Ring (8610) 6398 4901
- Sanyuanqiao (8610) 8453 8108
- Zhongguancun (8610) 6254 7457
- Chaoyang (8610) 6501 5588

ACCOMMODATION

★★★★★

NAME OF HOTEL	ADDRESS	TELEPHONE/FAX
Beijing Hotel	33 East Chang'an Ave	T(8610) 6513 7766 F(8610) 6513 7307
China World Hotel	1 Jianguomenwai Ave	T(8610) 6505 2266 F(8610) 6505 0828
Beijing Kempinski Hotel	50 Liangmaqiao Road, Chaoyang District	T(8610) 6465 3388 F(8610) 6465 3366
Tianlun Dynasty Hotel	50 Wangfujing Ave, Dongcheng District	T(8610) 6513 8888 F(8610) 6513 7866
Crowne Plaza	48 Wangfujing Ave, Dongcheng District	T(8610) 6513 3388 F(8610) 6513 2513
Beijing International Hotel	9 Jianguomennei Ave	T(8610) 6512 6688 F(8610) 6512 9972
Beijing Xiyuan Hotel	1 Sanlihe Road	T(8610) 6831 3388 F(8610) 6831 4577

★★★★

NAME OF HOTEL	ADDRESS	TELEPHONE/FAX
Fragrance Hill Hotel	Fragrance Hill Park, Haidian District	T(8610) 6259 1166 F(8610) 6259 1382
Rosedale Hotel Beijing	8 Jiangtai West Road, Chaoyang District	T(8610) 6436 2288 F(8610) 6436 1818
Central Garden Hotel	18 Gaoliangqiao xijie Xizhimenwai Ave, Haidian District	T(8610) 5156 8888 F(8610) 5156 6789
SCITECH Hotel	22 Jianguomenwai Avenue	T(8610) 6512 3388 F(8610) 6512 3542
Debao Hotel	22 Debao Xinyuan, Xicheng District	T(8610) 6831 8866 F(8610) 6833 4571
Millennium Hotel	338 Guanganmennei Street, XuanWu District	T(8610) 6357 8888 F(8610) 6357 4003

Serviced Apartments

NAME OF HOTEL	ADDRESS	TELEPHONE/FAX
China World Apartments	No.1, Jian Guo Men Wai Avenue	T(8610) 6505 2686 F(8610) 6505 0531
East Lake Villas	35 Dongzhimenwai Main Street	T(8610) 6467 7966 F(8610) 6467 7075
Landmark Towers	8 North Dongsanhuan Road, Chaoyang District	T(8610) 6590 6688 F(86 10) 6590 6922
Kerry Residence	Beijing Kerry Centre, 1 Guang Hua Road, Chaoyang District	T(8610) 8529 8255 F(8610) 8529 8278
The Tower Apartments at Oriental Plaza	No.1, East Chang An Ave, Dong Cheng District	T(8610) 8518 1188
The Ascott Beijing	108 B Jianguo Road Chaoyang District Beijing, 100022, China	T(8610) 6567 8100

MEDICAL/ DENTAL

FOREIGN HOSPITALS AND A-CLASS HEALTHCARE SERVICES

AEA International	(8610) 6462 9112
Beijing Hong Kong International Clinic	(8610) 6553 2288
Beijing International Medical Service Center	(8610) 6465 1384
Beijing United Family Hospital	(8610) 6433 3960
Friendship Hospital A-Class Division	(8610) 8316 9706
Guree Dental	(8610) 6505 9439
Peking Union Medical Hospital	(8610) 6529 5269
PLA General Hospital A-Class Division	(8610) 6693 7329
Sino-German Poly Clinic	(8610) 6501 1983
Vista Clinic	(8610) 8529 6618
Xiehe Hospital A-Class Division	(8610) 6529 5269
Bayley & Jackson Medical Centre	(8610) 68562 9998

LOCAL HOSPITALS

• Dongcheng District

Xiehe Hospital	(8610) 6529 6114
Tongren Hospital	(8610) 6512 9911
Beijing Hospital	(8610) 6513 2266
Gulou Hospital	(8610) 6401 2356
Beijing No. 6 Hospital	(8610) 6403 5566
Beijing General Military Hospital	(8610) 6672 1629
Beijing Traditional Chinese Medicines Hospital	(8610) 6401 6677

• Xicheng District

Fuwai Hospital	(8610) 6831 4466
PKU No. 1 Hospital	(8610) 6617 1122
PKU People's Hospital	(8610) 6831 4422
Beijing Emergence Medical Center	(8610) 6601 3877
China Children Health Guidance Center	(8610) 6802 5864

• Chongwen District

Tiantan Hospital	(8610) 6701 6611
Chongwen No. 1 Hospital	(8610) 6722 2060
Qianmen Hospital	(8610) 6702 1291

• Xuanwu District

Beijing Friendship Hospital	(8610) 6301 4411
Xuanwu Hospital	(8610) 6301 3355

• Chaoyang District

Sino-Japan Friendship Hospital	(8610) 6422 1122
Anzhen Hospital	(8610) 6441 2341
Chaoyang Hospital	(8610) 6500 7755
Beijing Armed Police General Hospital	(8610) 6416 1188
CAAC General Hospital	(8610) 8576 2244
• Haidian District	
PKU No. 3 Hospital	(8610) 6201 7691
Haidian Hospital	(8610) 6255 1593
PLA General Hospital	(8610) 6693 7329
General Navy Hospital	(8610) 6858 7733
General Air Force Hospital	(8610) 6843 7770
Armed Forces General Hospital	(8610) 6821 2211
Railway General Hospital	(8610) 6322 5544
Chinese Academy of Traditional Chinese Medicines	(8610) 6287 5599
• Fengtai District	
Fengtai Hospital	(8610) 6381 3667
Armed Forces No. 3 Hospital	(8610) 6821 2266
• Shijingshan	
Shijingshan Hospital	(8610) 6866 8131
Capital Iron & Steel Hospital	(8610) 6887 5731
• Fangshan	
Fangshan No.1 Hospital	(8610) 6931 3443
Yanshan Petrochemicals Corp. Hospital	(8610) 6934 2517
• Mentougou	
Mentougou Traditional Chinese Medicines Hospital	(8610) 6984 2182
• Tongzhou	
Tongzhou Traditional Chinese Medicines Hospital	(8610) 6954 2682
• Shunyi	
Shunyi Hospital	(8610) 6944 4548
• Huairou	
Huairou Hospital	(8610) 6964 4822
• Miyun	
Miyun Hospital	(8610) 6904 3990
• Yanqing	
Yanqing Hospital	(8610) 6914 4448

- Daxing
  Renhe Hospital (8610) 6924 2469

- Pinggu
  Pinggu Hospital (8610) 8999 2001

EDUCATIONAL INSTITUTIONS

INTERNATIONAL KINDERGARTENS

Beanstalk International Kindergarten	(8610) 6466 3311
Beijing Oxford Little Professor Kindergarten	(8610) 6493 6626
British Council	(8610) 6590 6903
Children's House	(8610) 6505 2288
Deutsche Schule Peking	(8610) 6532 2536
Lido Kindergarten	(8610) 6437 6688

PRIMARY INTERNATIONAL SCHOOLS

Fang Cao Di Primary School	(8610) 6509 4329
International Academy of Beijing	(8610) 6432 3151
The Montessori School of Beijing	(8610) 6532 6713
Western Academy of Beijing	(8610) 8456 4155
Yew Chung Beijing International School	(8610) 6594 1731

SECONDARY INTERNATIONAL SCHOOLS

Beijing BISS International School	(8610) 6443 3151
Beijing No. 55 Middle School	(8610) 6467 1356
International School of Beijing	(8610) 6437 6688
New School of Collaborative Learning	(8610) 6298 1620
The Western Academy of Beijing	(8610) 6437 5935

UNIVERSITIES AND COLLEGES

Peking University	(8610) 6275 2114
Tsinghua University	(8610) 6251 1361
People's University of China	(8610) 6251 1361
Beijing Normal University	(8610) 6220 6183
Beijing University of International Studies	(8610) 6842 2277
Beijing University of Language & Culture	(8610) 8230 3114
Beijing University of Aviation & Aerospace	(8610) 8231 6114
Beijing Industrial & Commercial University	(8610) 6890 4661
China Agricultural University	(8610) 6289 2406
Beijing Broadcasting College	(8610) 6577 9460

Beijing Institute of Technology	(8610) 6891 3333
Beijing University of Science & Technology	(8610) 6233 2312
Beijing University of Post & Telecom	(8610) 6228 2222
Beijing University of Chemical Technology	(8610) 6443 4771
Northern Jiaotong University	(8610) 6225 6622
Beijing Fashion College	(8610) 6428 8317
Beijing University of Traditional Chinese Medicines	(8610) 6428 6805
Central University of Finance & Economics	(8610) 6228 8114
Central University of Nationalities	(8610) 6893 2442
Beijing Forestry University	(8610) 6233 8222
Beijing Meteorological College	(8610) 6840 6114
Beijing No. 2 International Studies College	(8610) 6577 8564
China University of Politics & Law	(8610) 6974 5577
Central Institute of Arts & Painting	(8610) 6438 0462
Central Music Academy	(8610) 6642 5702
China Music Academy	(8610) 6487 4884
Central Opera Institute	(8610) 6404 3485
Central Chinese Opera Institute	(8610) 6344 5054
Beijing Film Academy	(8610) 8204 8899
China Mines University	(8610) 6233 1203
Beijing Printing College	(8610) 6924 3981
Beijing Diplomatic College	(8610) 6832 3367
Beijing Materials College	(8610) 8953 4000
Police University of China	(8610) 8390 3114
Northern China Electrical University	(8610) 8079 5666
University of International Business & Economy	(8610) 6449 2001
Institute of International Relations	(8610) 6286 1317
Beijing College of Electronic Science & Technology	(8610) 6370 055
Beijing Institute of Petrochemical Engineering	(8610) 6924 1138
China News Academy	(8610) 6862 3311
China Youth College of Politics	(8610) 6842 1144
Beijing Petroleum University	(8610) 6232 0066
Geological Science University of China	(8610) 8232 2222
Beijing Acupuncture College	(8610) 6436 1199
Beijing Mechanical Industry College	(8610) 6293 9189
Beijing Technological University	(8610) 6739 1765
Capital Normal University	(8610) 6890 1993
Capital Iron & Steel Technological College	(8610) 6887 4163
Beijing Information Engineering College	(8610) 6487 2255
Beijing Agriculture College	(8610) 8079 9313
Capital Sports Teachers College	(8610) 8209 9111
Beijing Medical Professional College	(8610) 6944 3147
Beijing United University	(8610) 6493 0052
Beijing Dancing Academy	(8610) 6841 1620
Capital Medical University	(8610) 6305 1503

Beijing Construction Engineering College	(8610) 6833 6376
Capital University of Economy & Commerce	(8610) 6597 6600
Beijing Education Academy	(8610) 8208 9116
Beijing Adults Education College	(8610) 8208 9116
Beijing Broadcasting & TV University	(8610) 6616 0522
Beijing Arts & Social Sciences University	(8610) 8049 4651

MBA PROGRAMS

Peking University Guanghua Management School	(8610) 6275 7784
People's University College of Business Administration	(8610) 6251 1342
Tsinghua University School of Economics & Management	(8610) 6278 9880
Northern Jiaotong University School of Economics	(8610) 6324 0153
Beijing Institute of Technology Graduate School	(8610) 6891 2286
University of International Business & Economy	(8610) 6449 2202
Beijing University of Aviation & Aerospace Management School	(8610) 8231 7839
Beijing University of Post & Telecommunication Management School	(8610) 6228 5713
Beijing University of Science & Technology Management School	(8610) 6232 9826
China Mines University Department of Economics & Management	(8610) 6233 1251

BUSINESS CLUBS

THE CAPITAL CLUB

50 F Capital Tower, 6 Xinyuan South Road, Chaoyang District
Tel: (8610) 8486 2225 Fax: (8610) 8486 3909

THE CHINA CLUB

51 Xirongxian Hutong, Xidan, Xicheng District
Tel: (8610) 6603 8855 Fax: (8610) 6603 9594

THE CHANG'AN CLUB

10 East Chang'an Boulevard, Dongcheng District
Tel: (8610) 6522 9988 Fax: (8610) 6522 6978

THE AMERICAN CLUB

China Resources Tower, 8 Jianguomenwai North Avenue, Dongcheng District
Tel: (8610) 8519 2888 Fax: (8610) 8519 2800

WINE & DINE

ASIAN

• Traditional Established Chinese Restaurants

Bianyifang	(8610) 6702 2405
Changzheng Restaurant	(8610) 6255 3995
Cuihualou	(8610) 6525 4581
Daoxiangcun	(8610) 6403 6257
Dasunzhai	(8610) 8952 2340
Donglaishun	(8610) 6407 8827
Dongxinlou	(8610) 6404 5972
Douyichu	(8610) 6702 1555
Fangshan Restaurant	(8610) 6404 3481
Fengze Garden	(8610) 6318 6688
Gongdelin	(8610) 6702 0867
Hangzhou Cuisine	(8610) 6597 2299
Hongbinlou	(8610) 6899 4566
Huaiyangcun	(8610) 6801 1117
Huifengtang	(8610) 6816 7897
Hundunhou	(8610) 6512 0059
Jingyang Restaurant	(8610) 6303 2120
Kaorouyuan	(8610) 6524 5223
Kaorouji	(8610) 6404 2554
Lao Shanghai	(8610) 6437 6688
Laijinyuxuan	(8610) 6605 6676
Laozhengxin	(8610) 6702 2686
Liuquanju	(8610) 6616 3137
Meifulin	(8610) 6303 2388
Moon Shanghai	(8610) 6506 9988
Oasis	(8610) 6418 1072
Shanghai Cuisine	(8610) 6590 3388
Shenlong Restaurant	(8610) 6404 4264
Snow Garden	(8610) 6523 3872
Songhelou	(8610) 6524 5223
Taifenglou	(8610) 6301 0153
Tingliguan	(8610) 6288 1608
Tongcunlou	(8610) 6714 3476
Tongcun Garden	(8610) 6235 4568
Tongheju	(8610) 6851 3377
Qingfeng Pao House	(8610) 6617 5487
Quanjude Roast Duck	(8610) 6304 8992
Quanshuzhai	(8610) 6404 4278
Quyuan Restaurant	(8610) 6831 8502
Wuxiangzhai	(8610) 6513 9661

Xiangjugong	(8610) 6762 8457
Xiaochang Chen	(8610) 6723 2902
Yitiaolong	(8610) 6304 4638
Yuhuatai Restaurant	(8610) 6200 4206
Zhonghouju	(8610) 6799 1505

• Taiwanese

Ban Mu Yuan	(8610) 6593 0428
Green Leaf Restaurant	(8610) 6597 2299
Shenglin Fu Restaurant	(8610) 6415 9274
Taiwan Pengji Hotpot Restaurant	(8610) 6492 3517

• Indian

Omar Khayam	(8610) 6513 9988
Rasa Sayang	(8610) 6437 6688
Shamiana	(8610) 6833 8822
Spices Restaurant	(8610) 6718 1188
TAJ Indian Restaurant	(8610) 6505 5866
The Tandoor-Shanghai Food Street, Jin Jiang Hotel, 59 Mao Ming Road (S). Shanghai	(8621) 6472 5494
The Tandoor-Beijing 1st Floor, Great Dragon (Zhaolong) Hotel, 2 Workers' Stadium Road (N). Beijing	(8610) 6597 2211
The Tandoor-Chengdu Sunjoy Inn, No.34, Section 4, Ren Ming Nan Lu, Chengdu	(8628) 8555 1958
The Spice Market West Building, Somerset Grand Shanghai, 8 Ji Nan Road, Shanghai	(8621) 6384 6838

• Japanese

Ago	(8610) 6508 8413
Genji	(8610) 6833 8822
Go Nin Byakusho	(8610) 6403 4003
Izumo	(8610) 6591 5381
Matsuko	(8610) 6582 5208
Miyako	(8610) 6436 2288
Sakura	(8610) 6500 4275
Unkai	(8610) 6466 2288

• Korean

Bobea Won	(8610) 6491 3371
Hanchuangong Korean Restaurant	(8610) 6463 0745
Hanjiayu	(8610) 6512 0873

Jinro Restaurant	(8610) 6499 3288
Korean BBQ Restaurant	(8610) 6603 9547
Korean Roast Restaurant	(8610) 6518 2324
Mapu	(8610) 6462 0316
Sorabol	(8610) 6590 6688

• Singaporean

Asian Star Restaurant	(8610) 6582 5306
Old Bazaar	(8610) 6415 7598

• Thai

Borom Piman Thai Restaurant	(8610) 6437 6688
Sawasdee	(8610) 6460 2339
Meinam River	(8610) 6513 3388

WESTERN

• American

AS&W All American Food	(8610) 8208 4248
American	(8610) 6416 2272
Apollo Coffee Garden	(8610) 6597 2299
Café California	(8610) 6436 2288
Frank's Place	(8610) 6507 2617
Hard Rock Café	(8610) 6590 6688
Henry J. Beans Bar & Grill	(8610) 6505 2266
Kaiss's	(8610) 6465 1798
Mrs Shannon's Bagels	(8610) 6435 9561
Sammies	(8610) 6506 6616
Sports City Café	(8610) 6515 8855
Texan Bar & Grill	(8610) 6437 6688
TGIF	(8610) 6597 5037
The Louisiana	(8610) 6466 2288
Waterside Café	(8610) 6424 9882

• French

Asia Coffee Shop	(8610) 6505 2266
Bistro des Chateaux	(8610) 6500 2266
Brasserie Flo	(8610) 6595 5139
Justine's	(8610) 6500 2233
La Fleur	(8610) 6417 1200
La Scene	(8610) 6593 5650
Le Ciel	(8610) 6590 5826
Le Gavroche	(8610) 6595 2485
Maxim's	(8610) 6512 1992

Plaza Grill	(8610) 6513 3388

• German

Bavaria Bierstube	(8610) 6559 2888
Deutsches Bierhaus	(8610) 6512 8333
Paulaner Brauhaus	(8610) 6465 3388
Schiller's	(8610) 6464 9016

• Italian

Adria 1	(8610) 6460 6896
Adria 2	(8610) 6500 6186
Angel Italian Food and Bar	(8610) 6415 7384
Danieli's	(8610) 6460 6688
Domino's	(8610) 6218 4995
Gisa	(8610) 6594 0938
Il Gallo Nero	(8610) 6500 7799
Napolis	(8610) 6251 0180
Peter Pan	(8610) 6595 1414
Pit Stop	(8610) 6436 2288
Pizza Factory	(8610) 6518 6840
Roma	(8610) 6559 2888
Roma Ristorante Italiano	(8610) 6512 8899
Trattoria La Gondola	(8610) 6465 3388
Trattoria La Gondola	(8610) 6460 0896

• Mexican

Cabo	(8610) 6515 6826
Ei Gaucho	(8610) 6502 2198
Mexican Restaurant	(8610) 6593 5972
Mexican Wave	(8610) 6506 3981

• Scandinavian

Laxen Oxen	(8610) 6466 3388

• Swiss

Café Swiss	(8610) 6456 5588

• Fast Food

A & W All American Food	(8610) 6238 6833
Hometown Food	(8610) 6862 5541
Japanese Noodle	(8610) 6374 6948
Kentucky Fried Chicken	(8610) 6554 5888
Lotteria	(8610) 6599 3388
McDonald's	(8610) 6528 1188
Pizza Hut	(8610) 6554 6511

Rogers	(8610) 6835 0888
The Subway Sandwich	(8610) 6435 6670
Tianjin Goubuli	(8610) 6404 3097
Yonghe	(8610) 8844 0088
Yonshinoya	(8610) 6651 5283
Xiangfei Fried Chicken	(8610) 6611 9967

INDUSTRIAL PARKS IN BEIJING

Beijing Economic & Technological Development Zone
4 Wanyuan Street Beijing 100076
Tel: (8610) 6788 124 Fax: (8610) 6788 1210

Zhongguancun Science Park
9 Daozhuomiao, Haidian District Beijing 100080
Tel: (8610) 8269 0500 Fax: (8610) 8269 0506

Zhongguancun Science Park, Changping Zone
9 Chaoqian Road, Changping District Beijing 102200
Tel: (8610) 6974 4527 Fax: (8610) 6974 5549

Zhongguancun Science Park Haidian Zone
3 Zhongguancun South Avenue, Haidian District Beijing 100081
Tel: (8610) 6891 5118 Fax: (8610) 6891 5214

Zhongguancun Electronics City
12 Jiuxianqiao Road, Chaoyang District Beijing 100016
Tel: (8610) 6437 7993 Fax: (8610) 6436 0367

Zhongguancun Science Park Fengtai Zone
2 Haiying Road, Fengtai District Beijing 100070
Tel: (8610) 6372 6083 Fax: (8610) 6373 6079

Zhongguancun Science Park Yizhuang Zone
4 Wanyuan Street Beijing 100076
Tel: (8610) 6788 0186 Fax: (8610) 6788 0267

Yanshan East Liushui Industrial Park
14 East Liushui Industrial Park, Fangshan District Beijing 102502
Tel: (8610) 6934 2270 Fax: (8610) 6934 2270

Liangxiang Satellite Town Industrial Park
2 Jinguang Road, Kaixuan Avenue, Liangxiang, Beijing 102488
Tel: (8610) 6935 1867 Fax: (8610) 6935 1867

Liantan Economic Development Zone
Liantan Village, Huangcun Town, Daxing District, Beijing 102600
Tel: (8610) 6125 8565 Fax: (8610) 6125 8565

Binhe Industrial Park
22 Fuqian West Street, Pinggu District, Beijing 101200
Tel: (8610) 6996 3791 Fax: (8610) 6996 3791

China Town & Village Enterprises City
23 Fuxin Road, Beijing 100036
Tel: (8610) 6829 8318 Fax: (8610) 6829 8318

Shangdi Information Industrial Base
Haidian District, Beijing 100085
Tel: (8610) 6298 1809 Fax: (8610) 6298 7268

Tianzhu Airport Industrial Park
Tianzhu Town, Shunyi District, Beijing 101312
Tel: (8610) 6456 7640 Fax: (8610) 6456 7640

Linhe Industrial Park
Shuntong Road East, Shunyi District, Beijing 101300
Tel: (8610) 8949 3610 Fax: (8610) 8949 2548

Badachu Science Park
#401 Wanshang Tower, Shijingshan District, Beijing 100043
Tel: (8610) 6868 6665 Fax: (8610) 6868 1188

Shilong Industrial Park
6 Shilong South Road, Mentougou District, Beijing 102308
Tel: (8610) 6980 3404 Fax: (8610) 6980 3414

Wangjing New Industrial Bank
3 Donghu Nanhuqu, Chaoyang District, Beijing 100102
Tel: (8610) 6471 25269 Fax: (8610) 6472 4723

Miyun Industrial Park
Wulijin, West Miyun, Beijing 101500
Tel: (8610) 6904 4661 Fax: (8610) 6904 4644

Xinggu Industrial Park
Pinggu South Street, Pinggu District, Beijing 101200
Tel: (8610) 6996 3464 Fax: (8610) 6996 3464

Daxing Industrial Park
Kangzhuang Road East, Huangcun, Daxing District, Beijing 102600
Tel: (8610) 6021 4645 Fax: (8610) 6127 2817

Tongzhou Industrial Park
Guanghua Road West, Zhangjiawang Town, Tongzhou District, Beijing 101113
Tel: (8610) 6957 1700 Fax: (8610) 6957 1700

Yanqi Industrial Park
Yanqing District, Beijing 101407
Tel: (8610) 6166 6616 Fax: (8610) 6166 3427

Badaling Industrial Park
2 West Avenue, Yanqing Town, Yanqing County, Beijing 102100
Tel: (8610) 6918 9371 Fax: (8610) 6914 1563

Chengguang Industrial Park
Capital International Airport North, Beijing 101300
Tel: (8610) 6947 2405 Fax: (8610) 6947 2495

Juyuan Industrial Park
Mapo Town, Shunyi District, Beijing 101300
Tel: (8610) 6940 1879 Fax: (8610) 6940 3524

Niulanshan Industrial Park
Niulanshan Town, Shunyi District, Beijing 101301
Tel: (8610) 6941 4015 Fax: (8610) 6941 4091

Hongda Industrial Park
North Xiaoying Town, Shunyi District, Beijing 101305
Tel: (8610) 6048 3615 Fax: (8610) 6048 5838

Fulida Industrial Park
Beiwu Town, Shunyi District, Beijing 101300
Tel: (8610) 6142 1808 Fax: (8610) 6142 1808

Yongle Industrial Pak
Caichangtun, Yongledian, Tongzhou District, Beijing 101105
Tel: (8610) 8051 2919 Fax: (8610) 8051 1573

Yanqing Nancaiyuan Industrial Park
1 Hunan East Road, Yanqing County, Beijing 102100
Tel: (8610) 6914 3476 Fax: (8610) 0 6914 2562

COURIER SERVICES

City56 Express Service	(8610) 8575 6152
DHL	(8610) 6466 5566
Eastern Express System	(8610) 6415 9818
Federal Express	(8610) 6468 5566
New Railway Express Service	(8610) 6717 9115
Pony Express Service	(8610) 6217 6195
Senfeng Express Service	(8610) 84566109
TNT Skypack Sinotrans	(8610) 6467 7877
UPS	(8610) 6505 5005

FOREIGN EXECUTIVE SEARCH FIRMS

Alliance Consulting Ltd.	(8610) 6500 7994
Beijing Foreign Enterprise Service Corporation	(8610) 6501 6677
China International Enterprise Cooperation Corporation	(8610) 8838 2449
China Star International Economic & Technological Cooperation Corporation	(8610) 8527 1201
China International Technological & Intellectual Cooperation Corporation	(8610) 6561 3920
China International Talents Development Center	(8610) 5532 0262
CIASE Headhunting & Consultation Company	(8610) 6492 6210
CyberOrient Headhunting Services (Beijing) Co., Ltd.	(8610) 6275 0983
TMP Worldwide	(8610) 8453 8833
Wang & Li Asia Resources Online	(8610) 6515 5960

EXECUTIVE SEARCH FIRMS

Beijing Top Jobway Center	(8610) 6489 7710
Beijing Tailai Headhunter Consulting Agency	(8610) 6200 5458
Beijing Yanbo Consulting Company	(8610) 6612 8496
Beijing Shuanggao Talents Development Service Center	(8610) 6214 0639
Beijing Ciasehe Management Consultancy Company	(8610) 6492 6210
Beijing Sinotalents	(8610) 6216 1436
Beijing Person Consulting Company	(8610) 6508 2228
Beijing MTCS Consulting Service	(8610) 8207 9121
Beijing Career Information Consulting Co. Ltd.	(8610) 6599 2546
Beijing CEMC	(8610) 6463 6378

HUMAN RESOURCE MARKETS & CENTERS IN BEIJING

Beijing HR Service Center	(8610) 6512 3374

Dongcheng District HR Service Center	(8610) 6425 7248
Xicheng District HR Service Center	(8610) 8806 4343
Chongwen District HR Service Center	(8610) 6714 2756
Xuanwu District HR Service Center	(8610) 6317 0716
Chaoyang District HR Service Center	(8610) 6509 4894
Haidian District HR Service Center	(8610) 6894 5136
Fengtai District HR Service Center	(8610) 6383 0805
Shijingshan District HR Service Center	(8610) 6886 3630
Mengtougou District HR Service Center	(8610) 6984 4345
Fangshan District HR Service Center	(8610) 6936 5740
Shunyi District HR Service Center	(8610) 6944 2549
Tongzhou District HR Service Center	(8610) 6951 6795
Daxing District HR Service Center	(8610) 6924 1884
Changping District HR Service Center	(8610) 6974 6282
Pinggu District HR Service Center	(8610) 6998 3705
Yanqing County HR Service Center	(8610) 6910 -2383
Miyun District HR Service Center	(8610) 6904 2577

COMMERCIAL SPACE

DONGCHENG DISTRICT

Fuhua Tower
8 Chaoyangmen North Avenue, Dongcheng District
Tel: (8610) 6554 1605 Fax: (8610) 6554 3181

Overseas Chinese Tower
2 Wangfujing Avenue, Dongcheng District
Tel: (8610) 6513 6666 Fax: (8610) 6513 4248

Guanghua Chang'an Tower
7 JianguomenneiAvenue, Dongcheng District
Tel: (8610) 6510 1100 Fax: (8610) 6510 1002

Chang'an Plaza
10 Chang'an Avenue, Dongcheng District
Tel: (8610) 6522 9988 Fax: (8610) 6522 6978

Intercontinental Tower
16 Ande Road, Dongcheng District
Tel: (8610) 8425 2288 Fax: (8610) 6420 9068

Shenbo Business Park Center
2 Jianguomen South Avenue, Dongcheng District
Tel: (8610) 6526 3775

New Dongan Plaza
138 Wangfujing Avenue, Dongcheng District
Tel: (8610) 6528 0186 Fax: (8610) 6529 0361

The Tower Offices at Oriental Plaza
No.1, East Chang An Ave, Dong Cheng District, Beijing, 100738, China
Tel: (8610) 8518 6688

Hung Kee Center
18 Jianguomennei Avenue, Dongcheng District
Tel: (8610) 6518 6518 Fax: (8610) 6518 3329

Xingtong Plaza
8 Beijing Railway Station East Street, Dongcheng District
Tel: (8610) 6527 4980 Fax: (8610) 6526 8768

Poly Plaza
14 Dongzhimen South Avenue, Dongcheng District
Tel: (8610) 6500 1188 Fax: (8610) 6501 0268

Beijing Hotel Business Center
33 East Chang'an Road, Dongcheng District
Tel: (8610) 6513 7304 Fax: (8610) 6513 7703

China Aviation Plaza
10A Dongzhimen South Avenue, Dongcheng District
Tel: (8610) 6415 7788 Fax: (8610) 6415 4640

COFCO Plaza
8 Jianguomennei Avenue, Dongcheng District
Tel: (8610) 6526 6666 Fax: (8610) 6526 3980

Century Plaza
99 Wangfujing Avenue, Dongcheng District
Tel: (8610) 6513 8899 Fax: (8610) 6527 1258

Capital Trust Plaza
2A East 3rd Ring North Road, Dongcheng District
Tel: (8610) 6466 1681 Fax: (8610) 6466 1681

Wangfujing Plaza
251 Wangfujing Avenue, Dongcheng District
Tel: (8610) 6528 0491 Fax: (8610) 6559 5508

Hong Kong & Macau Center
2 Chaoyangmen North Avenue, Dongcheng District
Tel: (8610) 6501 2288 Fax: (8610) 6501 1250

Huacheng Plaza
2 Dahua Road, Dongcheng District
Tel: (8610) 6526 6830 Fax: (8610) 6526 6771

XICHENG DISTRICT

COSCO Plaza
158 Fuxinmennei Avenue, Xicheng District
Tel: (8610) 6606 6626 Fax: (8610) 6649 3214

Sichuan Plaza
1 Fuwai Avenue, Xicheng District
Tel: (8610) 6836 4645 Fax: (8610) 6846 3645

Parkson Tower
111 Fuxinmennei Avenue, Xicheng District
Tel: (8610) 6607 3718 Fax: (8610) 6607 3524

Sinochem Tower
2A Fuxinmenwai Avenue, Xicheng District
Tel: (8610) 6856 8818 Fax: (8610) 6856 8189

International Finance Plaza
156 Fuxingmennei Avenue, Xicheng District
Tel: (8610) 6642 6110 Fax: (8610) 6642 6100

Xidan International Plaza
111 Xidan North Avenue, Xicheng District

Tel: (8610) 6615 5566 Fax: (8610) 6615 0221

Ping'an Plaza
23 Financial Avenue, Xicheng District
Tel: (8610) 6621 0332 Fax: (8610) 6621 0308

State Enterprise Tower
35 Financial Avenue, Xicheng District
Tel: (8610) 8809 1000 Fax: (8610) 8809 1028
Jingyu Plaza
129A Xuanwumen West Avenue, Xicheng District
Tel: (8610) 6641 6688 Fax: (8610) 6641 6572

Jiangwei Plaza
66 South Lishi Road, Xicheng District
Tel: (8610) 6802 9797 Fax: (8610) 6802 3975

Yuetan Plaza
2 Yuetan North Street, Xicheng District
Tel: (8610) 6088 5999 Fax: (8610) 6808 3333

Wantong New World Plaza
2 Fuchengmenwai Avenue, Xicheng District
Tel: (8610) 6857 8944 Fax: (8610) 6857 8610

CHONGWEN DISTRICT

Taikang Plaza
80 Chongwenmenwai Avenue, Chongwen District
Tel: (8610) 6712 0378

Jinglun Plaza
40 Chongwai Avenue, Chongwen District
Tel: (8610) 6712 0109 Fax: (8610) 6712 3921

Taoran Plaza
1 Majiabao Road, Chongwen District
Tel: (8610) 8728 6688 Fax: (8610) 6722 0060

China Brand Tower
1 Anhua North Street
Guangqumennei Avenue, Chongwen District
Tel: (8610) 67156688

XUANWU DISTRICT

High-tech Tower
1 South Binhe Road, Guanganmen, Xuanwu District
Tel: (8610) 6346 0020 Fax: (8610) 6349 7653

Xiaoxiang Tower
42 Beiwei Road, Xuanwu District
Tel: (8610) 8316 1188 Fax: (8610) 6303 2674
Greatwall Plaza
88 Xuanwumenwai Avenue, Xuanwu District
Tel: (8610) 6301 7766 Fax: (8610) 8316 3116

Suyuan Jinjiang Tower
2 Guanganmenwai Avenue, Xuanwu District
Tel: (8610) 6326 7788 Fax: (8610) 6345 1696

Zhongjinxin International Plaza
338 Guanganmennei Avenue, Xuanwu District
Tel: (8610) 6537 8888 Fax: (8610) 6357 4783

Parco Plaza
6 Xuanwumen Avenue, Xuanwu District
Tel: (8610) 6310 3366 Fax: (8610) 6310 1036

HAIDIAN DISTRICT

Digital Tower
48 North 3rd Ring West Road, Haidian District
Tel: (8610) 6217 5100 Fax: (8610) 6218 0999

Beijing Telecom Hotel Business Center
6 Shifangyuan, Haidian District
Tel: (8610) 6390 1947 Fax: (8610) 6396 8680

Pacific International Plaza
106 Zhicun Road, Haidian District
Tel: (8610) 6252 5323 Fax: (8610) 6257 8318

PKU Pacific Tech Center
52 Haidian Road, Haidian District
Tel: (8610) 8266 7102 Fax: (8610) 8266 7107

Zhongguancun Tower
27 Zhongguancun Avenue, Haidian District
Tel: (8610) 8285 6666 Fax: (8610) 8285 6680

Jingyu Tower
100 West 3rd Ring North Road, Haidian District
Tel: (8610) 6845 4460 Fax: (8610) 6872 5588

Shangdi Plaza
16 Information Road
Shanghai Information Industry Base, Haidian District
Tel: (8610) 6297 1740 Fax: (8610) 6297 1434
Modern Plaza
40 Zhongguancun Avenue, Haidian District
Tel: (8610) 6256 2188

Haidian New Tech Plaza
7 Chaoqiao, Haidian District
Tel: (8610) 6258 4355 Fax: (8610) 6258 4353

Ideal Tower
111 Zhicun Road, Haidian District
Tel: (8610) 8266 5807 Fax: (8610) 8266 5159

China Electronic Information Tower
6 Zhongguancun South Avenue, Haidian District
Tel: (8610) 6250 1818

BIT Tech Plaza
9 Zhongguancun South Avenue, Haidian District
Tel: (8610) 6848 1257 Fax: (8610) 6846 7126

Aviation Greatwall Plaza
30 Haidian South Road, Haidian District
Tel: (8610) 6874 8188 Fax: (8610) 6874 8133

Stone Plaza
2 Haidian Avenue, Haidian District
Tel: (8610) 6261 0168 Fax: (8610) 6261 0104

Lotus Plaza
16 Lianhuaci West Road, Haidian District
Tel: (8610) 6398 2083 Fax: (8610) 6396 3138

International Enterprise Cooperation Business Plaza
20 Zhicun Road, Haidian District
Tel: (8610) 6204 5455

Flower Technology Garden Center
11 Zhongguancun South Avenue, Haidian District
Tel: (8610) 6848 5173 Fax: (8610) 6842 3472

Tsinghua Unisplendor Business Center
East Gate, Tsinghua University
Haidian District
Tel: (8610) 6255 6539 Fax: (8610) 6278 6008

Guangda Guoxin Tower
11 Zhongguancun South Avenue, Haidian District
Tel: (8610) 6846 4616 Fax: (8610) 6846 4618

China Science & Technology Hall
3 Fuxin Road, Haidian District
Tel: (8610) 6851 8822 Fax: (8610) 6852 5845

Huazhong Science & Technology Plaza
4 Zhongguancun South Road, Haidian District
Tel: (8610) 6261 0016 Fax: (8610) 6261 0019

China Land Tower
6 Beifengwo, Haidian District
Tel: (8610) 6324 6666 Fax: (8610) 6361 108

Media Center
11 Fuxing Road, Haidian District
Tel: (8610) 6851 4422 Fax: (8610) 6851 5255

CHAOYANG DISTRICT

Jingguan Center
Hujialou Road, Chaoyang District
Tel: (8610) 6597 8888 Fax: (8610) 6597 8200

Full-link Plaza
18 Chaoyangmen Avenue, Chaoyang District
Tel: (8610) 6588 1997

Sung Hung Kee International Plaza
3 Maizidian West Road, Chaoyang District
Tel: (8610) 6467 3299 Fax: (8610) 6460 9678

Huixing Plaza
8 Beicheng East Road, Chaoyang District

Tel: (8610) 6491 1808 Fax: (8610) 6491 0678

Asia Pacific Plaza
8 Yabao Road, Haidian District
Tel: (8610) 6513 9988 Fax: (8610) 6512 1524

Tongguang Plaza
12 Agriculture Exhibition South Road, Chaoyang District
Tel: (8610) 6538 9011 Fax: (8610) 6538 0066
CTS Plaza
2 North 3rd Ring East Road, Chaoyang District
Tel: (8610) 6462 2288 Fax: (8610) 6461 2412

Kerry Center
1 Guanghua Road, Chaoyang District
Tel: (8610) 8529 8226 Fax: (8610) 8529 8278

Huapu International Plaza
19 Chaoyangmenwai Avenue, Chaoyang District
Tel: (8610) 6599 1908 Fax: (8610) 6599 1968

Huabin International Plaza
8 Yongan East Street, Chaoyang District
Tel: (8610) 8528 8528

Landmark Tower
8 East 3rd Ring North Road, Chaoyang District
Tel: (8610) 6590 6688 Fax: (8610) 6590 0501

South Silver Plaza
2 East 3rd Ring North Road, Chaoyang District
Tel: (8610) 6410 7001 Fax: (8610) 6410 6628

Jingtai Center
24 Jianguomenwai Avenue, Chaoyang District
Tel: (8610) 6515 6454 Fax: (8610) 6515 6447

Anhui Tower
1 Huixing West Street, Chaoyang District
Tel: (8610) 6496 5588 Fax: (8610) 6495 6177

Capital Tower
6 Xinyuan South Road, Chaoyang District
Tel: (8610) 6466 0088 Fax: (8610) 8486 2092

International Tower
19 Jianguomenwai Avenue, Chaoyang District
Tel: (8610) 6500 1159 Fax: (8610) 6500 7243

Lufthansa Center
50 Liangmaqiao Road, Chaoyang District
Tel: (8610) 6465 3388 Fax: (8610) 6465 1564

China World Trade Center
1 Jianguomenwai Avenue, Chaoyang District
Tel: (8610) 6505 2288 Fax: (8610) 6505 1009

Hanwei Tower
7 Guanghua Road, Chaoyang District
Tel: (8610) 6561 1155 Fax: (8610) 6561 3989

Kelun Tower
12A Guanghua Road, Chaoyang District
Tel: (8610) 6581 9195 Fax: (8610) 6851 1874

United Tower
20 Chaowai Avenue, Chaoyang District
Tel: (8610) 6588 3395 Fax: (8610) 6588 5831

Jingri Plaza
17 East 3rd Ring South Road, Chaoyang District
Tel: (8610) 6766 8866 Fax: (8610) 6765 6108

Sci-tech Tower
22 Jianguomenwai Avenue, Chaoyang District
Tel: (8610) 6512 2288 Fax: (8610) 6512 3678

China Insurance Tower
20 Chaowai Market Street, Chaoyang District
Tel: (8610) 6592 22299 Fax: (8610) 6503 5110

Fortune Plaza
3 East 3rd Ring North Road, Chaoyang District
Tel: (8610) 6466 9812 Fax: (8610) 6466 7008

Changfugong Office Building
26 Jianguomenwai Avenue, Chaoyang District
Tel: (8610) 6513 8570 Fax: (8610) 6513 9830

Overseas Chinese Merchants Tower
2 Chaowai Yanjing West Street, Chaoyang District
Tel: (8610) 6594 9885 Fax: (8610) 6500 5692

China International Science & Technology Exhibition Center
12 Yuming Road, Chaoyang District
Tel: (8610) 6235 1678 Fax: (8610) 6235 1677

China Minerals Tower
15 Anhui Street Zone 4, Chaoyang District
Tel: (8610) 6491 6821 Fax: (8610) 6491 6666

Panly Plaza
22 Chaoyangmenwai, Chaoyang District
Tel: (8610) 6588 6355 Fax: (8610) 6588 2928

REAL ESTATE AGENTS/DEVELOPERS

Yosemite Villa
Next to the Beijing International School
Shunyi/ No. 4 Yu Yang Road, Oushayu Town, Shunyi District, Beijing, P.R. China
Tel: (8610) 8046 5770 Fax: (8610) 8046 5776

Beijing Bel-property Investment Ltd
Room 616, Silver Tower, 2 East 3rd Ring North Road, Chaoyang District 100027
Tel: (8610) 6410 7078 Fax: (8610) 6410 7070

CB Richard Ellis
15F, Units 10A-18, IBM Tower, Pacific Century Place
2A Worker's Stadium Road Beijing 100027
Tel: (8610) 6539 1288 Fax: (8610) 6539 1178

Chesterton Petty
Suite 206, COFCO Plaza Tower B, 8 Jianguomennei Avenue, Dongcheng District 100005
Tel: (8610) 6526 4146 Fax: (8610) 6526 4149

Colliers Jardine
#1606 Capital Towe, 6 Xinyuan South Road, Chaoyang District 100004
Tel: (86 (10) 8486 3099 Fax: (8610) 8486 3789

Cushman & Wakefield
#403, The Gateway Building, 10 Yabao Road, Chaoyang District 100020
Tel: (8610) 6591 5697 Fax: (8610) 6591 5699

DTZ Debenham Tie Leung
#16-22 Bright China Chang An Building, 7 Jianguomennei Avenue, Dongcheng District, Beijing 100005
Tel: (8610) 6510 1388 Fax: (8610) 6510 1368

FPD Savillis
415 China World Trade Center Tower B, 1 Jianguomenwai Avenue, Beijing 100004
Tel: (8610) 6505 2348 Fax: (8610) 6505 2350

Insignia Brooke
209 Building B, Beijing BITIC Leasing Center, 1 Xingfusancun North Road, Chaoyang District 100027
Tel: (8610) 6462 5384 Fax: (8610) 6462 5385

Jones Lang Lasalle
#08-12 Full Link Plaza Tower B, 18 Chaoyangmenwai Avenue, Beijing 100020
Tel: (8610) 6588 1300 Fax: (8610) 6588 1330

ADVERTISING AND PR FIRMS

B & B International Ltd.	(8610) 8526 1228
Bates China	(8610) 6597 3999
BBDO CNUAC	(8610) 6526 3961
Beijing Guo'an Advertising Group	(8610) 6505 0028
Burson Marsteller	(8610) 6505 6363
China Global Public Relations Co. Ltd.	(8610) 6307 2690
China International Advertising	(8610) 6506 1172
D'Arcy, Masius, Benton & Bowles	(8610) 8545 4177
DDB Worldwide	(8610) 8519 2486
Dentsu	(8610) 65611926
Dentsu Yong & Rubicam	(8610) 6505 9922
Euro RSCG Partnership	(8610) 6597 5180
FCB China	(8610) 8391 5088
Grey Worldwide	(8610) 6505 5127
J. Walter Thompson	(8610) 6581 5050
Leo Burnett Shanghai Advertising	(8610) 6505 8838
Mindshare China	(8610) 6444 0088
Ogilvy & Mather	(8610) 6443 6488
Optimum Media Direction	(8610) 6561 2198
Public Ad-Link	(8610) 6561 0293

Saatchi & Saatchi	(8610) 6510 2255
TBWA LeeDavis	(8610) 8529 9120

ACCOUNTING FIRMS

FOREIGN ACCOUNTING FIRMS

Andersen Hua Qiang
Tel: (8610) 6505 3333 Fax: (8610) 6505 1828

Deloitte Touche Tohmatsu
Tel: (8610) 6528 1599 Fax: (8610) 6528 1598
Grant Thornton
Tel: (8610) 6522 7483 Fax: (8610) 6451 23454

HLB International
Tel: (8610) 6595 0411 Fax: (8610) 6595 5570

Howarth International
Tel: (8610) 6522 7520 Fax: (8610) 6522 7521

KPMG
Tel: (8610) 6505 6300 Fax: (8610) 6505 6306

Price Waterhouse Coopers
Tel: (8610) 65612233 Fax: (8610) 8529 9000

Salustro Reydel
Tel: (8610) 6526 3769 Fax: (8610) 6526 3770

LOCAL ACCOUNTING FIRMS

China Auditing CPA Co. Ltd.
Tel: (8610) 6842 2248 Fax: (8610) 6841 5997

China Excellence CPA Co. Ltd.
Tel: (8610) 6515 0408 Fax: (8610) 6515 0407

Huasong CPA Co. Ltd.
Tel: (8610) 8421 0769 Fax: (8610) 8421 0762

New Century Tax Firm
Tel: (8610) 8285 6056 Fax: (8610) 8225 6560

Probity CPA Co. Ltd.
Tel: (8610) 6554 5271 Fax: (8610) 6554 5078

Reanda CPA Co. Ltd.
Tel: (8610) 6526 3760 Fax: (8610) 6526 3767

Shine Wing CPA Co. Ltd.
Tel: (8610) 6554 2288 Fax: (8610) 6554 1612

Tingxinlei Accounting Firm
Tel: (8610) 6328 8538 Fax: (8610) 6328 8538

Topson CPA Firm
Tel: (8610) 6218 3557 Fax: (8610) 6217 6133
ULCPAS Accounting Firm
Tel: (8610) 6851 0084 Fax: (8610) 6876 7540

User Tax Agent Firm
Tel: (8610) 6621 0980 Fax: (8610) 6621 0987

Xinchengwanda CPA Co. Ltd.
Tel: (8610) 6385 1976 Fax: (8610) 6389 1975

Xingzhonghai CPA Co. Ltd.
Tel: (8610) 6804 2129 Fax: (8610) 0 6804 2130

Xinyi CPA Co. Ltd.
Tel: (8610) 6964 2769 Fax: (8610) 6964 2769

Zhongchengxin CPA Co. Ltd.
Tel: (8610) 6848 3287 Fax: (8610) 6842 4097

Zhongda Anyong Accounting Co. Ltd.
Tel: (8610) 8352 9829 Fax: (8610) 8364 6520

Zhongjia CPA Firm
Tel: (8610) 6301 5264 Fax: (86) (100 6301 5180

Zhonglihua CPA Co. Ltd.
Tel: (8610) 6588 4746 Fax: (8610) 6588 4745

Zhongpingjian CPA Co. Ltd.
Tel: (8610) 6552 2440 Fax: (8610) 6552 8913

LAW FIRMS

Anderson Mori	(8610) 6590 9064
Allen & Overy	(8610) 6510 2368
Baker & Mckenzie	(8610) 6505 0591
Beiten Burkhardt Mittl & Wegener	(8610) 8529 8110
Blake Cassels & Graydon Barristers & Solicitors	(8610) 6561 1515
Brown & Wood LLP	(8610) 6505 5359
Bruckhaus Westrick Heller Lober	(8610) 6410 6338
Cameron Mckenna Solicitors	(8610) 6505 3399
Cha & Pan Attorney	(8610) 6466 3866
Coudert Brothers	(8610) 6597 3851
Denton Hall International Lawyers	(8610) 6505 4891
Denton Wide Sapte	(8610) 8518 6680
DS Paris Law Firm	(8610) 6587 2329
Freshfields Solicitors	(8610) 6410 6338
Gide Loyrette Nouel	(8610) 6597 4511
Goodman Phillips & Vineberg	(8610) 6518 6201
Graham & James	(8610) 6507 8857
Hayth & Curley	(8610) 6566 9088
Jewkes Chan & Partners	(8610) 6522 3061
J. Nassir &Partners Law Firm	(8610) 6460 3167
Komatsu, Koma & Nishikawa	(8610) 6518 3858
Koo Partners	(8610) 6554 2740
Leboeuf, Lamb, Greene & Macrae	(8610) 6561 0422
Livasiri & Co. Solicitors	(8610) 6505 2618
Linklaters & Alliance	(8610) 6505 8590
Lovell White Durrant	(8610) 6526 3490
Morisogo Law Offices	(8610) 6590 9292
Morrison & Foerter LLP	(8610) 6505 9090
Paragon Law Offices	(8610) 6512 9809
Paul Weiss Rifkind Wharton & Garrison	(8610) 6505 6822
Richards Butler	(8610) 6599 2690
Shearman & Sterling	(8610) 6505 3399
Somatatsuo Law Office	(8610) 6526 6648
Sullivan & Cromwell	(8610) 6505 6120
Vivien Chan & Co.	(8610) 6522 7069
Vinson & Elkins	(8610) 6410 6300

LOCAL LAW FIRMS

Beacon Law Firm	(8610) 8498 4678
Borong Law Firm	(8610) 6407 3379

C&M China Law Firm	(8610) 6468 5454
C&X Law Firm	(8610) 6712 3931
Century Link & Xinjiyuan Law Office	(8610) 6515 0284
Dacheng Law Firm	(8610) 6858 8098
Finance & Business Law Firm	(8610) 6708 8104
GH Partners	(8610) 8453 4055
Global Law Office	(8610) 6467 2007
Great Wall Law Firm	(8610) 6461 2601
Huanzhong Law Firm	(8610) 6489 6300
Initiative Law Firm	(8610) 8835 5571
J&A Law Firm	(8610) 6846 1010
Keyuan Law Firm	(8610) 6768 5672
King & Capital Lawyers	(8610) 8525 3399
Liwen & Partners	(8610) 6592 3356
New Era Law Firm	(8610) 8261 0005
Ocean Law Firm	(8610) 6568 6310
P&H Law Firm	(8610) 8813 1230
Zhonglun Law Firm	(8610) 6568 1188

INSURANCE

CHINA LIFE INSURANCE SUBSIDIARIES

• Dongcheng District	(8610) 6417 5724
• Xicheng District	(8610) 6612 8778
• Xidan Avenue	(8610) 6605 7481
• Chongwen District	(8610) 8728 1262
• Xuanwu District	(8610) 8316 0049
• Chaoyang District	(8610) 6591 0575
• Haidian District	(8610) 6205 6997
• Fengtai District	(8610) 6381 2306
• Mentougou District	(8610) 6985 2034
• Shijingshan District	(8610) 6886 3148
• Fangshan District	(8610) 8935 0154
• Daxing District	(8610) 6929 5431
• Tongzhou District	(8610) 6952 2523
• Shunyi District	(8610) 6944 5704
• Changping District	(8610) 6974 7244
• Yanqing County	(8610) 6914 4178
• Huairou County	(8610) 6962 1678

People's Insurance Corporation of China Beijing	(8610) 6503 5001
• Dongcheng District	(8610) 8425 4315

• Huairou County	(8610) 6964 4466
• Yanqing County	(8610) 6914 4641
China Pacific Insurance Beijing	(8610) 6641 8855
• Haidian District	(8610) 6203 4108
• Dongcheng District	(8610) 6422 9788
• Xicheng District	(8610) 6836 1774
• Chaoyang District	(8610) 6461 9254
• Shunyi District	(8610) 6944 0524
• Changping District	(8610) 6974 3292
• Tongzhou District	(8610) 6051 1067
• Fengtai District	(8610) 6344 3870
China Pingan Insurance Beijing	(8610) 6621 0453
• Chaoyang District	(8610) 6599 2397
• Fengtai District	(8610) 6389 9988
• Fangshan District	(8610) 8936 3579
• Xicheng District	(8610) 6832 6593
• Xuanwu District	(8610) 6357 8888
• Haidian District	(8610) 6239 4326
Xinhua Life Insurance	(8610) 6390 3399
• Haidian District	(8610) 6202 7287
• Xuanwu District	(8610) 6355 1166
• Shijingshan District	(8610) 6883 0638
• Chongwen District	(8610) 6715 1798
• Xicheng District	(8610) 6830 3766
• Chaoyang District	(8610) 8451 4921
• Fangshan District	(8610) 6934 5917
• Tongzhou District	(8610) 6953 4501
• Daxing District	(8610) 6929 9932
• Shunyi District	(8610) 6942 6445
Huatai Property Insurance	(8610) 6621 8833
• Xicheng District	(8610) 8836 3369
• Chongwen District	(8610) 6775 8718
• Chaoyang District	(8610) 6505 2071
• Fengtai District	(8610) 6328 8655
• Tongzhou District	(8610) 6955 8399
• Fangshan District	(8610) 8935 4988
• Haidian District	(8610) 8261 7258
Taikang Life Insurance	(8610) 8401 8270
• Dongcheng District	(8610) 66791430
• Shijingshan District	(8610) 6395 4662

• Fengtai District	(8610) 6381 7611
• Daxing District	(8610) 6923 1931
• Tongzhou District	(8610) 6952 7547
• Changping District	(8610) 6972 4971
• Huairou District	(8610) 6965 0140
• Xuanwu District	(8610) 6310 2154
• Fangshan District	(8610) 8936 2945
• Haidian District	(8610) 6395 4653
• Chaoyang District	(8610) 6585 0638
• Xicheng District	(8610) 6833 0452
• Shunyi District	(8610) 8148 2774

Product Order For

Please indicate the title and quantity that you wish to order:

China Knowledge Press Titles	ISBN	Price (US$)	Quantity	Total
CHINA BUSINESS GUIDE / DIRECTORY				
• China Business Guide (Second Edition)	981-41-6300-7	US$ 35.00		
• Investment Opportunities in China's Tourism Industry	981-41-6304-X	US$ 105.00		
• Branding in China	981-41-6305-8	US$ 59.00		
INSIDER'S GUIDE: DOING BUSINESS SERIES				
• Doing Business in Shanghai All New 2nd Edition	981-41-6301-5	US$ 49.95		
• Doing Business in Beijing New Edition	981-41-6302-3	US$ 49.95		
INDUSTRY GUIDE / DIRECTORY				
• Building a Successful Plant in China 2nd Edition	981-41-6303-1	US$ 90.00		

China Knowledge Market Research Reports Titles	Price (US$)	Quantity	Total

China Knowledge Media Titles	ISBN	Price (US$)	Quantity	Total
• Inside the World's Largest Factory VCD (5 episodes)	981-05-1483-2	US$ 90.00		

Shipping & Delivery charges to*:		
	Asia/Australia/New Zealand	US$ 15
	US, UK & Europe	US$ 25
	Other Countries	US$ 30

***Shipping & Delivery charges are waived for orders above US$1,000**
***Free Delivery within Singapore**

Sub Total ____________

Shipping & Delivery Charges* ____________

TOTAL ____________

Payment Method: ☐ **Telegraphic Transfer** ☐ **Credit Card** ☐ **Cheque Payment**

All Telegraphic Transfer or Cheque payable to " **China Knowledge Press Pte Ltd** " USD Current A/C 260-841465-181
SGD Current A/C 141-268441-001

Bank Details: **HSBC Bank** Ocean Building Branch Singapore, 20 Raffles Place, #02-00 Ocean Towers, Singapore 048620

Bank Code: 7232 Branch Code: 141 Swift Address: HSBCSGSG

Credit Card Details - AMEX/MASTERCARD/VISA *Please delete where appropriate

Card No. : |_|_|_|_|_|_|_|_|_|_|_|_|_|_|_|_|

Expiry Date: |_|_|_|_| Signature: ____________

Name: ____________

Company Name: ____________

Business Activity: ____________

Delivery Address: ____________

Telephone: ____________(Mobile) ____________(Office) Email: ____________

Please send or fax your completed order form with payment to:

China Knowledge Pte Ltd

8 Temasek Boulevard, #37-01A Suntec Tower 3, Singapore 038988

Tel +65 6235 8468 **Fax** +65 6235 2374

www.chinaknowledge.co